Frommer's™

Portable Acapulco, Ixtapa & Zihuatanejo

6th Edition

by Shane Christensen

with "Inland to Old Mexico: Taxco, Cuernavaca & Tepoztlán" by Joy Hepp

Wiley Publishing, Inc.

Published by:
WILEY PUBLISHING, INC.
111 River St.
Hoboken, NJ 07030-5774

ISBN 978-0-470-48721-1

Editor: Jessica Langan-Peck
Production Editor: Erin Amick
Cartographer: Nick Trotter
Photo Editor: Richard Fox
Production by Wiley Indianapolis Composition Services

Front cover photo: Cliff Diving in Acapulco © Steve Allen / JupiterImages / Brand X / Alamy Images

For information on our other products and services or to obtain technical support, please contact our Customer Care Department within the U.S. at 877/762-2974, outside the U.S. at 317/572-3993 or fax 317/572-4002.

Wiley also publishes its books in a variety of electronic formats. Some content that appears in print may not be available in electronic formats.

Manufactured in the United States of America

5 4 3 2 1

CONTENTS

3 NORTHWARD TO ZIHUATANEJO & IXTAPA 73

4 THE OAXACA COAST: FROM PUERTO ESCONDIDO TO HUATULCO 97

5 INLAND TO OLD MEXICO: TAXCO, CUERNAVACA & TEPOZTLÁN 129

6 FAST FACTS 163

7 SURVIVAL SPANISH 172

INDEX 178

LIST OF MAPS

ABOUT THE AUTHOR

A former resident of Mexico City, **Shane Christensen** has written extensively for Frommer's throughout Mexico, and is also the author of *Frommer's Dubai* and *Frommer's Grand Canyon.* He resides in New York, and goes back to Mexico every chance he gets.

A Mexico City–based writer and blogger, **Joy Hepp** writes for several print and online publications including her own blog, www.chilangabacha.com.

HOW TO CONTACT US

In researching this book, we discovered many wonderful places—hotels, restaurants, shops, and more. We're sure you'll find others. Please tell us about them, so we can share the information with your fellow travelers in upcoming editions. If you were disappointed with a recommendation, we'd love to know that, too. Please write to:

Frommer's Acapulco, Ixtapa & Zihuatanejo, 6th Edition
Wiley Publishing, Inc. • 111 River St. • Hoboken, NJ 07030-5774

AN ADDITIONAL NOTE

Please be advised that travel information is subject to change at any time—and this is especially true of prices. We therefore suggest that you write or call ahead for confirmation when making your travel plans. The authors, editors, and publisher cannot be held responsible for the experiences of readers while traveling. Your safety is important to us, however, so we encourage you to stay alert and be aware of your surroundings. Keep a close eye on cameras, purses, and wallets, all favorite targets of thieves and pickpockets.

FROMMER'S STAR RATINGS, ICONS & ABBREVIATIONS

Every hotel, restaurant, and attraction listing in this guide has been ranked for quality, value, service, amenities, and special features using a **star-rating system.** In country, state, and regional guides, we also rate towns and regions to help you narrow down your choices and budget your time accordingly. Hotels and restaurants are rated on a scale of zero (recommended) to three stars (exceptional). Attractions, shopping, nightlife, towns, and regions are rated according to the following scale: zero stars (recommended), one star (highly recommended), two stars (very highly recommended), and three stars (must-see).

In addition to the star-rating system, we also use **seven feature icons** that point you to the great deals, in-the-know advice, and unique experiences that separate travelers from tourists. Throughout the book, look for:

Finds	Special finds—those places only insiders know about
Fun Facts	Fun facts—details that make travelers more informed and their trips more fun
Kids	Best bets for kids and advice for the whole family
Moments	Special moments—those experiences that memories are made of
Overrated	Places or experiences not worth your time or money
Tips	Insider tips—great ways to save time and money
Value	Great values—where to get the best deals

The following **abbreviations** are used for credit cards:

AE American Express **DISC** Discover **V** Visa
DC Diners Club **MC** MasterCard

TRAVEL RESOURCES AT FROMMERS.COM

Frommer's travel resources don't end with this guide. Frommer's website, **www.frommers.com,** has travel information on more than 4,000 destinations. We update features regularly, giving you access to the most current trip-planning information and the best airfare, lodging, and car-rental bargains. You can also listen to podcasts, connect with other Frommers.com members through our active-reader forums, share your travel photos, read blogs from guidebook editors and fellow travelers, and much more.

1

Planning Your Trip to Southern Pacific Mexico

Though Pacific Mexico may be uniform in its often exotic tropical beaches and jungle scenery, the resorts along this coast couldn't be more varied in personality. From high-energy seaside cities to pristine, primitive coves, this is the Mexico that first lured vacationers from around the globe. Spanish conquistadors were attracted to this coast for its numerous sheltered coves and protected bays from which they set sail to the Far East. Years later, Mexico's first tourists found the same elements appealing, but for different reasons—they were seeking escape in the warm sunshine, and stretches of blue coves nicely complemented the heady tropical landscape of the adjacent coastal mountains.

Time at the beach is generally the top priority for most travelers to this part of Mexico. Each of the beach towns detailed in this book is capable of satisfying your sand-and-surf needs for a few days, or even a week or more. You could also combine several coastal resorts into a single trip, or mix the coastal with the colonial, say, with visits to both Puerto Escondido and Oaxaca City, or Acapulco and Taxco.

The resorts have distinct personalities, but you get the requisite beach wherever you go, whether you choose a city that offers virtually every luxury imaginable or a rustic town providing little more than basic (but charming) seaside relaxation.

Over the years, a diverse selection of resorts has evolved in the area. Each is distinct, yet together they offer an ideal attraction for almost any type of traveler. The region encompasses the country's oldest, largest, and most decadent resort, **Acapulco,** one-time playground of Hollywood's biggest celebrities. Of all the resorts, Acapulco has the best airline connections, the broadest range of late-night entertainment, the most savory dining, and the widest range of accommodations—from hillside villas and luxury resort hotels to modest inns on the beach and in the city center.

The resort of **Ixtapa** and its neighboring seaside village, **Zihuatanejo,** offer beach-bound tourist attractions, but on a smaller, newer, and less hectic scale than Acapulco. They attract travelers for their complementary contrasts—international high-rise hotels in one, plus the local color and leisurely pace of the other. To get here, many people fly into Acapulco, then make the 4- to 5-hour trip north (by rental car or bus), although one can fly directly into Ixtapa/Zihuatanejo, as well.

South of Acapulco, along the Oaxacan Coast, lie the small, laid-back beach towns of **Puerto Escondido** and **Puerto Angel,** both on picturesque bays bordered by relaxed communities. The region's most upscale resort community, **Bahías de Huatulco,** couples an unspoiled, slow-paced nature with the kind of modern infrastructure and luxurious facilities you'd find in the country's more crowded megaresorts. Nine bays encompass 36 beaches—many are isolated stretches of pure white sand—and countless inlets and coves. Huatulco has become increasingly known for its ecotourism attractions; you won't find much in the way of shopping or nightlife, but for most visitors, the clear blue waters and quiet, restful beaches are reason enough to come.

From Acapulco a road leads inland to **Taxco,** a colonial city that clings to the side of a mountain and is famed for its hundreds of silver shops. And verdant **Cuernavaca,** known as the land of eternal spring, has gained a reputation for exceptional spa facilities, while also boasting a wealth of cultural and historic attractions.

The whole region is graced with a stunning coastline and tropical mountains. Outside the urban centers, however, paved roads are few, and these two states remain among Mexico's poorest, despite decades-long influx of U.S. tourist dollars (and many other currencies).

For additional help in planning your trip and for more on-the-ground resources in Southern Pacific Mexico, please turn to chapter 6, "Fast Facts," on p. 163.

1 WHEN TO GO

SEASONS

Mexico has two principal travel seasons: high and low. High season begins around December 20 and continues through Easter, although in some places high season can begin as early as mid-November. Low season begins the day after Easter and continues through mid-December; during low season, prices may drop 20% to 50%. In beach destinations, the prices may also increase during the months of July and August, the traditional national summer vacation period. Prices in inland cities, such as Guadalajara, seldom fluctuate from high to low season, but may rise dramatically during Easter and Christmas weeks.

Southern Pacific Mexico

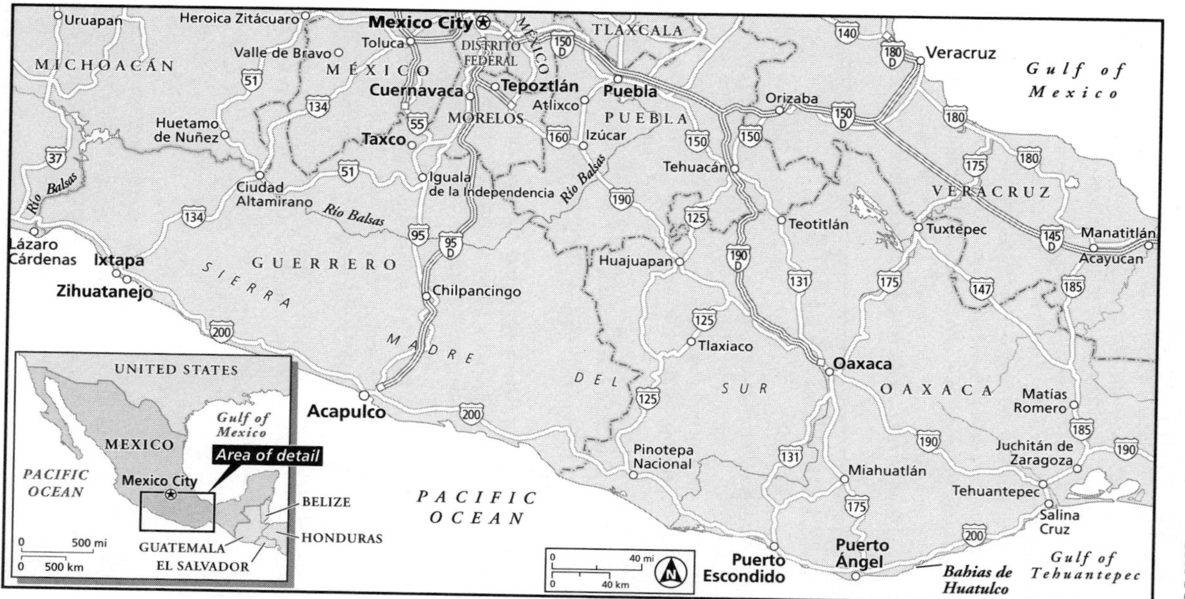

CLIMATE

Mexico's central Pacific coast offers one of the world's most perfect winter climates—dry and balmy with temperatures ranging from the 80s during the day to the 60s at night. From Ixtapa/Zihuatanejo down south, you can swim year-round. High mountains shield Pacific beaches from *nortes* ("northers"—freezing blasts out of Canada via the Texas Panhandle).

Summers are hot and sunny, with an increase in humidity during the rainy season, between May and October. Rains come almost every afternoon in June and July, and are usually brief but strong—just enough to cool off the air for evening activities. In September, heat and humidity are least comfortable and rains heaviest.

CALENDAR OF EVENTS

For an exhaustive list of events beyond those listed here, check http://events.frommers.com, where you'll find a searchable, up-to-the-minute roster of what's happening in cities all over the world. During national holidays, Mexican banks and governmental offices—including immigration—are closed.

JANUARY

New Year's Day (Año Nuevo). National holiday. Parades, religious observances, parties, and fireworks welcome in the New Year everywhere. January 1.

Three Kings Day (Día de los Reyes). Commemorates the Three Kings' bringing of gifts to the Christ Child. Children receive gifts, and friends and families gather to share the *Rosca de Reyes,* a special cake. Inside the cake is a small doll representing the Christ Child; whoever receives the doll in his or her piece must host a tamales and atole party the next month. January 6.

FEBRUARY

Candlemas. Music, dances, processions, food, and other festivities lead up to a blessing of seed and candles, a ritual that mixes pre-Hispanic and European traditions marking the end of winter. All those who attended the Three Kings' Celebration reunite to share atole and tamales at a party hosted by the recipient of the doll found in the Rosca. February 2.

Carnaval. Carnaval takes place the 3 days preceding Ash Wednesday and the start of Lent. It is celebrated with special gusto in Mazatlán. Here, the celebration resembles New Orleans's Mardi Gras, with festivities and parades. Transportation and hotels are packed, so it's best to make reservations 6 months in advance and arrive a couple of days ahead of the beginning of celebrations.

Ash Wednesday. The start of Lent and time of abstinence. It's a day of reverence nationwide, but some towns honor it with folk dancing and fairs. Lent begins on February 25 in 2009, and February 17 in 2010

March

Benito Juárez's Birthday. National holiday. March 21.

April

Holy Week. Celebrates the last week in the life of Christ, from Palm Sunday to Easter Sunday, with somber religious processions almost nightly, spoofings of Judas, and reenactments of specific biblical events, plus food and craft fairs. Businesses close during this week of Mexican national vacations.

If you plan on traveling to or around Mexico during Holy Week, make your reservations early. Airline seats on flights in and out of the country are reserved months in advance. Buses to almost anywhere in Mexico will be full, so try arriving on the Wednesday or Thursday before Good Friday. Easter Sunday is quiet.

May

Labor Day (May Day). Nationwide parades; everything closes. May 1.

Holy Cross Day (Día de la Santa Cruz). Workers place a cross on top of unfinished buildings and celebrate with food, bands, folk dancing, and fireworks around the work site. May 3.

Cinco de Mayo. A national holiday that celebrates the defeat of the French in the Battle of Puebla. May 5.

June

Día de San Pedro (St. Peter and St. Paul's Day). Celebrated wherever St. Peter is the patron saint, and honors anyone named Pedro or Peter. It's especially festive at San Pedro Tlaquepaque, near Guadalajara, with numerous mariachi bands, folk dancers, and parades with floats. In Mexcatitlan, Nayarit, shrimpers hold a regatta to celebrate the season opening. June 29.

September

Independence Day. Celebrates Mexico's independence from Spain. A day of parades, picnics, and family reunions throughout the country. At 11pm on September 15, the president of Mexico gives the famous independence *grito* (shout) from the National Palace in Mexico City, which is duplicated by every *presidente municipal* (mayor) in every town plaza in Mexico.

November

Day of the Dead. The Day of the Dead is actually 2 days, All Saints' Day (honoring saints and deceased children) and All Souls' Day (honoring deceased adults). Relatives gather at cemeteries carrying candles and food, and often spend the night beside the graves of loved ones. Weeks before, bakers begin producing bread shaped like mummies or round loaves decorated with bread "bones." Decorated sugar skulls emblazoned with glittery names are sold everywhere. Many days ahead, homes and churches erect special altars laden with Day of the Dead bread, fruit, flowers, candles, and favorite foods and photographs of saints and of the deceased. Children, dressed in costumes and masks, carry mock coffins and pumpkin lanterns through the streets at night, expecting people to drop money in them. November 1 and 2.

Revolution Day. Commemorates the start of the Mexican Revolution in 1910 with parades, speeches, rodeos, and patriotic events. November 20.

December

Feast of the Virgin of Guadalupe. Throughout the country, the patroness of Mexico is honored with religious processions, street fairs, dancing, fireworks, and Masses. It is one of Mexico's most moving and beautiful displays of traditional culture. The Virgin of Guadalupe appeared to a young man, Juan Diego, in December 1531, on a hill near Mexico City. He convinced the bishop that he had seen the apparition by revealing his cloak, upon which the Virgin was emblazoned. Children dress up as Juan Diego, wearing mustaches and red bandannas. December 12.

Christmas Posadas. On each of the 9 nights before Christmas, it's customary to reenact the Holy Family's search for an inn, with door-to-door candlelit processions in cities and villages nationwide. Most business and community organizations host them in place of the northern tradition of a Christmas party. December 15 to 24.

Christmas. Mexicans extend this celebration, often starting 2 weeks before Christmas, through New Year's. Many businesses close, and resorts and hotels fill up. December 24 and 25.

New Year's Eve. As in the rest of the world, New Year's Eve is celebrated with parties and fireworks.

2 ENTRY REQUIREMENTS

PASSPORTS

All travelers to Mexico are required to present **photo identification** and **proof of citizenship,** such as a valid passport, naturalization papers, or an original birth certificate with a raised seal, along with a driver's license or official ID, such as a state or military-issued ID. Driver's licenses and permits, voter registration cards, affidavits, and similar documents are not sufficient to prove citizenship for readmission into the United States. If the last name on the birth certificate is different from your current name, bring a photo identification card *and* legal proof of the name change, such as the original marriage license or certificate. ***Note:*** Photocopies are *not* acceptable.

New regulations issued by the Department of Homeland Security now require virtually every air traveler **entering the U.S.** to show a passport. All U.S. and Canadian citizens traveling by **air** to Mexico are required to present a valid passport or other valid travel document to enter or reenter the United States. Other valid travel documents (known as WHTI-compliant documents; visit www.travel.state.gov for more information) include the new **Passport Card** and SENTRI, NEXUS, FAST, and Global Entry Programs. Members of the U.S. Armed Forces on active duty traveling on orders are exempt from the passport requirement. The limited-use, wallet-size **Passport Card** is valid only for frequent travel for U.S. citizens who live in border communities, and only covers land and sea travel (and not air travel) between the U.S. and Canada, Mexico, the Caribbean region, and Bermuda.

As of January 31, 2008, U.S. and Canadian citizens traveling between the United States and Mexico by **land** or **sea** need to present either a WHTI-compliant document (see above), or a government-issued photo ID, such as a driver's license, plus proof of citizenship such as a birth certificate. Effective June 1, 2009, all U.S. citizens are required to present a passport book, passport card, or WHTI-compliant document when re-entering the United States. Children under age 16 are able to continue crossing land and sea borders using only a U.S. birth certificate (or other form of U.S. citizenship such as a naturalization certificate). The original birth certificate or a copy may be used.

From our perspective, it's easiest just to travel with a valid passport. Safeguard your passport in an inconspicuous, inaccessible place, like a money belt, and keep a copy of the critical pages with your passport number in a separate place. If you lose your passport, visit the nearest consulate of your native country as soon as possible for a replacement.

For information on how to get a passport, see p. 167 ("Passports," in chapter 6, "Fast Facts"). The websites listed provide downloadable passport applications and current fees for processing passport applications. The "Foreign Entry Requirements" brochure no longer exists. For information on entry requirements for Mexico, see the Entry/Exit Requirements section in the Country Specific Information for Mexico at **http://travel.state.gov/travel/cis_pa_tw/cis/cis_970.html**. You may also contact the U.S. embassy or consulate of Mexico for further information.

VISAS

For detailed information regarding visas to Mexico, visit the National Immigration Institute at **www.inm.gob.mx**.

American and Canadian tourists do not require a visa or a tourist card for stays of 72 hours or less within the border zone (20–30km/12–19 miles from the U. S. border). For travel to Mexico beyond the border zone, Americans must be in possession of a tourist card, also called Tourist Migration Form (FMTTV: Migration Form for Tourists, Transmigrants, Visiting Businesspersons or Visiting Consultants). This document is provided by airlines or by immigration authorities at the country's points of entry. If you enter Mexico by land, it is your responsibility to stop at the immigration module located at the border.

Authorities can demand to see your tourist card at any time. You must therefore carry the original or a copy at all times and must surrender the original upon leaving Mexico. Failure to do so will result in a fine and/or expulsion.

In order to obtain a tourist card, Americans and Canadians are required to present a valid passport or valid official photo identification (such as a passport or driver's license) and proof of citizenship (such as a passport, birth certificate, or citizenship card).

Your tourist card is stamped on arrival. Travelers who fail to have their tourist card stamped may be fined, detained, or expelled from the country.

An immigration official will determine the number of days you can remain in Mexico. Do not assume that you will be granted the full 180 days. An extension of your stay can be requested for a fee at the National Institute of Immigration of the Ministry of the Interior or its local offices.

Note on travel of minors: Mexican law requires that any non-Mexican citizen under the age of 18 departing Mexico without both parents must carry notarized written permission from the parent or guardian who is not traveling with the child to or from Mexico. This permission must include the name of the parent, the name of the child, the name of anyone traveling with the child, and the notarized signature(s) of the absent parent(s). The U.S. Department of State recommends that permission include travel dates, destinations, airlines, and a summary of the circumstances surrounding the travel. The child must be carrying the original letter (not a facsimile or scanned copy), and proof of the parent/child relationship (usually a birth certificate or court document) and an original custody decree, if applicable. Travelers should contact the Mexican Embassy or closest Mexican Consulate for current information.

CUSTOMS

Mexican Customs inspection has been streamlined. At most points of entry, tourists are requested to press a button in front of what looks like a traffic signal, which alternates on touch between red and green. Green light and you go through without inspection; red light and your luggage or car may be inspected. If you have an unusual amount of luggage or an oversized piece, you may be subject to inspection anyway.

What You Can Bring into Mexico

When you enter Mexico, Customs officials will be tolerant if you are not carrying illegal drugs or firearms. Tourists are allowed to bring in their personal effects duty-free. A laptop computer, camera equipment, and sports equipment that could feasibly be used during your stay are also allowed. The underlying guideline is: Don't bring anything that looks as if it's meant to be resold in Mexico. **U.S. citizens** entering Mexico by the land border can bring in gifts worth up to $50 duty-free, except for alcohol and tobacco products. Those entering Mexico by air or sea can bring in gifts worth a value of up to $300 duty-free. The website for Mexican Customs ("Aduanas") is **www.aduanas.gob.mx**.

What You Can Take Home from Mexico

U.S. Citizens: Returning U.S. citizens who have been away for at least 48 hours are allowed to bring back, once every 30 days, $800 worth of merchandise duty-free. You'll pay a flat rate of duty on the next $1,000 worth of purchases. Any dollar amount beyond that is subject to duties at whatever rates apply. On mailed gifts, the duty-free limit is $200. Be sure to keep your receipts for purchases accessible to expedite the declaration process. ***Note:*** If you owe duty, you are required to pay on your arrival in the United States—either by cash, personal check, government or traveler's check, or money order (and, in some locations, a Visa or MasterCard).

To avoid paying duty on foreign-made personal items you owned before your trip, bring along a bill of sale, insurance policy, jeweler's appraisal, or receipts of purchase. Or before you leave, you can register with Customs items that can be readily identified by a permanently affixed serial number or marking—think laptop computers, cameras, and CD players. Take the items to the nearest Customs office or register them with Customs at the airport from which you're departing. You'll receive, at no cost, a Certificate of Registration, which allows duty-free entry for the life of the item.

For specifics on what you can bring back and the corresponding fees, download the invaluable free pamphlet "Know Before You Go" online at **www.cbp.gov** (click on "Travel," and then click on "Know Before You Go"). Or contact the **U.S. Customs & Border Protection (CBP),** 1300 Pennsylvania Ave. NW, Washington, DC 20229 (✆ **877/287-8667**) and request the pamphlet.

Canadian Citizens: For a clear summary of Canadian rules, write for the booklet "I Declare," issued by the **Canada Border Services Agency** (✆ **800/461-9999** in Canada, or 204/983-3500; www.cbsa-asfc.gc.ca/cpr-crp-eng.html).

U.K. Citizens: For information, contact **HM Revenue & Customs** at ✆ **0845/010-9000** (from outside the U.K., 44/2920501261), or consult their website at www.hmrc.gov.uk.

Australian Citizens: A helpful brochure available from Australian consulates or Customs offices is "Know Before You Go." For more information, call the **Australian Customs Service** at ✆ **1300/363-263** (or 61262756666 outside Australia), or log on to **www.customs.gov.au**.

New Zealand Citizens: Most questions are answered in a free pamphlet available at New Zealand consulates and Customs offices: "New Zealand Customs Guide for Travellers, Notice no. 4." For more information, contact **New Zealand Customs Service,** The Customhouse, 6140 Whitmore St., Box 2218, Wellington (✆ **006493005399** or 0800/428-786 (0800/4 CUSTOMS); www.customs.govt.nz).

Medical Requirements

No special vaccinations are required for entry into Mexico. For other medical requirements and health-related recommendations, see "Health," p. 19.

3 GETTING THERE & GETTING AROUND

GETTING THERE

By Plane

Mexico has dozens of international and domestic airports. Among the airports in the southern Pacific coast region are Acapulco (ACA),

Huatulco (HUX), Ixtapa/Zijuatanejo (ZIH), and Puerto Escondido (PXM).

The main departure points in North America for international airlines are Atlanta, Chicago, Dallas/Fort Worth, Denver, Houston, Las Vegas, Los Angeles, Miami, New York, Orlando, Philadelphia, Phoenix, Raleigh/Durham, San Antonio, San Francisco, Seattle, Toronto, and Washington, D.C.

Arriving at the Airport

Immigration and customs clearance at Mexican airports is generally efficient. Expect longer lines during peak seasons, but you can usually clear immigration and customs within an hour. For more on what to expect when passing through Mexican customs, see "Customs," p. 9.

By Car

Driving is not the cheapest way to get to Mexico, and it is definitely not the easiest way to get to the southern Pacific coast. While driving is a convenient way to see the country, you may think twice about taking your own car south of the border once you've pondered the bureaucracy involved. One option is to rent a car once you arrive and tour around a specific region. Rental cars in Mexico are generally clean and well maintained, although they are often smaller than rentals in the U.S., may have manual rather than automatic transmission, and are comparatively expensive due to pricey mandatory insurance. Discounts are often available for rentals of a week or longer, especially when you make arrangements in advance online or from the United States. Be careful about estimated online rates, which often fail to include the price of the mandatory insurance. (See "Car Rentals," later in this chapter, for more details.)

To check on road conditions or to get help with any travel emergency while in Mexico, call ✆ **01-800/482-9832,** or 55/5089-7500 in Mexico City. English-speaking operators staff both numbers.

In addition, check with the **U.S. Department of State** (see "Safety," later in this chapter) for warnings about dangerous driving areas.

By Ship

Numerous cruise lines serve Mexico. Some (such as Carnival) cruise to Acapulco, Ixtapa/Zihuatanejo, and Manzanillo. Several cruise-tour specialists sometimes offer last-minute discounts on unsold cabins. One such company is **CruisesOnly** (✆ **800/278-4737;** www.cruisesonly.com).

GETTING AROUND

Mexico has two large private national carriers: **Mexicana** (✆ **800/531-7921;** www.mexicana.com) and **AeroMéxico** (✆ **866/275-6419;**

www.aeromexico.com), in addition to several up-and-coming low-cost carriers. Mexicana and AeroMéxico offer extensive connections to the United States as well as within Mexico.

Up-and-coming low-cost carriers include **Aviacsa** (www.aviacsa.com), **Click Mexicana** (www.click.com.mx), **InterJet** (www.interjet.com.mx), and **Volaris** (www.volaris.com.mx). Regional carriers include **Aerovega** (www.oaxaca-mio.com/aerovega.htm), **Aero Tucán** (www.aero-tucan.com), and **AeroMéxico Connect** (www.amconnect.com). The regional carriers can be expensive, but they go to difficult-to-reach places. In each applicable section of this book, we've mentioned regional carriers with all pertinent telephone numbers.

Because major airlines may book some regional carriers, check your ticket to see if your connecting flight is on one of these smaller carriers—they may use a different airport or a different counter.

AIRPORT TAXES Mexico charges an airport tax on all departures. Passengers leaving the country on international flights pay about $24 in dollars or the peso equivalent. It has become a common practice to include this departure tax in your ticket price. Taxes on each domestic departure within Mexico are around $17, unless you're on a connecting flight and have already paid at the start of the flight.

RECONFIRMING FLIGHTS Although Mexican airlines say it's not necessary to reconfirm a flight, it's still a good idea. To avoid getting bumped on popular, possibly overbooked flights, check in for an international flight 1½ hours in advance of travel.

By Car

Most Mexican roads are not up to U.S. standards of smoothness, hardness, width of curve, grade of hill, or safety markings. Driving at night is dangerous—the roads are rarely lit; trucks, carts, pedestrians, and bicycles usually have no lights; and you can hit potholes, animals, rocks, dead ends, or uncrossable bridges without warning.

The spirited style of Mexican driving sometimes requires keen vision and reflexes. Be prepared for new customs, as when a truck driver flips on his left turn signal when there's not a crossroad for miles. He's probably telling you the road's clear ahead for you to pass. Another custom that's very important to respect is turning left. Never turn left by stopping in the middle of a highway with your left-turn signal on. Instead, pull onto the right shoulder, wait for traffic to clear, and then proceed across the road.

GASOLINE There's one government-owned brand of gas and one gasoline station name throughout the country—**Pemex** (Petroleras Mexicanas). There are two types of gas in Mexico: *magna,* 87-octane unleaded gas, and *premio* 93 octane. In Mexico, fuel and oil are sold by the liter, which is slightly more than a quart (1 gal. equals about 3.8L). Many franchise Pemex stations have bathroom facilities and convenience stores—a great improvement over the old ones. Gas stations accept both credit and debit cards for gas purchases.

TOLL ROADS Mexico charges some of the highest tolls in the world for its network of new toll roads, so they are rarely used. Generally, though, using toll roads cuts travel time. Older toll-free roads are generally in good condition, but travel times tend to be longer.

BREAKDOWNS If your car breaks down on the road, help might already be on the way. Radio-equipped green repair trucks, run by uniformed English-speaking officers, patrol major highways during daylight hours. These **"Green Angels"** perform minor repairs and adjustments free, but you pay for parts and materials.

Your best guide to repair shops is the Yellow Pages. For repairs, look under *Automóviles y Camiones: Talleres de Reparación y Servicio;* auto-parts stores are under *Refacciones y Accesorios para Automóviles.* To find a mechanic on the road, look for the sign TALLER MECÁNICO.

Places called *vulcanizadora* or *llantera* repair flat tires, and it is common to find them open 24 hours a day on the most traveled highways.

MINOR ACCIDENTS When possible, many Mexicans drive away from minor accidents, or try to make an immediate settlement, to avoid involving the police. If the police arrive while the involved persons are still at the scene, the cars will likely be confiscated and both parties will likely have to appear in court. Both parties may also be taken into custody until liability is determined. Foreigners who don't speak fluent Spanish are at a distinct disadvantage when trying to explain their version of the event. Three steps may help the foreigner who doesn't wish to do as the Mexicans do: If you were in your own car, notify your Mexican insurance company, whose job it is to intervene on your behalf. If you were in a rental car, notify the rental company immediately and ask how to contact the nearest adjuster. (You did buy insurance with the rental, right?) Finally, if all else fails, ask to contact the nearest Green Angel, who may be able to explain to officials that you are covered by insurance. See also "Getting There," earlier in this chapter.

CAR RENTALS You'll get the best price if you reserve a car at least a week in advance in the United States. U.S. car-rental firms include **Advantage** (✆ 800/777-5500 in the U.S. and Canada; www.advantage.com); **Avis** (✆ 800/331-1212 in the U.S., 800/879-2847 in Canada; www.avis.com); **Budget** (✆ 800/527-0700 in the U.S. and Canada; www.budget.com); **Hertz** (✆ 800/654-3131 in the U.S. and Canada; www.hertz.com); **National** (✆ 800/227-7368 in the U.S. and Canada; www.nationalcar.com); and **Thrifty** (✆ 800/847-4389 in the

Warning! Bus Hijackings

The U.S. Department of State notes that bandits target long-distance buses traveling at night, but daylight robberies have occurred as well. First-class buses on toll *(cuota)* roads sustain a markedly lower crime rate than second-class and third-class buses that travel the less secure "free" *(libre)* highways.

U.S. and Canada; www.thrifty.com), which often offers discounts for rentals in Mexico. For European travelers, **Kemwel Holiday Auto** (© 877/820-0665; www.kemwel.com.au/car-hire-guides/Mexico.cfm) and **Auto Europe** (© 800/223-5555; www.autoeurope.com) can arrange Mexican rentals, sometimes through other agencies.

Cars are easy to rent if you are 25 or older and have a major credit card, valid driver's license, and passport with you. Without a credit card, you must leave a cash deposit, usually a big one. One-way rentals are usually simple to arrange, but they are more costly.

Car-rental costs are high in Mexico because cars are more expensive. The condition of rental cars has improved greatly over the years, and clean new cars are the norm. You will pay the least for a manual car without air-conditioning. Prices may be considerably higher if you rent around a major holiday. Also double-check charges for insurance—some companies will increase the insurance rate after several days. Always ask for detailed information about all charges you will be responsible for.

Car-rental companies usually write credit card charges in U.S. dollars.

DEDUCTIBLES Be careful—these vary greatly; some are as high as $2,500 which comes out of your pocket immediately in case of damage.

INSURANCE Insurance is offered in two parts: **Collision and damage** insurance covers your car and others if the accident is your fault, and **personal accident** insurance covers you and anyone in your car. Read the fine print on the back of your rental agreement and note that insurance may be invalid if you have an accident while driving on an unpaved road.

DAMAGE Inspect your car carefully and note every damaged or missing item, no matter how minute, on your rental agreement, or you may be charged.

By Taxi

Taxis are the preferred way to get around almost all of Mexico's resort areas. Fares for short trips within towns are generally preset by zone, and are quite reasonable compared with U.S. rates. For longer trips or excursions to nearby cities, taxis can generally be hired for around $15 to $20 per hour, or for a negotiated daily rate. A negotiated one-way price is usually much less than the cost of a rental car for a day, and a taxi travels much faster than a bus. For anyone who is uncomfortable driving in Mexico, this is a convenient, comfortable alternative. A bonus is that you have a Spanish-speaking person with you in case you run into trouble. Many taxi drivers speak at least some English. Your hotel can assist you with the arrangements.

By Bus

Mexican buses run frequently, are readily accessible, and can transport you almost anywhere you want to go. Taking the bus is much more common in Mexico than in the U.S., and the executive and first-class coaches can be as comfortable as business class on an airline. Buses are often the only way to get from large cities to other nearby cities and small villages. Don't hesitate to ask questions if you're confused about anything, but note that little English is spoken in bus stations.

Dozens of Mexican companies operate large, air-conditioned, Greyhound-type buses between most cities. Classes are *segunda* (second), *primera* (first), and *ejecutiva* (deluxe), which goes by a variety of names. Deluxe buses often have fewer seats than regular buses, show video movies, are air-conditioned, and make few stops. Many run express from point to point. They are well worth the few dollars more. In rural areas, buses are often of the school-bus variety, with lots of local color.

Whenever possible, it's best to buy your reserved-seat ticket, often using a computerized system, a day in advance on long-distance routes and especially before holidays.

4 MONEY & COSTS

The Value of the Mexican Peso vs. Other Popular Currencies

Pesos	US$	Can$	UK£	Euro (€)	Aus$	NZ$
100	$7.55	C$8.90	£4.98	€5.60	A$10.09	NZ$12.92

Frommer's lists exact prices in the local currency. The currency conversions quoted above were correct at press time. However, rates fluctuate, so before departing consult a currency exchange website such as **www.oanda.com/convert/classic** to check up-to-the-minute rates.

Money Matters

The **universal currency sign ($)** is used to indicate pesos in Mexico. The use of this symbol in this book, however, denotes U.S. currency.

In general, the southern region of Mexico is considerably cheaper, not just than most U.S. and European destinations, but also than many other parts of Mexico, although prices vary significantly depending on the specific location. The most expensive destinations are those with the largest number of foreign visitors, such as Cancún. The least expensive are those off the beaten path and in small rural villages, particularly in the poorer states of Tabasco and Chiapas. In the major cities, prices vary greatly depending on the neighborhood. As you might imagine, tourist zones tend to be much more expensive than local areas.

The currency in Mexico is the **peso.** Paper currency comes in denominations of 20, 50, 100, 200, and 500 pesos. Coins come in denominations of 1, 2, 5, 10, and 20 pesos, and 20 and 50 **centavos** (100 centavos = 1 peso).

Getting **change** is a problem. Small-denomination bills and coins are hard to come by, so start collecting them early in your trip. Shopkeepers and taxi drivers everywhere always seem to be out of change and small bills; that's doubly true in markets. There seems to be an expectation that the customer should provide appropriate change, rather than the other way around.

Many establishments that deal with tourists, especially in coastal resort areas, quote prices in U.S. dollars. To avoid confusion, they use the abbreviations "Dlls." for dollars and "M.N." (*moneda nacional,* or national currency) for pesos.

Don't forget to have enough pesos to carry you over a weekend or Mexican holiday, when banks are closed. In general, avoid carrying the U.S. $100 bill, the bill most commonly counterfeited in Mexico and therefore the most difficult to exchange, especially in smaller towns. Because small bills and coins in pesos are hard to come by in Mexico, the $1 bill is very useful for tipping. ***Note:*** A tip of U.S. coins, which cannot be exchanged into Mexican currency, is of no value to the service provider.

Casas de cambio (exchange houses) are generally more convenient than banks for money exchange because they have more locations and longer hours; the rate of exchange may be the same as at a bank or slightly lower. Before leaving a bank or exchange-house window, count your change in front of the teller before the next client steps up.

Large airports have currency-exchange counters that often stay open whenever flights are operating. Though convenient, they generally do not offer the most favorable rates.

A hotel's exchange desk commonly pays less favorable rates than banks; however, when the currency is in a state of flux, higher-priced hotels are known to pay higher rates than banks, in an effort to attract dollars. ***Note:*** In almost all cases, you receive a better rate by changing money first, then paying.

The bottom line on exchanging money: Ask first, and shop around. Banks generally pay the top rates.

You'll avoid lines at airport ATMs by exchanging at least some money—just enough to cover airport incidentals and transportation to your hotel—before you leave home (though don't expect the exchange rate to be ideal). You can exchange money at your local American Express or Thomas Cook office or at your bank. American Express also dispenses traveler's checks and foreign currency via www.americanexpress.com or ✆ **800/221-7282.**

Banks in Mexico have expanded and improved services. Except in the smallest towns, they tend to be open weekdays from 9am until 5pm, and often for at least a half day on Saturday. In larger resorts and cities, they can generally accommodate the exchange of dollars (which used to stop at noon) anytime during business hours. Some, but not all, banks charge a 1% fee to exchange traveler's checks. But you can pay for most purchases directly with traveler's checks at the establishment's stated exchange rate. Don't even bother with personal checks drawn on a U.S. bank—the bank will wait for your check to clear, which can take weeks, before giving you your money.

Travelers to Mexico can easily withdraw money from **ATMs** in most major cities and resort areas. The U.S. Department of State recommends caution when you're using ATMs in Mexico, stating that they should only be used during business hours and in large protected facilities, but this pertains primarily to Mexico City, where crime remains a significant problem. In most resorts in Mexico, the use of ATMs is perfectly safe—just use the same precautions you would at any ATM. Universal bank cards (such as the Cirrus and PLUS systems) can be used. This is a convenient way to withdraw money and avoid carrying too much with you at any time. The exchange rate is generally more favorable than at *casas de cambio.* Most machines offer Spanish/English menus and dispense pesos, but some offer the option of withdrawing dollars.

The **Cirrus** (✆ **800/424-7787;** www.mastercard.com) and **PLUS** (✆ **800/843-7587;** www.visa.com) networks span the globe. Go to

Tips A Few Words About Prices

Prices in this book have been converted to the U.S. dollar at 13 pesos. Most hotels in Mexico—except places that receive little foreign tourism—quote prices in U.S. dollars. Thus, currency fluctuations are unlikely to affect the prices most hotels charge.

Mexico has a **value-added tax** of 15% (*Impuesto de Valor Agregado*, or IVA; pronounced "*ee*-bah") on most everything, including restaurant meals, bus tickets, and souvenirs. Hotels charge the usual 15% IVA, plus a locally administered bed tax of 2% (in most areas), for a total of 17%. The prices quoted by hotels and restaurants do not necessarily include IVA. You may find that upper-end properties (three or more stars) quote prices without IVA included, while lower-priced hotels include IVA. Ask to see a printed price sheet and ask if the tax is included.

your bank card's website to find ATM locations at your destination. Be sure you know your daily withdrawal limit before you depart. ***Note:*** Many banks impose a fee every time you use a card at another bank's ATM, and that fee can be higher for international transactions (although seldom more than $2 in Mexico) than for domestic ones. In addition, the bank from which you withdraw cash may charge its own fee. For international withdrawal fees, ask your bank.

Credit cards are another safe way to carry money. They also provide a convenient record of all your expenses, and they generally offer relatively good exchange rates. You can withdraw cash advances from your credit cards at banks or ATMs, but high fees make credit-card cash advances a pricey way to get cash. Keep in mind that you'll pay interest from the moment of your withdrawal, even if you pay your monthly bills on time. Also, note that many banks now assess a 1% to 3% "transaction fee" on **all** charges you incur abroad (whether you're using the local currency or your native currency).

In Mexico, Visa, MasterCard, and American Express are the most accepted cards. You'll be able to charge most hotel, restaurant, and store purchases, as well as almost all airline tickets, on your credit card. Pemex gas stations have begun to accept credit card purchases for gasoline, though this option may not be available everywhere and often not at night—check before you pump. You can get cash advances of several hundred dollars on your card, but there may be a wait of 20 minutes to 2 hours. Charges will be made in pesos, then converted into dollars by the bank issuing the credit card. Generally you receive the favorable bank rate when paying by credit card. However, be aware that some establishments in Mexico add a 5% to 7% surcharge when you pay with a credit card. This is especially true when using American Express. Many times, advertised discounts will not apply if you pay with a credit card.

5 HEALTH

GENERAL AVAILABILITY OF HEALTH CARE

In most of Mexico's resort destinations, you can usually find health care that meets U.S. standards. Care in more remote areas is limited. Standards of medical training, patient care, and business practices vary greatly among medical facilities in beach resorts throughout Mexico. Puerto Vallarta has first-rate hospitals, for example, but other cities along the Pacific Coast generally do not. In recent years, some U.S. citizens have complained that certain health-care facilities in beach resorts have taken advantage of them by overcharging or providing unnecessary medical care.

Prescription medicine is broadly available at Mexican pharmacies; however, be aware that you may need a copy of your prescription or to obtain a prescription from a local doctor.

Contact the **International Association for Medical Assistance to Travellers (IAMAT; ✆ 716/754-4883** or, in Canada, 416/652-0137; www.iamat.org) for tips on travel and health concerns in the countries you're visiting and for lists of local, English-speaking doctors. The United States **Centers for Disease Control and Prevention** (**✆ 800/ CDC INFO;** www.cdc.gov) provides up-to-date information on health hazards by region or country, and offers tips on food safety. **Travel Health Online** (www.tripprep.com), sponsored by a consortium of travel medicine practitioners, may also offer helpful advice on traveling abroad. You can find listings of reliable medical clinics overseas at the **International Society of Travel Medicine** (www.istm.org).

SWINE FLU

As of June 12, 2009, the WHO had reported nearly 30,000 A(H1N1) ("swine flu") cases in 74 countries, including 145 deaths, with Mexico among the most heavily affected countries. The number of cases continued to rise worldwide, and it was too early to tell how far or for how long the virus would spread. The **World Health Organization (WHO)** pandemic alert reached level 6 at press time, signaling pandemic, although with moderate severity. According to the **Centers for Disease Control and Prevention (CDC),** the symptoms of this contagious virus are similar to those of seasonal flu and include fever, cough, sore throat, runny or stuffy nose, body aches, headache, chills, and fatigue. Many people who have been infected with this virus also reported diarrhea and vomiting. Like seasonal flu, severe symptoms and death have occurred as a result of illness associated with this virus. It is important to note, however, that most cases of influenza are not the A(H1N1) virus. For the latest information regarding the risks of swine flu when traveling to Mexico, and what to do if you get sick, please consult the **U.S. State Department's** website at www.travel.state.gov, the **CDC** website at www.cdc.gov, or the website of the **World Health Organization** at www.who.int.

COMMON AILMENTS

SUN/ELEMENTS/EXTREME WEATHER EXPOSURE Mexico is synonymous with sunshine; most of the country is bathed in intense sunshine for much of the year. Avoid excessive exposure, especially in the tropics where UV rays are more dangerous. The hottest months in Mexico's south are April and May, but the sun is intense most of the year.

DIETARY RED FLAGS Travelers' diarrhea (locally known as *turista,* the Spanish word for "tourist")—persistent diarrhea, often accompanied by fever, nausea, and vomiting—used to attack many travelers to Mexico. (Some in the U.S. call this "Montezuma's revenge," but you won't hear it called that in Mexico.) Widespread improvements in infrastructure, sanitation, and education have greatly diminished this ailment, especially in well-developed resort areas. Most travelers make a habit of drinking only bottled water, which also helps to protect against unfamiliar bacteria. In resort areas, and generally throughout Mexico, only purified ice is used. If you do come down with this ailment, nothing beats Pepto Bismol, readily available in Mexico. Imodium is also available in Mexico and is used by many travelers for a quick fix. A good high-potency (or "therapeutic") vitamin supplement and even extra vitamin C can help; yogurt is good for healthy digestion.

Since dehydration can quickly become life-threatening, the Public Health Service advises that you be careful to replace fluids and electrolytes (potassium, sodium, and the like) during a bout of diarrhea. Drink Pedialyte, a rehydration solution available at most Mexican pharmacies, or natural fruit juice, such as guava or apple (stay away from orange juice, which has laxative properties), with a pinch of salt added.

The U.S. Public Health Service recommends the following measures for preventing travelers' diarrhea: **Drink only purified water** (boiled water, canned or bottled beverages, beer, or wine). **Choose**

Over-the-Counter Drugs in Mexico

Antibiotics and other drugs that you'd need a prescription to buy in the States are often available over the counter in Mexican pharmacies. Mexican pharmacies also carry a limited selection of common over-the-counter cold, sinus, and allergy remedies.

food carefully. In general, avoid salads (except in first-class restaurants), uncooked vegetables, undercooked protein, and unpasteurized milk or milk products, including cheese. Choose food that is freshly cooked and still hot. Avoid eating food prepared by street vendors. In addition, something as simple as **clean hands** can go a long way toward preventing *turista.*

HIGH-ALTITUDE HAZARDS Travelers to certain regions of Mexico occasionally experience **elevation sickness,** which results from the relative lack of oxygen and the decrease in barometric pressure that characterizes high elevations (more than 1,500m/5,000 ft.). Symptoms include shortness of breath, fatigue, headache, insomnia, and even nausea. Mexico City is at 2,240m (7,349 ft.) above sea level, as are a number of other central and southern cities, such as San Cristóbal de las Casas (even higher than Mexico City). At high elevations, it takes about 10 days to acquire the extra red blood corpuscles you need to adjust to the scarcity of oxygen. To help your body acclimate, drink plenty of fluids, avoid alcohol, and don't overexert yourself during the first few days. If you have heart or lung trouble, consult your doctor before flying above 2,400m (7,872 ft.).

BUGS, BITES & OTHER WILDLIFE CONCERNS **Mosquitoes** are prevalent along the coast. *Repelente contra insectos* (insect repellent) is a must, and it's not always available in Mexico. If you'll be in these areas and are prone to bites, bring along a repellent that contains the active ingredient DEET. Avon's Skin So Soft also works extremely well. Another good remedy to keep the mosquitoes away is to mix citronella essential oil with basil, clove, and lavender essential oils. If you're sensitive to bites, pick up some antihistamine cream from a drugstore at home.

Most readers won't ever see an *alacrán* (scorpion). But if one stings you, go immediately to a doctor. The one lethal scorpion found in some parts of Mexico is the *Centruroides,* part of the Buthidae family, characterized by a thin body, thick tail, and triangular-shaped sternum. Most deaths from these scorpions result within 24 hours of the sting as a result of respiratory or cardiovascular failure, with children and elderly people most at risk. Scorpions are not aggressive (they don't hunt for prey), but they may sting if touched, especially in their hiding places. In Mexico, you can buy scorpion toxin antidote at any drugstore. It is an injection, and it costs around $25. This is a good idea if you plan to camp in a remote area, where medical assistance can be several hours away.

TROPICAL ILLNESSES You shouldn't be overly concerned about tropical diseases if you stay on the normal tourist routes and don't eat street food. However, both dengue fever and cholera have appeared in Mexico in recent years. Talk to your doctor or to a medical specialist in tropical diseases about precautions you should take. You can also get medical bulletins from the U.S. Department of State and the Centers for Disease Control and Prevention (see "General Availability of Health Care," earlier in this chapter). You can protect yourself by taking some simple precautions: Watch what you eat and drink; don't swim in stagnant water (ponds, slow-moving rivers, or wells); and avoid mosquito bites by covering up, using repellent, and sleeping under netting. The most dangerous areas seem to be on Mexico's west coast, away from the big resorts.

On occasion, coastal waters from the Gulf of Mexico can become contaminated with rapid growth in algae (phytoplankton), leading to a phenomenon known as harmful algal bloom or a "red tide." The algal release of neurotoxins threatens marine life and can cause rashes and even flu-like symptoms in exposed humans. Although red tides happen infrequently, you should not enter the water if you notice a reddish-brown color or are told there is a red tide.

WHAT TO DO IF YOU GET SICK AWAY FROM HOME

Any English-speaking embassy or consulate staff in Mexico can provide a list of area doctors who speak English. The U.S. Embassy's consular section, for example, keeps a list of reliable English-speaking doctors. If you get sick in Mexico, consider asking your hotel concierge to recommend a local doctor—even his or her own. You can also try the emergency room at a local hospital or urgent care facility. Many hospitals also have walk-in clinics for emergency cases that are not life-threatening; you may not get immediate attention, but you won't pay emergency room prices.

For travel to Mexico, you may have to pay all medical costs upfront and be reimbursed later. Medicare and Medicaid do not provide coverage for medical costs outside the U.S. (that means neither Medicare nor Medicaid reimburses for emergency health care in Mexico, either). Before leaving home, find out what medical services your

Smoke-Free Mexico?

In early 2008, the Mexican president signed into law a nationwide smoking ban in workplaces and public buildings, and on public transportation. Under this groundbreaking law, private businesses are permitted to allow public smoking only in enclosed ventilated areas. Hotels may maintain up to 25% of guest rooms for smokers. Violators face stiff fines, and smokers refusing to comply could receive up to 36-hour jail sentences. Despite some uncertainty over how thoroughly the legislation is being followed and enforced throughout different parts of the country, they place Mexico—where a significant percentage of the population smokes—at the forefront of efforts to curb smoking and improve public health in Latin America. So before you light up, be sure to ask about the application of local laws in Mexican public places and businesses you visit.

health insurance covers. To protect yourself, consider buying medical travel insurance.

Very few health insurance plans pay for medical evacuation back to the U.S. (which can cost $10,000 and more). A number of companies offer global medical evacuation services. If you're ever hospitalized more than 150 miles from home, **MedjetAssist** (© **800/527-7478;** www.medjetassist.com) will pick you up and fly you to the hospital of your choice, virtually anywhere, in a medically equipped and staffed aircraft—24 hours day, 7 days a week. Annual memberships are $250 individual, $385 family; you can also purchase short-term memberships.

It is generally less expensive and more reliable to contract a U.S.-based company for a medical evacuation from Mexico to the U.S. than to contract a Mexican-based company. Contact the consular affairs section of the U.S. Embassy in Mexico City or nearest consulate for suggestions.

6 SAFETY

Although the vast majority of visitors to Mexico return home unharmed, it should be noted that taxi robberies, kidnappings, highway carjackings, and other crimes have beset tourists as well as locals in recent years. And in border regions and some other parts of Mexico—including Acapulco and the state of Guerrero—drug-related violence and organized crime have escalated significantly.

Throughout Mexico, precautions are necessary, but travelers should be realistic. You can generally trust a person whom you approach for help or directions, but be wary of anyone who approaches you offering the same. The more insistent the person is, the more cautious you should be.

Exercise caution when you're in unfamiliar areas, and be aware of your surroundings at all times. Leave valuables and irreplaceable items in a safe place, or don't bring them at all. A significant number of pickpocket incidents, purse snatchings, and hotel-room thefts do occur. Use hotel safes when available. And remember that public transportation is a popular place for wallet thefts and purse snatchings.

Enjoy the ocean, but don't swim alone in isolated beach areas because of strong currents and powerful waves. Try to swim where a lifeguard is present. All beaches in Mexico are public by law, and it is best not to be out on the beaches at night. In Acapulco, it's best to avoid swimming outside the bay area. According to the U.S. State Department, several people have died while swimming in rough surf at the Revolcadero Beach near Acapulco. Several people have also drowned in the area of Zipolite Beach in Puerto Angel, Oaxaca because of sudden waves and strong currents.

Before you travel to any notable hot spots in Mexico (see below), consult **www.travel.state.gov** for the U.S. Department of State's country specific information and travel alerts.

CRIME IN RESORT TOWNS

There have been a number of rapes reported in Mexico's resort areas, usually at night or in the early morning. Armed street crime is a serious problem in all the major cities. Some bars and nightclubs, especially in resort cities such as Acapulco, can be havens for drug dealers and petty criminals.

HIGHWAY SAFETY

Travelers should exercise caution while traveling Mexican highways, avoiding travel at night, and using toll *(cuota)* roads rather than the less secure free *(libre)* roads whenever possible. It is also advised that you should not hike alone in backcountry areas nor walk alone on less-frequented beaches, ruins, or trails.

Travelers are advised to cooperate with official checkpoints when traveling on Mexican highways. Avoid driving along coastal roads at night, and try not to drive alone.

Bus travel should take place during daylight hours on first-class conveyances. Although bus hijackings and robberies have occurred on toll roads, buses on toll roads have a markedly lower rate of incidents than second-class and third-class buses that travel the less secure "free" highways.

BRIBES & SCAMS

As is the case around the world, there are the occasional bribes and scams in Mexico, targeted at people believed to be naive, such as telltale tourists. For years, Mexico was known as a place where bribes—called *mordidas* (bites)—were expected; however, the country is rapidly changing. Frequently, offering a bribe today, especially to a police officer, is considered an insult, and it can land you in deeper trouble.

When you are crossing the border, should the person who inspects your car ask for a tip, you can ignore this request—but understand that the official may suddenly decide that a complete search of your belongings is in order. If you sense you're being asked for a bribe, understand that although it may be common, offering a bribe to a public official to avoid a ticket or other penalty is officially a crime in Mexico.

Many tourists have the impression that everything works better in Mexico if you "tip"; however, in reality, this only perpetuates the *mordida* tradition. If you are pleased with a service, feel free to tip. But you shouldn't tip simply to attempt to get away with something illegal or inappropriate—whether it is evading a ticket that's deserved or a car inspection as you're crossing the border.

Whatever you do, avoid impoliteness; you won't do yourself any favors if you insult a Mexican official. Extreme politeness, even in the face of adversity, rules Mexico. In Mexico, *gringos* have a reputation for being loud and demanding. By adopting the local custom of excessive courtesy, you'll have greater success in negotiations of any kind. Stand your ground, but do it politely.

As you travel in Mexico, you may encounter several types of scams, which are typical throughout the world. One involves some kind of a distraction or feigned commotion. While your attention is diverted, for example, a pickpocket makes a grab for your wallet. In another common scam, an unaccompanied child pretends to be lost and frightened and takes your hand for safety. Meanwhile the child or an accomplice plunders your pockets. A third involves confusing currency. A shoeshine boy, street musician, guide, or other individual might offer you a service for a price that seems reasonable—in pesos. When it comes time to pay, he or she tells you the price is in dollars, not pesos. Be very clear on the price and currency when services are involved.

7 SPECIALIZED TRAVEL RESOURCES

In addition to the destination-specific resources listed below, please visit Frommers.com for additional specialized travel resources.

GAY & LESBIAN TRAVELERS

Mexico is a conservative country, with deeply rooted Catholic religious traditions. Public displays of same-sex affection are rare and still considered shocking for men, especially outside of urban or resort areas. Women in Mexico frequently walk hand in hand, but anything more would cross the boundary of acceptability. However, gay and lesbian travelers are generally treated with respect and should not experience harassment, assuming they give the appropriate regard to local customs.

Acapulco is one of Mexico's most gay friendly resort cities, including hotels, bars and clubs that cater to the community. For more information, visit **MexGay Vacations** at www.mexgay.com. Information about gay-friendly accommodations is available at www.gayplaces2stay.com.

The International Gay and Lesbian Travel Association (**IGLTA;** ✆ **800/448-8550** or 954/776-2626; www.iglta.org) is the trade association for the gay and lesbian travel industry, and offers an online directory of gay- and lesbian-friendly travel businesses and tour operators.

Many agencies offer tours and travel itineraries specifically for gay and lesbian travelers. Among them are **Above and Beyond Tours** (✆ **800/397-2681;** www.abovebeyondtours.com); **Now, Voyager** (✆ **800/255-6951;** www.nowvoyager.com); and **Olivia Cruises & Resorts** (✆ **800/631-6277;** www.olivia.com).

Gay.com Travel (✆ **415/834-6500;** www.gay.com/travel or www.outandabout.com) is an excellent online successor to the popular ***Out & About*** print magazine. It provides regularly updated information about gay-owned, gay-oriented, and gay-friendly lodging, dining, sightseeing, nightlife, and shopping establishments in every important destination worldwide. British travelers should click on the "Travel" link at **www.gaybritain.co.uk/flash5/player.asp** for advice and gay-friendly trip ideas.

The Canadian website **GayTraveler** (www.gaytraveler.ca) offers ideas and advice for gay travel all over the world.

The following travel guides are available at many bookstores, or you can order them from any online bookseller: ***Spartacus International***

Gay Guide, 35th Edition (Bruno Gmünder Verlag; www.spartacus world.com/gayguide), and the *Damron* guides (www.damron.com), with separate, annual books for gay men and lesbians.

For more gay and lesbian travel resources, see **www.frommers.com/planning**.

TRAVELERS WITH DISABILITIES

Mexico may seem like one giant obstacle course to travelers in wheelchairs or on crutches. At airports, you may encounter steep stairs before finding a well-hidden elevator or escalator—if one exists. Airlines will often arrange wheelchair assistance to the baggage area. Porters are generally available to help with luggage at airports and large bus stations, once you've cleared baggage claim.

Mexican airports are upgrading their services, but it is not uncommon to board from a remote position, meaning you either descend stairs to a bus that ferries you to the plane, which you board by climbing stairs, or you walk across the tarmac to your plane and ascend the stairs. Deplaning presents the same problem in reverse.

Escalators (and there aren't many in the country) are often out of order. Stairs without handrails abound. Few restrooms are equipped for travelers with disabilities; when one is available, access to it may be through a narrow passage that won't accommodate a wheelchair or a person on crutches. Many deluxe hotels (the most expensive) now have rooms with bathrooms designed for people with disabilities. Those traveling on a budget should stick with one-story hotels or hotels with elevators. Even so, there will probably still be obstacles somewhere. Generally speaking, no matter where you are, someone will lend a hand, although you may have to ask for it.

Most disabilities shouldn't stop anyone from traveling. There are more options and resources out there than ever before.

Organizations that offer a vast range of resources and assistance to travelers with disabilities include **MossRehab** (www.mossresourcenet.org); the **American Foundation for the Blind (AFB; ✆ 800/232-5463;** www.afb.org); and **SATH (Society for Accessible Travel & Hospitality; ✆ 212/447-7284;** www.sath.org). **AirAmbulanceCard.com** (**✆ 800/631-6565**) is now partnered with SATH and allows you to pre-select top-notch hospitals in case of an emergency.

Access-Able Travel Source (www.access-able.com) offers a comprehensive database on travel agents from around the world with experience in accessible travel; destination-specific access information; and links to such resources as service animals, equipment rentals, and access guides.

Many travel agencies offer customized tours and itineraries for travelers with disabilities. Among them are **Flying Wheels Travel**

(✆ **507/451-5005;** www.flyingwheelstravel.com) and **Accessible Journeys** (✆ **800/846-4537** or 610/521-0339; www.disabilitytravel.com).

Flying with Disability (www.flying-with-disability.org) is a comprehensive information source on airplane travel. **Avis Rent a Car** (✆ **888/879-4273**) offers services for customers with special travel needs. These include specially outfitted vehicles with swivel seats, spinner knobs, and hand controls; mobility scooter rentals; and accessible bus service. Be sure to reserve well in advance.

Also check out the quarterly magazine ***Emerging Horizons*** (www.emerginghorizons.com), available by subscription ($16.95 inside the U.S.; $21.95 outside the U.S.).

The "Accessible Travel" link at **Mobility-Advisor.com** (www.mobility-advisor.com) offers a variety of travel resources to people with disabilities.

British travelers should contact **Holiday Care** (✆ **0845/124-9971** in the U.K. only; www.holidaycare.org.uk) to access a wide range of travel information and resources for people with disabilities and elderly people.

For more on organizations that offer resources to travelers with disabilities, go to **www.frommers.com/planning**.

FAMILY TRAVEL

If you have trouble getting your kids out of the house in the morning, dragging them thousands of miles away may seem like an insurmountable challenge. But family travel can be immensely rewarding, giving you new ways of seeing the world through the eyes of children.

Children are considered the national treasure of Mexico, and Mexicans will warmly welcome and cater to your children. Many parents were reluctant to bring young children into Mexico in the past, primarily due to health concerns, but I can't think of a better place to introduce children to the exciting adventure of exploring a different culture. Hotels can often arrange for a babysitter.

Before leaving, ask your doctor which medications to take along. Disposable diapers cost about the same in Mexico but are of poorer quality. You can get Huggies Supreme and Pampers identical to the ones sold in the United States, but at a higher price. Many stores sell Gerber's baby foods. Dry cereals, powdered formulas, baby bottles, and purified water are easily available in midsize and large cities or resorts.

Cribs may present a problem; only the largest and most luxurious hotels provide them. However, rollaway beds are often available. Child seats or high chairs at restaurants are common.

Consider bringing your own car seat; they are not readily available for rent in Mexico.

Every country's regulations differ, but in general children traveling abroad should have plenty of documentation on hand, particularly if they're traveling with someone other than their own parents (in which case a notarized form letter from a parent is often required). For details on entry requirements for children traveling abroad, go to the U.S. Department of State website (www.travel.state.gov); click on "International Travel," "Travel Brochures," and "Foreign Entry Requirements."

Recommended family travel websites include **Family Travel Forum** (www.familytravelforum.com), a comprehensive site that offers customized trip planning; **Family Travel Network** (www.familytravelnetwork.com), an online magazine providing travel tips; and **TravelWithYourKids.com** (www.travelwithyourkids.com), a comprehensive site written by parents for parents, offering sound advice for long-distance and international travel with children.

For a list of more family-friendly travel resources, visit **www.frommers.com/planning**.

To locate accommodations, restaurants, and attractions that are particularly kid friendly, refer to the "Kids" icon throughout this guide.

WOMEN TRAVELERS

Mexicans in general, and men in particular, are nosy about single travelers, especially women. If a taxi driver or anyone else with whom you don't want to become friendly asks about your marital status, family, and so forth, my advice is to make up a set of answers (regardless of the truth): "I'm married, traveling with friends, and I have three children." Saying you are single and traveling alone may send the wrong message. U.S. television—widely viewed now in Mexico—has given many Mexican men the image of American single women as being sexually promiscuous. Check out the award-winning website **Journeywoman** (www.journeywoman.com), a "real-life" women's travel information network where you can sign up for a free e-mail newsletter and get advice on everything from etiquette and dress to safety; or the travel guide ***Safety and Security for Women Who Travel,*** by Sheila Swan and Peter Laufer (Travelers' Tales, Inc.), offering common-sense tips on safe travel.

For general travel resources for women, go to www.frommers.com/planning.

SENIOR TRAVEL

Mexico is a popular country for retirees. For decades, North Americans have been living indefinitely in Mexico by returning to the border and recrossing with a new tourist permit every 6 months. Mexican immigration officials have caught on, and now limit the maximum time in the country to 6 months within any year. This is to encourage even partial residents to acquire proper documentation.

AIM-Adventures in Mexico, Apartado Postal 31–70, 45050 Guadalajara, Jalisco, is a well-written, informative newsletter for prospective retirees. Issues have evaluated retirement in Pacific Mexico destinations such as Puerto Angel, Puerto Escondido and Huatulco, Oaxaca, Taxco. Subscriptions are $29 to the United States.

Sanborn Tours, 2015 S. 10th St., P.O. Drawer 519, McAllen, TX 78505-0519 (© **800/395-8482;** www.sanborns.com), offers a "Retire in Mexico" orientation tour.

Mention the fact that you're a senior citizen when you make your travel reservations. Although all the major U.S. airlines have canceled their senior discount and coupon book programs, many hotels still offer lower rates for seniors. In most cities, people older than 60 qualify for reduced admission to theaters, museums, and other attractions, and discounted fares on public transportation.

Members of **AARP,** 601 E St. NW, Washington, DC 20049 (© **888 /687-2277;** www.aarp.org), get discounts on hotels, airfares, and car rentals. AARP offers members a wide range of benefits, including *AARP: The Magazine* (www.aarpmagazine.org) and a monthly newsletter. Anyone over 50 can join.

Many reliable agencies and organizations target the 50-plus market. **Elderhostel** (© **800/454-5768;** www.elderhostel.org) arranges study programs for those age 55 and older. **ElderTreks** (© **800/741-7956;** U.K. 0808/234-1714; international 416/588-5000; www.eldertreks.com) offers small-group tours to off-the-beaten-path or adventure-travel locations, restricted to travelers 50 and older.

Recommended publications offering travel resources and discounts for seniors include: the quarterly magazine ***Travel 50 & Beyond*** (www.travel50andbeyond.com) and the bestselling paperback ***Unbelievably Good Deals and Great Adventures That You Absolutely Can't Get Unless You're Over 50 2005–2006, 16th Edition*** (McGraw-Hill), by Joann Rattner Heilman.

For more information and resources on travel for seniors, see **www.frommers.com/planning**.

STUDENT TRAVEL

Because Mexicans consider higher education a luxury rather than a birthright, there is no formal network of student discounts and programs. Most Mexican students travel with their families rather than with other students, so student discount cards are not commonly recognized.

However, more hostels have entered the student travel scene. **Hostels.com.mx** offers a list that includes hostels in Acapulco, Oaxaca, and Puerto Escondido.

8 SUSTAINABLE TOURISM

Sustainable tourism is conscientious travel. It means being careful with the environments you explore and respecting the communities you visit. Two overlapping components of sustainable travel are **ecotourism** and **ethical tourism. The International Ecotourism Society (TIES)** defines ecotourism as responsible travel to natural areas that conserves the environment and improves the well-being of local people. TIES suggests that ecotourists follow these principles:

- Minimize environmental impact.
- Build environmental and cultural awareness and respect.
- Provide positive experiences for both visitors and hosts.
- Provide direct financial benefits for conservation and for local people.
- Raise sensitivity to host countries' political, environmental, and social climates.
- Support international human rights and labor agreements.

You can find some eco-friendly travel tips and statistics, as well as touring companies and associations—listed by destination under "Travel Choice"—at the **TIES** website, **www.ecotourism.org**. Also check out **www.ecotravel.com**, which lets you search for sustainable touring companies in several categories (water-based, land-based, spiritually oriented, and so on).

While much of the focus of ecotourism is about reducing impacts on the natural environment, ethical tourism concentrates on ways to preserve and enhance local economies and communities, regardless of location. You can embrace ethical tourism by staying at a locally owned hotel or shopping at a store that employs local workers and sells locally produced goods.

Responsible Travel (www.responsibletravel.com) is a great source of sustainable travel ideas; the site is run by a spokesperson for ethical tourism in the travel industry. **Sustainable Travel International** (www.sustainabletravelinternational.org) promotes ethical tourism practices, and manages an extensive directory of sustainable properties and tour operators around the world.

In the U.K., **Tourism Concern** (www.tourismconcern.org.uk) works to reduce social and environmental problems connected to tourism. The **Association of Independent Tour Operators (AITO;**

www.aito.co.uk) is a group of specialist operators leading the field in making holidays sustainable.

Volunteer travel has become increasingly popular among those who want to venture beyond the standard group-tour experience to learn languages, interact with locals, and make a positive difference while on vacation. Volunteer travel usually doesn't require special skills—just a willingness to work hard—and programs vary in length from a few days to a number of weeks. Some programs provide free housing and food, but many require volunteers to pay for travel expenses, which can add up fast.

For general information on volunteer travel, visit **www.volunteer abroad.org** and **www.idealist.org**. Specific volunteer options in Mexico are listed under "Special Interest Trips," later in this chapter.

Before you commit to a volunteer program, it's important to make sure any money you're giving is truly going back to the local community, and that the work you'll be doing will be a good fit for you. **Volunteer International** (www.volunteerinternational.org) has a helpful list of questions to ask to determine the intentions and the nature of a volunteer program.

SUSTAINABLE TOURISM IN SOUTHERN PACIFIC MEXICO

The coast of Oaxaca State is one of Mexico's most diverse regions, with more indigenous languages spoken than any other state in Mexico. Economically though, Oaxaca is also one of Mexico's least developed states. The region depends largely on tourism, yet despite the huge government investment at Huatulco with hopes to duplicate Cancún, tourism has yet to really boom along the coast. This can be great for the independent traveler looking to avoid crowds. The Oaxaca Coast is isolated from the interior, cut off by the Sierra Madre del Sur mountain range. It's a treacherous and tortuous 8-hour journey over a twisting mountain highway from the capital of Oaxaca City, a jewel in Mexico's tourism cache, and a 5-hour drive south of Acapulco.

This piece of Pacific Coast, known as "El País de la Tortuga," or Turtle Country, is home to 10 of the world's 11 varieties of sea turtle. For decades, the primary source of income for the coastal Oaxaqueño villages was sea turtle poaching. The communities just south of Puerto Escondido are said to have killed 1,000 turtles a day in the 1980s, which threatened the very existence of the entire species. A heavily enforced federal law passed in 1990 made the killing of turtles illegal. While this immediately halted the slaughter, it left dozens of villages without any means of monetary support practically overnight.

The town of **Mazunte,** approximately 64km (40 miles) south of Puerto Escondido, was one such community. In 1991 the government turned the town's shuttered cannery into the **Centro Mexicano de la Tortuga** (Mexican Center for the Turtle; Spanish-only website, **www.centromexicanodelatortuga.org**, or **www.tomzap.com/turtle.html**), with the intention of attracting tourism. Today, this is Mexico's premier turtle research center and sanctuary. Visitors tour the facility with a researcher or volunteer whose main focus is to discuss the fragility of the turtle life cycle and foster respect for their ecosystem which is shared by the coastal Oaxaqueño communities.

A sea turtle reaches reproductive age at 15, which means the turtle population on the Oaxca Coast will only have the potential to grow after 2009. Thus, much emphasis is placed on caring for the turtles' nests. While traveling throughout this region you will likely see armed troops shuttling back and forth to the beaches to prevent looters and poachers from stealing eggs. Near Puerto Escondido, Playa Escobilla is a favorite nesting ground. Here, visitors can make overnight trips from July to September, when the turtles heave themselves on shore to lay their eggs. The cost is a mere 20 pesos ($1.80) and must be arranged in person at the **Centro Mexicano de la Tortuga.**

Turtle tourism isn't the only eco-tourism to be found in the region. The coast here is also a magnet for migratory birds, and visitors can bird watch in two nearby lagoons. The presence of birds will permeate any trip to the region, even if the traveler does not intentionally seek them out. You can hear them singing even while you swim in the ocean, they're that prevalent. **Parque Nacional Lagunas Chacahua** is a 32km-long (20 miles) brackish mangrove lagoon which was overfished by locals some 30 years ago and subsequently protected by the government. Today, you can take a noisy motorboat tour with one of the former fishermen, who will ferry you to the isolated towns and beaches on the lagoon. In Puerto Escondido, contact either **Rutas de Aventura,** run by Gustavo Boltjes at the Hotel Santa Fe (✆ **954/588-0457;** Spanish-only website www.rutasdeaventura.com.mx), or **Agencia de Viajes Dimar,** for Michael Malone's Hidden Voyages Ecotours (✆ **954/582-0734;** www.viajesdimar.com).

AMTAVE (Asociación Mexicana de Turismo de Aventura y Ecoturismo, A.C.) is an active association of ecotourism and adventure tour operators. It publishes an annual catalog of participating firms and their offerings, all of which must meet certain criteria for security, quality, and training of the guides, as well as for sustainability of natural and cultural environments. For more information, contact **AMTAVE** (✆ **55/5688-3883;** www.amtave.org).

General Resources for Green Travel

In addition to the resources for the Southern Pacific Coast listed above, the following websites provide valuable wide-ranging information on sustainable travel. For a list of even more sustainable resources, as well as tips and explanations on how to travel greener, visit www.frommers.com/planning.

- **Responsible Travel** (www.responsibletravel.com) is a great source of sustainable travel ideas; the site is run by a spokesperson for ethical tourism in the travel industry. **Sustainable Travel International** (www.sustainabletravel international.org) promotes ethical tourism practices, and manages an extensive directory of sustainable properties and tour operators around the world.
- In the U.K., **Tourism Concern** (www.tourismconcern.org.uk) works to reduce social and environmental problems connected to tourism. The **Association of Independent Tour Operators (AITO)** (www.aito.co.uk) is a group of specialist operators leading the field in making holidays sustainable.
- In Canada, **www.greenlivingonline.com** offers extensive content on how to travel sustainably, including a travel and transport section and profiles of the best green shops and services in Toronto, Vancouver, and Calgary.
- In Australia, the national body which sets guidelines and standards for ecotourism is **Ecotourism Australia** (www.ecotourism.org.au). **The Green Directory** (www.thegreen directory.com.au), **Green Pages** (www.thegreenpages.com.au), and **Eco Directory** (www.ecodirectory.com.au) offer sustainable travel tips and directories of green businesses.

ANIMAL RIGHTS ISSUES

The Pacific Coast presents many opportunities to swim with dolphins. The capture of wild dolphins was outlawed in Mexico in 2002. The only dolphins added to the country's dolphin swim programs since then were born in captivity. This law may have eased concerns about the death and implications of capturing wild dolphins, but the controversy is not over. Marine biologists who run the dolphin swim

- **Carbonfund** (www.carbonfund.org), **TerraPass** (www.terrapass.org), and **Carbon Neutral** (www.carbonneutral.org) provide info on "carbon offsetting," or offsetting the greenhouse gas emitted during flights.
- **Greenhotels** (www.greenhotels.com) recommends green-rated member hotels around the world that fulfill the company's stringent environmental requirements. **Environmentally Friendly Hotels** (www.environmentallyfriendlyhotels.com) offers more green accommodation ratings. The **Hotel Association of Canada** (www.hacgreenhotels.com) has a Green Key Eco-Rating Program, which audits the environmental performance of Canadian hotels, motels, and resorts.
- **Sustain Lane** (www.sustainlane.com) lists sustainable eating and drinking choices around the U.S.; also visit **www.eatwellguide.org** for tips on eating sustainably in the U.S. and Canada.
- For information on animal-friendly issues throughout the world, visit **Tread Lightly** (www.treadlightly.org). For information about the ethics of swimming with dolphins, visit the **Whale and Dolphin Conservation Society** (www.wdcs.org).
- **Volunteer International** (www.volunteerinternational.org) has a list of questions to help you determine the intentions and the nature of a volunteer program. For general info on volunteer travel, visit **www.volunteerabroad.org** and **www.idealist.org**.

programs say the mammals are thriving and that the programs provide a forum for research, conservation, education, and rescue operations. Animal rights advocates maintain that keeping these intelligent mammals in captivity is nothing more than exploitation. Their argument is that these private dolphin programs don't qualify as "public display" under the Marine Mammal Protection Act because the entry fees bar most of the public from participating.

Visit the website of the **Whale and Dolphin Conservation Society** at www.wdcs.org or the **American Cetacean Society,** www.acsonline.org, for further discussion on the topic.

Bullfighting is considered an important part of Latin culture, but you should know, before you attend a *correo,* that the bulls (at least four) will ultimately be killed in a gory spectacle. This is not the case in some countries, such as France and Portugal, but the Mexicans follow the Spanish model. That said, a bullfight is a portal into understanding Mexico's Spanish colonial past, although nowadays bullfights are more of a tourist attraction, especially in tourist laden Cancún. To read more about the implications of attending a bullfight, visit **www.peta.org**, the website of People for the Ethical Treatment of Animals (PETA) (or see specifically: www.peta.org/mc/factsheet_display.asp?ID=64).

For information on animal-friendly issues throughout the world, visit **Tread Lightly** (www.treadlightly.org).

9 SPECIAL INTEREST TRIPS & ESCORTED GENERAL INTEREST TOURS

ACADEMIC TRIPS & LANGUAGE CLASSES

For Spanish-language instruction, **Instituto de Lenguajes Puerto Escondido** (**© 954/582 2055;** www.puertoschool.com) combines language classes with ecotours, active excursions, workshops and even surf classes. Homestays are available.

To explore your inner Frida or Diego while in Mexico, look into **Mexico Art Tours,** 1233 E. Baker Dr., Tempe, AZ 85282 (**© 888/783-1331** or 480/730-1764; www.mexicanarttours.com). Typically led by Jean Grimm, a specialist in the arts and cultures of Mexico, these unique tours feature compelling speakers who are themselves respected scholars and artists. Itineraries include visits to Chiapas, Guadalajara, Guanajuato, Puebla, Puerto Vallarta, Mexico City, San Miguel de Allende, and Veracruz—and other cities. Special tours involve archaeology, architecture, interior design, and culture—such as a Day of the Dead tour.

The **Archaeological Conservancy,** 5301 Central Ave. NE, Suite 402, Albuquerque, NM 87108 (**© 505/266-1540;** www.americanarchaeology.com), presents various trips each year, led by an expert, usually an archaeologist. The trips change from year to year and space is limited; make reservations early.

ATC Tours and Travel, Av. 16 de Septiembre 16, 29200 San Cristóbal de las Casas, Chis. (✆ **967/678-2550** or 678-2557; fax 967/678-3145; www.atctours.com), a Mexico-based tour operator with an excellent reputation, offers specialist-led trips, primarily in southern Mexico. In addition to trips to the ruins of Palenque and Yaxchilán (extending into Belize and Guatemala by river, plane, and bus if desired), ATC runs horseback tours to Chamula or Zinacantán, and day trips to the ruins of Toniná around San Cristóbal de las Casas; birding in the rainforests of Chiapas and Guatemala (including in the El Triunfo Reserve of Chiapas); hikes to the shops and homes of textile artists of the Chiapas highlands; and walks from the Lagos de Montebello in the Montes Azules Biosphere Reserve, with camping and canoeing. The company can also prepare custom itineraries.

ADVENTURE & WELLNESS TRIPS

Oaxaca Reservations/Zapotec Tours, 4955 North Claremont Ave., Suite B, Chicago, IL 60625 (✆ **800/446-2922** or 773/506-2444; fax 773/506-2445; www.oaxacainfo.com), offers a variety of tours to Oaxaca City and the Oaxaca coast (including Puerto Escondido and Huatulco). Its specialty trips include Day of the Dead in Oaxaca and the Food of the Gods Tour of Oaxaca. The coastal trips emphasize nature, while the Oaxaca City tours focus on the immediate area, with visits to weavers, potters, markets, and archaeological sites. This is also the U.S. contact for several hotels in Oaxaca City that offer a 10% discount for reserving online.

Trek America, P.O. Box 189, Rockaway, NJ 07866 (✆ **800/221-0596** or 973/983-1144; fax 973/983-8551; www.trekamerica.com), organizes lengthy, active trips that combine trekking, hiking, van transportation, and camping in the Yucatán, Chiapas, Oaxaca, the Copper Canyon, and Mexico's Pacific coast, and a trip that covers Mexico City, Teotihuacán, Taxco, Guadalajara, Puerto Vallarta, and Acapulco.

FOOD & WINE TRIPS

If you're looking to eat your way through Mexico, sign up with **Culinary Adventures,** 6023 Reid Dr. NW, Gig Harbor, WA 98335 (✆ **253/851-7676;** fax 253/851-9532; www.marilyntausend.com). It runs a short but select list of cooking tours in Mexico. Culinary Adventures features well-known cooks, with travel to regions known for excellent cuisine. Destinations vary each year. The owner, Marilyn Tausend, is the author of *Cocinas de la Familia* (Family Kitchens), *Savoring Mexico,* and *Mexican,* and co-author of *Mexico the Beautiful Cookbook.*

VOLUNTEER & WORKING TRIPS

For numerous links to volunteer and internship programs throughout Mexico involving teaching, caring for children, providing health care, feeding the homeless, and doing other community and public service, visit **www.volunteerabroad.com**.

10 STAYING CONNECTED

TELEPHONES

Mexico's telephone system is slowly but surely catching up with modern times. Most telephone numbers have 10 digits. Every city and town that has telephone access has a two-digit (Mexico City, Monterrey, and Guadalajara) or three-digit (everywhere else) area code. In Mexico City, Monterrey, and Guadalajara, local numbers have eight digits; elsewhere, local numbers have seven digits. To place a local call, you do not need to dial the area code. Many fax numbers are also regular phone numbers; ask whoever answers for the fax tone *("me da tono de fax, por favor").*

The **country code** for Mexico is **52.**

To call Mexico: If you're calling Mexico from the United States:

1. Dial the international access code: 011 from the U.S.; 00 from the U.K., Ireland, or New Zealand; or 0011 from Australia.
2. Dial the country code: 52.
3. Dial the two- or three-digit area code, then the eight- or seven-digit number. For example, if you wanted to call the U.S. consulate in Acapulco, the entire number would be 011-52-744-469-0556. If you wanted to dial the U.S. embassy in Mexico City, the entire number would be 011-52-55-5209-9100.

To make international calls: To make international calls from Mexico, dial 00, then the country code (U.S. or Canada 1, U.K. 44, Ireland 353, Australia 61, New Zealand 64). Next, dial the area code and number. For example, to call the British Embassy in Washington, you would dial 00-1-202-588-7800.

For directory assistance: Dial ✆ **040** if you're looking for a number inside Mexico. ***Note:*** Listings usually appear under the owner's name, not the name of the business, and your chances to find an English-speaking operator are slim.

For operator assistance: If you need operator assistance in making a call, dial ✆ **090** to make an international call, and ✆ **020** to call a number in Mexico.

Toll-free numbers: Numbers beginning with 800 within Mexico are toll-free, but calling a U.S. toll-free number from Mexico costs the same as an overseas call. To call an 800 number in the U.S., dial 001-880 and the last seven digits of the toll-free number. To call an 888 number in the U.S., dial 001-881 and the last seven digits of the toll-free number. For a number with an 887 prefix, dial 882; for 866, dial 883.

CELLPHONES

Telcel is Mexico's expensive, primary cellphone provider. It has upgraded its systems to GSM and offers good coverage in much of the country, including the major cities and resorts. Most Mexicans buy their cellphones without a specific coverage plan and then pay as they go or purchase pre-paid cards with set amounts of air-time credit. These cellphone cards with scratch-off pin numbers can be purchased in Telcel stores as well as many newspaper stands and convenience stores.

Many U.S. and European cellphone companies offer networks with roaming coverage in Mexico. Rates can be very high, so check with your provider before committing to making calls this way. An increasing number of Mexicans, particularly among the younger generation, prefer the less expensive rates of **Nextel** (www.nextel.com.mx), which features push-to-talk service. **Cellular Abroad** (www.cellularabroad.com) offers cellphone rentals and purchases as well as SIM cards for travel abroad. Whether you rent or purchase the cellphone, you need to purchase a SIM card that is specific for Mexico.

To call a Mexican cellular number in the same area code, dial 044 and then the number. To dial the cellular phone from anywhere else in Mexico, first dial 01, and then the three-digit area code and the seven-digit number. To place an international call to a cellphone (for example, from the U.S.), you now must add a "1" after the country code; for example, 011-52-1 + 10-digit number.

VOICE-OVER INTERNET PROTOCOL (VOIP)

If you have Web access while traveling, consider a broadband-based telephone service (in technical terms, **Voice over Internet Protocol,** or **VoIP**) such as Skype (www.skype.com) or Vonage (www.vonage.com), which allow you to make free international calls from your laptop or in a cybercafe. Neither service requires the people you're calling to have that service (though fees apply if they do not). Check the websites for details.

INTERNET & E-MAIL

With Your Own Computer

Wireless Internet access is increasingly common in Mexico's major cities and resorts. Mexico's largest airports offer Wi-Fi access provided for a fee by Telcel's Prodigy Internet service. Most five-star hotels now offer Wi-Fi in the guest rooms, although you will need to check in advance whether this service is free or for a fee. Hotel lobbies often have Wi-Fi, as well. To find public Wi-Fi hotspots in Mexico, go to **www.jiwire.com**; its Hotspot Finder holds the world's largest directory of public wireless hotspots.

Without Your Own Computer

Many large Mexican airports have **Internet kiosks,** and quality Mexican hotels usually have business centers with Internet access. You can also check out such copy stores as **Kinko's** or **OfficeMax,** which offer computer stations with fully loaded software (as well as Wi-Fi).

11 TIPS ON ACCOMMODATIONS

MEXICO'S HOTEL RATING SYSTEM

The hotel rating system in Mexico is called "Stars and Diamonds." Stars are given for the quality of the facilities, and diamonds for the service. Hotels may qualify to earn one to five stars or diamonds. The guidelines relate to service, facilities, and hygiene more than to prices. Many, but not all, hotels in Mexico volunteer to be part of this strict rating system.

Five-diamond hotels meet the highest requirements for rating: The beds are comfortable, bathrooms are in excellent working order, all facilities are renovated regularly, infrastructure is top-tier, and services and hygiene meet the highest international standards.

Five-star hotels usually offer similar quality, but with lower levels of service and detail in the rooms. For example, a five-star hotel may have less luxurious linens or, perhaps, room service during limited hours rather than 24 hours.

Four-star hotels are less expensive and more basic, but they still guarantee cleanliness and basic services such as hot water and purified drinking water. Three-, two-, and one-star hotels are at least working to adhere to certain standards: Bathrooms are cleaned and linens are washed daily, and you can expect a minimum standard of service. Two- and one-star hotels generally provide bottled water rather than purified water.

The nonprofit organization Calidad Mexicana Certificada, A.C., known as **Calmecac** (www.calmecac.com.mx), is responsible for hotel ratings; visit their website for additional details about the rating system.

HOTEL CHAINS

In addition to the major international chains, you'll run across a number of less-familiar brands as you plan your trip to Mexico. They include:

- **Brisas Hotels & Resorts** (www.brisas.com.mx). These were the hotels that originally attracted jet-set travelers to Mexico. Spectacular in a retro way, these properties offer the laid-back luxury that makes a Mexican vacation so unique.
- **Fiesta Americana** and **Fiesta Inn** (www.posadas.com). Part of the Mexican-owned Grupo Posadas company, these hotels set the country's midrange standard for facilities and services. They generally offer comfortable, spacious rooms and traditional Mexican hospitality. Fiesta Americana hotels offer excellent beach-resort packages. Fiesta Inn hotels are usually more business oriented. Grupo Posadas also owns the more luxurious Caesar Park hotels and the eco-oriented Explorean hotels.
- **Hoteles Camino Real** (www.caminoreal.com). Once known as the premier Mexican hotel chain, Camino Real still maintains a high standard of service at its properties, although the company was sold in 2005, and many of the hotels that once formed a part of it have been sold off or have become independent. Its beach hotels are traditionally located on the best beaches in the area. This chain also focuses on the business market. The hotels are famous for their vivid and contrasting colors.
- **NH Hoteles** (www.nh-hotels.com). The NH hotels are noted for their family-friendly facilities and quality standards. The beach properties' signature feature is a pool, framed by columns, overlooking the sea.
- **Quinta Real Grand Class Hotels and Resorts** (www.quintareal.com). These hotels, owned by Summit Hotels and Resorts, are noted for architectural and cultural details that reflect their individual regions. At these luxury properties, attention to detail and excellent service are the rule. Quinta Real is the top line Mexican hotel brand.

HOUSE RENTALS & SWAPS

House and villa rentals and swaps are becoming more common in Mexico, but no single recognized agency or business provides this service exclusively for Mexico. In the chapters that follow, we have provided information on independent services that we have found to be reputable.

You'll find the most extensive inventory of homes at **Vacation Rentals by Owner (VRBO;** www.vrbo.com). They have more than

Finds Boutique Lodgings

Mexico lends itself beautifully to the concept of small, private hotels in idyllic settings. They vary in style from grandiose estate to palm-thatched bungalow. **Mexico Boutique Hotels** (www.mexicoboutiquehotels.com) specializes in smaller places to stay with a high level of personal attention and service. Most options have less than 50 rooms, and the accommodations consist of entire villas, *casitas,* bungalows, or a combination.

33,000 homes and condominiums worldwide, including a large selection in Mexico. Another good option is **VacationSpot** (✆ **888/903-7768;** www.vacationspot.com), owned by Expedia and a part of its sister company Hotels.com. It has fewer choices, but the company's criteria for adding inventory is much more selective and often includes on-site inspections. They also offer toll-free phone support.

For tips on surfing for hotel deals online, visit **www.frommers.com**.

2

Acapulco

I like to think of Acapulco as a diva—a little past her prime, perhaps overly made up, but still capable of captivating an audience. It's tempting to dismiss Acapulco as a passé resort: Drug-related violence, underinvestment, and poverty in some parts of this huge city have led many tourists to head for glitzier Mexican resorts such as Cancún and Cabo San Lucas. But Acapulco surprisingly retains its appeal, and its temptations are hard to resist. This is a place where beautiful bodies pack the sun-soaked beaches, daring men dive from cliffs into the sea, romantic couples dine alongside unforgettable views of the bay, and uninhibited revelers dance the rest of the night away. Acapulco has world-class resorts, yet they're often much less expensive than comparable hotels elsewhere. Though most beach resorts are made for relaxing, Acapulco offers nonstop, 24-hours-a-day energy. Its perfectly sculpted bay is an adult playground filled with water-skiers in sexy *tanga* swimsuits and darkly tanned, mirror-shaded guys on jet skis. Visitors play golf and tennis with intensity, but the real sport is the nightlife, which has made this city famous for decades. Back in the days when there was a jet set, they came to Acapulco—filmed it, sang about it, wrote about it, and lived it.

It's not hard to understand why: The view of Acapulco Bay, framed by mountains and beaches, is breathtaking day or night. Playa Diamante (Diamond Beach), just south of the bay, is by far the best beach within driving distance of Mexico City. At night, a trendy set of upper-class Mexicans and international visitors fills the top restaurants, bars, and nightclubs, which are some of the hottest in the country.

Acapulco tries hard to hold on to its image as the ultimate party town, and remains a top weekend and vacation destination for affluent residents of Mexico City, who can reach the city in a few hours via a major highway. Don't expect small-town charm or undiscovered beaches, but do expect breathtaking bay views, wide-ranging tourist services, and good values. Acapulco's still the top choice for those who want to have dinner at midnight, dance until dawn, and sleep all day on a sun-soaked beach.

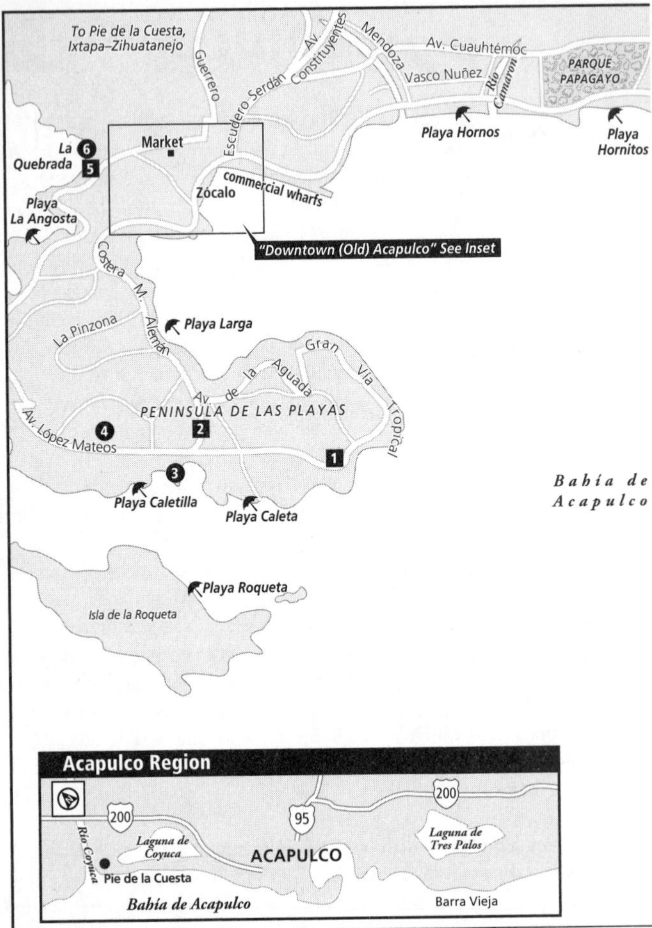

Acapulco Bay Area

To Pie de la Cuesta, Ixtapa–Zihuatanejo
Guerrero
Av. Constituyentes
Mendoza
Av. Cuauhtémoc
Vasco Nuñez
Río Camarón
PARQUE PAPAGAYO
Escudero
Serdán
Playa Hornos
Playa Hornitos
Market
La Quebrada
commercial wharfs
Zócalo
Playa La Angosta
"Downtown (Old) Acapulco" See Inset
Costera M. Alemán
La Pinzona
Playa Larga
Gran Vía Tropical
Av. de la Aguada
PENINSULA DE LAS PLAYAS
Av. López Mateos
Playa Caletilla
Playa Caleta
Bahía de Acapulco
Playa Roqueta
Isla de la Roqueta

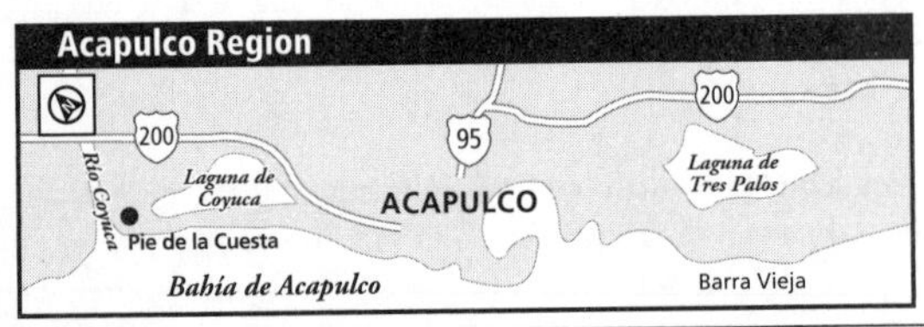

ACCOMMODATIONS ■

Calinda Beach Acapulco **9**
Camino Real Acapulco Diamante **13**
Casa Yal'ma Ka'an **14**
Fairmont Acapulco Princess **14**
Fairmont Pierre Marques **14**
Fiesta Americana Villas **8**
Hotel Costa Linda **2**
Hotel Elcano **10**
Hotel El Mirador Acapulco **5**
Hotel Los Flamingos **1**
Hotel Misión **15**
Las Brisas **12**
Quinta Real **14**
Sand's Acapulco **7**

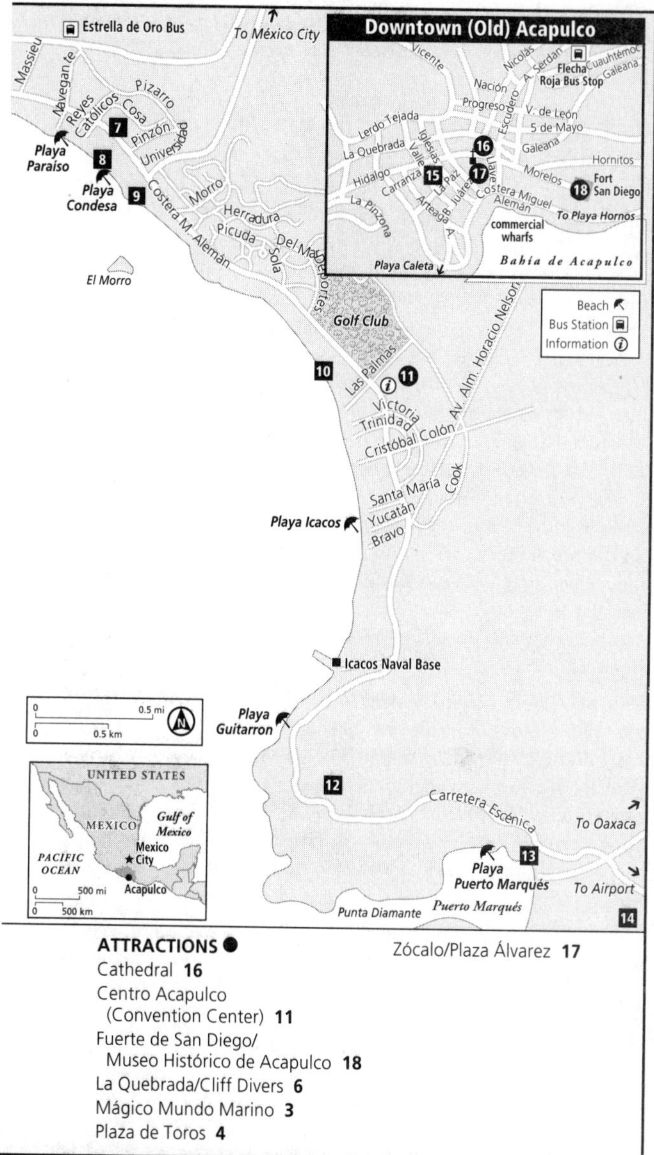
Downtown (Old) Acapulco
Estrella de Oro Bus
To México City
Massieu
Navegante
Reyes Católicos
Cosa
Pizarro
Pinzón
Universidad
Playa Paraíso
Playa Condesa
Costera M. Alemán
Morro
Herradura
Picuda
Sola
Del Mar
Deportes
El Morro
Golf Club
Las Palmas
Victoria
Trinidad
Cristóbal Colón
Av. Alm. Horacio Nelson
Cook
Santa María
Yucatán
Bravo
Playa Icacos
Icacos Naval Base
Playa Guitarron
Carretera Escénica
To Oaxaca
To Airport
Playa Puerto Marqués
Puerto Marqués
Punta Diamante
Vicente
Nicolás
A. Serdán
Cuauhtémoc
Galeana
Flecha Roja Bus Stop
Nación
Progreso
Escudero
V. de León
5 de Mayo
Lerdo Tejada
La Quebrada
Iglesias
Valle
Galeana
Hornitos
Hidalgo
Carranza
La Paz
Llave
Morelos
Fort San Diego
La Pinzona
Arteaga
B. Juárez
A.
Costera Miguel Alemán
To Playa Hornos
commercial wharfs
Bahía de Acapulco
Playa Caleta
Beach
Bus Station
Information
0.5 mi
0.5 km
UNITED STATES
MEXICO
Gulf of Mexico
Mexico City
PACIFIC OCEAN
Acapulco
500 mi
500 km
ATTRACTIONS
Cathedral 16
Centro Acapulco (Convention Center) 11
Fuerte de San Diego/ Museo Histórico de Acapulco 18
La Quebrada/Cliff Divers 6
Mágico Mundo Marino 3
Plaza de Toros 4
Zócalo/Plaza Álvarez 17

ACAPULCO

2

1 ESSENTIALS

366km (227 miles) S of Mexico City; 272km (169 miles) SW of Taxco; 979km (607 miles) SE of Guadalajara; 253km (157 miles) SE of Ixtapa/Zihuatenejo; 752km (466 miles) NW of Huatulco

GETTING THERE & DEPARTING

BY PLANE See chapter 1 for information on flying from the United States or Canada to Acapulco. Local numbers for major airlines with nonstop or direct service to Acapulco are **AeroMéxico** (✆ **744/485-1600** inside Mexico), **American** (✆ **744/481-0161,** or 01-800/904-6000 inside Mexico for reservations), **Continental** (✆ **744/466-9063**), **Delta** (✆ **01-800/123-4710**), **Mexicana** (✆ **744/466-9138** or 486-7585), and **US Airways** (✆ **744/466-9257**).

AeroMéxico flies from Guadalajara, Mexico City, Tijuana, and Monterrey; **Aviacsa** (✆ **01-800/711-6733**) flies from Mexico City; **InterJet** (✆ **01-800/01-12345**) is a low-cost carrier that flies from Toluca, about an hour from Mexico City; **Mexicana** flies from Mexico City. Check with a travel agent about **charter** flights.

The airport (airport code: ACA) is 22km (14 miles) southeast of town, over the hills east of the bay. Private **taxis** are the fastest way to get downtown; they cost $30 to $50. The major **rental-car** agencies all have booths at the airport. **Millinium** and **Movilaca** have desks at the front of the airport where you can buy tickets for minivan *colectivo* transportation into town ($10). You can reserve return service to the airport through your hotel.

BY CAR From Mexico City, take either the curvy toll-free **Hwy. 95D** south (6 hr.) or scenic **Hwy. 95,** the four- to six-lane toll highway (3½ hr.), which costs around $50 one-way. The free *(libre)* road from Taxco is in good condition; you'll save around $40 in tolls from there through Chilpancingo to Acapulco. From points north or south along the coast, the only choice is **Hwy. 200,** where you should always try (as on all Mexican highways) to travel by day.

BY BUS The **Estrella de Oro** terminal is at Av. Cuauhtémoc 1490, and the **Estrella Blanca** terminal (also called Central de Autobuses) is at Av. Cuauhtémoc 1605. **Turistar, Estrella de Oro,** and **Estrella Blanca** have almost hourly service for the 5- to 7-hour trip to Mexico City ($35–$55), and daily service to Zihuatanejo ($20). Buses also serve other points in Mexico, including Chilpancingo, Cuernavaca, Iguala, Manzanillo, Puerto Vallarta, and Taxco.

Tips **Car & Bus Travel Warning Eases**

Car robberies and bus hijackings on Hwy. 200, south of Acapulco on the way to Puerto Escondido and Huatulco, used to be common, and you may have heard warnings about the road. The trouble has all but disappeared, thanks to military patrols and greater police protection. However, as in most of Mexico, it's advisable to travel the highways during daylight hours only—not so much because of carjackings, but because highways are unlit, and animals can wander onto them.

ORIENTATION

VISITOR INFORMATION The **State of Guerrero Tourism Office** operates the **Procuraduría del Turista** (✆/fax **744/484-4416**), on the street level of the **Convention Center (Centro Acapulco),** set back from the main Costera Alemán, down a lengthy walkway with fountains. The office offers maps and information about the city and state, as well as police assistance for tourists; it's open daily from 8am to 11pm.

CITY LAYOUT Acapulco stretches more than 6km (3¾ miles) around the huge bay, so trying to take it all in by foot is impractical. The tourist areas are roughly divided into three sections. On the western end of the bay is **Acapulco Viejo (Old Acapulco),** the original town that attracted the jet-setters of the 1950s and 1960s—and today it looks as if it's still locked in that era, though a renaissance is slowly getting under way.

The second section, in the center of the bay, is the **Zona Hotelera (Hotel Zone);** it follows the main boulevard, **Costera Miguel Alemán** (or just "the Costera"), as it runs east along the bay from downtown. Towering hotels, restaurants, shopping centers, and strips of open-air beach bars line the street. At the far eastern end of the Costera lie the golf course and the International Center (a convention center). **Avenida Cuauhtémoc** is the major artery inland, running roughly parallel to the Costera.

The third major area begins just beyond the Gran Hotel Acapulco (previously the Hyatt), where the name of the Costera changes to **Carretera Escénica (Scenic Hwy.),** which continues all the way to the airport. The hotels along this section of the road are lavish, and extravagant private villas, gourmet restaurants, and flashy nightclubs built into the hillside offer dazzling views. The area fronting the beach here is **Acapulco Diamante,** Acapulco's most desirable address.

Street names and numbers in Acapulco can be confusing and hard to find. Many streets are not well marked or change names unexpectedly. Street numbers on the Costera are illogical, so don't assume that similar numbers will be close together.

GETTING AROUND **By Taxi** Taxis are more plentiful than tacos in Acapulco—and practically as inexpensive, if you're traveling in the downtown area only. Just remember that you should always establish the price with the driver before starting out. Hotel taxis may charge three times the rate of a taxi hailed on the street, and nighttime taxi rides cost extra, too. Taxis are also more expensive if you're staying in the Diamante section or south. The minimum fare is $2.50 per ride for a roving VW Bug–style taxi in town; the fare from Puerto Marqués to the hotel zone is $10, or $12 into downtown. *Sitio* taxis are nicer cars, but more expensive, with a minimum fare of $4. Acapulco taxis are easily recognizable by their flashy, blue neon lights.

By Bus Even though the city has a confusing street layout, using city buses is amazingly easy and inexpensive. Two kinds of buses run along the Costera: pastel color-coded buses and regular "school buses." The difference is the price: New air-conditioned tourist buses (Aca Tur Bus) are $1; old buses are 50¢. Covered bus stops line the Costera, with handy maps on the walls showing routes to major sights and hotels.

The best place near the *zócalo* to catch a bus is next to Sanborn's, 2 blocks east. CALETA DIRECTO or BASE-CALETA buses will take you to the Hornos, Caleta, and Caletilla beaches along the Costera. Some buses return along the same route; others go around the peninsula and return to the Costera.

For expeditions to more distant destinations, there are buses to **Puerto Marqués** to the east (marked PUERTO MARQUES–BASE) and **Pie de la Cuesta** to the west (marked ZOCALO–PIE DE LA CUESTA). Be sure to verify the time and place of the last bus back if you hop on one of these.

By Car Rental cars are available at the airport and at hotel desks along the Costera. Unless you plan on exploring outlying areas, trust me, you're better off taking taxis or using the easy and inexpensive public buses.

Fast Facts Acapulco

Area Code The telephone area code is **744.**

Climate Acapulco boasts sunshine 360 days a year, with average daytime temperatures of 27°C (80°F). Humidity varies, with approximately 59 inches of rain per year. June through October is the rainy season, though July and August are relatively dry. Tropical showers are brief and usually occur at night.

Consular Agents The **United States** has an agent at the Hotel Continental Emporio, Costera Alemán 121, Loc. 14 (✆ **744/469-0556**); the office is open Monday through Friday from 10am to 2pm. The **Canadian** office is at the Centro Comercial Marbella, Loc. 23 (✆ **744/484-1305**). The toll-free emergency number inside Mexico is ✆ **01-800/706-2900.** The office is open Monday through Friday from 9am to 5pm.

Currency Exchange Numerous banks along the Costera are open Monday through Friday from 9am to 6pm, Saturday from 10am to 2pm. Banks and their ATMs generally have the best rates. *Casas de cambio* (currency-exchange booths) along the street may have better rates than hotels.

Drugstores One of the largest drugstores in town is **Farmacía Daisy,** Francia 49, across the traffic circle from the convention center (✆ **744/48126350**). It's open daily from 9am to 11pm. Sam's Club and Wal-Mart, both on the Costera, have pharmacy services and lower prices on medicine.

Hospital **Hospital Magallanes,** Av. Wilfrido Massieu 2, Fracc. Magallanes (✆ **744/469-0270**), has an English-speaking staff and doctors. For local emergencies, call the **Cruz Roja (Red Cross),** Av. Ruiz Cortines s/n (✆ **065**).

Internet Access **@canet,** Costera Alemán 1632 Int., La Gran Plaza, Loc. D-1, lower floor (✆/fax **744/486-9186,** 486-8182), is open weekdays from 10am to 9pm and weekends from 11:30am to 9pm. Internet access costs about $2.50 per hour. This is a computer shop that also offers Internet access and has a very helpful staff. Also along the Costera strip is the **Santa Clara Cafe,** Costera Alemán 136, serving coffee, pastries, and ice cream, along with Internet service for $1 for 20 minutes. It's open 9am to 11pm.

Parking It is illegal to park on the Costera at any time. Try parking along side streets or in one of the few covered parking lots, such as in Plaza Bahía and in Plaza Mirabella.

Post Office The *correo* is next door to Sears, close to the Fideicomiso office. It's open Monday through Friday from 9am to 5pm, Saturday from 9am to 2pm. Other branches are in the Estrella de Oro bus station on Cuauhtémoc, inland from the Acapulco Qualton Hotel, and on the Costera near Caleta Beach.

Safety Riptides claim a few lives every year, so pay close attention to warning flags posted on Acapulco beaches. Red or black flags warn swimmers to stay out of the water, yellow flags signify caution, and white or green flags mean it's safe to swim. As is the case anywhere, tourists are vulnerable to thieves. This is especially true when shopping in a market, lying on the beach, wearing jewelry, or visibly carrying a camera, purse, or bulging wallet. Don't walk on Acapulco's beaches at night.

Telephone Acapulco phone numbers seem to change frequently. The most reliable source for telephone numbers is the **Procuraduría del Turista,** on the Costera in front of the convention center (✆ **744/484-4416**), which has an exceptionally friendly staff. It's open daily from 8am to 11pm.

Tourist Police Policemen in white and light-blue uniforms belong to the Tourist Police (✆ **066** for emergencies, or 744/485-0490), a special corps of English-speaking police established to assist tourists.

2 ACTIVITIES ON & OFF THE BEACH

Acapulco is known for its great beaches and watersports, and few visitors bother to explore its traditional downtown area. But the shaded ***zócalo*** (also called Plaza Alvarez) is worth a trip, to experience a glimpse of local life and color. Inexpensive cafes and shops border the plaza. At its far north end is the **cathedral Nuestra Señora de la Soledad,** with blue, onion-shaped domes and Byzantine towers. Though reminiscent of a Russian Orthodox church, it was originally (and perhaps appropriately) built as a movie set, then later adapted into a house of worship. From the church, turn east along the side street going off at a right angle (Calle Carranza, which doesn't have a marker) to find an arcade with newsstands and more shops. The hill behind the cathedral provides an unparalleled view of Acapulco. Take a taxi to the top of the hill from the main plaza, and follow signs to **El Mirador (lookout point).**

Local travel agencies book city tours, day trips to Taxco, cruises, and other excursions and activities. Taxco is about a 3-hour drive inland from Acapulco (see chapter 6 for more information).

Tips To Swim or Not to Swim in the Bay?

In the past decade, the city has gone to great lengths (and great expense) to clean up the waters off Acapulco. Nevertheless, this is an industrial port that was once heavily polluted, so many choose to stick to their hotel pool. The bay beaches that remain most popular are **Caleta** and **Caletilla beaches,** as well as **Playa Puerto Marqués.**

THE BEACHES Here's a rundown on the beaches, going from west to east around the bay. **Playa la Angosta** is a small, sheltered, often-deserted cove just around the bend from **La Quebrada** (where the cliff divers perform).

South of downtown on the Peninsula de las Playas lie the beaches **Caleta** and **Caletilla.** Separating them is a small outcropping of land that contains the aquarium and water park **Mágico Mundo Marino,** which is open daily from 9am to 6pm (© **744/483-1215**) and costs 60 pesos to enter. You'll find thatched-roofed restaurants, watersports equipment for rent, and brightly painted boats that ferry passengers to **Roqueta Island.** You can rent beach chairs and umbrellas for the day. Mexican families favor these beaches because they're close to several good value hotels. In the late afternoon, fishermen pull their colorful boats up on the sand; you can buy the fresh catch of the day and, occasionally, oysters on the half-shell.

Pleasure boats dock at **Playa Manzanillo,** south of the *zócalo.* Charter fishing trips sail from here. In the old days, the downtown beaches—Manzanillo, Honda, Caleta, and Caletilla—were the focal point of Acapulco. Today beaches and resort developments stretch along the 6.5km (4-mile) length of the shore.

East of the *zócalo,* the major beaches are **Hornos** (near Papagayo Park), **Hornitos, Paraíso, Condesa,** and **Icacos,** followed by the naval base (La Base) and **Punta del Guitarrón.** After Punta del Guitarrón, the road climbs to the legendary Las Brisas hotel. Past Las Brisas, the road continues to the small, clean bay of **Puerto Marqués,** followed by **Punta Diamante,** about 20km (12 miles) from the *zócalo.* The fabulous Acapulco Princess, the Quinta Real, and the Pierre Marqués hotels dominate the landscape, which fronts the open Pacific.

Playa Puerto Marqués, in the bay of Puerto Marqués, is an attractive area for swimming. The Camino Real and a large residential development are located here. The water is calm and the bay sheltered. Water-skiing and WaveRunner rentals can also be arranged.

Warning! Riptides

Each year, at least one or two unwary swimmers drown in Acapulco because of deadly riptides and undertow (see "Safety" in "Fast Facts," above). Check for warning flags posted by the lifeguards and be careful of the undertow no matter where you go. If you find yourself caught in the undertow, head back to shore at an angle instead of trying to swim straight back.

Past the bay lies **Revolcadero Beach,** a magnificent wide stretch of beach on the open ocean, where many of Acapulco's grandest resorts are found.

Other beaches lie farther north and are best reached by car, though buses also make the trip. **Pie de la Cuesta** is 13km (8 miles) west of town. Buses along the Costera leave every 5 or 10 minutes; a taxi costs about $20. The water is too rough for swimming, but it's a great spot for checking out big waves and the spectacular sunset, especially over *coco locos* (drinks served in fresh coconuts with the tops whacked off) at a rustic beachside restaurant. The area is known for excellent birding and surrounding coconut plantations.

If you're driving, continue west along the peninsula, passing **Coyuca Lagoon** on your right, until almost to the small air base at the tip. Along the way, various private entrepreneurs, mostly young boys, will invite you to park near different sections of beach. You'll also find *colectivo* boat tours of the lagoon offered for about $10.

BAY CRUISES & ROQUETA ISLAND The waters of Acapulco are dotted with virtually every kind of boat—yachts, catamarans, and trimarans (single- and double-deckers). Cruises run morning, afternoon, and evening. Some offer buffets, open bars, and live music; others just snacks, drinks, and taped music. Prices range from $26 to $50. Cruise operators come and go, and their phone numbers change so frequently from year to year that it's pointless to list them here; to find out what cruises are currently operating, contact any Acapulco travel agency or your hotel's tour desk, and ask for brochures or recommendations.

Boats from Caletilla Beach to **Roqueta Island**—a good place to snorkel, sunbathe, hike to a lighthouse, visit a small zoo, or have lunch—leave every 15 minutes from 9am until the last one returns at 5:30pm for under $10 round-trip. There are also primitive-style glass-bottom boats that circle the bay as you look down at a few fish and watch a diver swim down to the underwater sanctuary of the Virgin of Guadalupe, patron saint of Mexico. The statue of the Virgin—created by sculptor Armando Quesado—was placed there in 1958, in memory of a group of divers who lost their lives at the spot. You can purchase tickets ($5) directly from any boat that's loading.

WATERSPORTS & BOAT RENTALS An hour of **water-skiing** at Coyuca Lagoon can cost as little as $35 or as much as $70.

Scuba diving costs about $80 for 4 hours of instruction, when you book through a hotel or travel agency. Dive trips start at around $90 per person for one- or two-tank dives. One reputable shop, near Club de Esquís, is **Divers de México** (**✆ 744/482-1398**). We also recommend **Fish-R-Us** (**✆ 744/482-8282;** www.fish-r-us.com), which offers shore and boat dives, usually to Roqueta Island. Sunken ships, sea mountains, and cave rock formations are all on display around the area. **Boat rentals** are cheapest on Caletilla Beach, where you can usually find inner tubes, small boats, canoes, paddleboats, and chairs for rent.

For **deep-sea fishing** excursions, go to the boat cooperative's pink building opposite the *zócalo,* or book a day in advance (**✆ 744/482-1099**). Charter trips run $250 to $450 for 6 to 7 hours, tackle and bait included, with an extra charge for ice, drinks, and lunch. Credit cards are accepted, but you're likely to get a better deal by paying cash. Boats leave at 7am and return at 2pm. **Fish-R-Us** (**✆ 744/482-8282**) also books quality excursions. If you book through a travel agent or hotel, prices start at around $250 for four people. In addition to traditional fishing charters, they offer private yacht charters, scuba diving, and a 3-hour Night of Delight cruise, with dinner served on board. Prices vary per the service requested and number of people; call for details.

Parasailing, though not free from risk (the occasional thrill-seeker has collided with a palm tree or even a building), can be brilliant. Floating high over the bay hanging from a parachute towed by a motorboat costs about $35. Most of these rides operate on Condesa Beach, but they also can be found independently operating on the beach in front of most hotels along the Costera.

GOLF & TENNIS Both the **Acapulco Princess** (**✆ 744/469-1000**) and **Pierre Marqués** (**✆ 744/466-1000**) hotels share top-notch golf courses. The Princess's course is a rather narrow, level, Ted Robinson design. The Marques course, redesigned by Robert Trent Jones. Jr. in 1980 for the World Cup Golf Tournament, is longer and more challenging. A morning round of 18 holes at the Princess course costs $125 for guests and $135 for nonguests (discounted rates for afternoon rounds); prices are $10 more at the Marques course. American Express, Visa, and MasterCard are accepted, and the cart is included in the fee. Tee times begin at 7:30am, and reservations should be made at least a day in advance. Club rental is available for an extra $40. The **Mayan Palace Golf Club,** Geranios 22 (✆ **744/469-6043** or 466-2260), designed by Latin American golf great Pedro Guericia, lies farther east. Greens fees are $145 for visitors, and caddies are available for an additional $20. At the **Club de Golf Acapulco,** off the Costera next to the convention center (✆ **744/484-0781**), you can play 9 holes for $50 and 18 holes for $80, with equipment renting for $10.

The Robert von Hagge–designed course at the exclusive **Tres Vidas Golf Club,** Carretera a Barra Vieja Km 7 (✆ **744/444-5126**), is spectacular. The par-72, 18-hole course, right on the edge of the ocean, is landscaped with nine lakes, dotted with palms, and home to a flock of ducks and other birds. The club is open only to members, guests of members, and guests at Tres Vidas or a few other participating hotels. Greens fees are $200, including cart; a caddy is $20. Also here is a clubhouse with a restaurant (daily 7am–10pm), as well as a pool. American Express, Visa, and MasterCard are accepted.

The **Club de Tenis Gran Hotel Acapulco,** Costera Alemán 1 (✆ **744/484-1225**), is open daily from 7am to 11pm. Outdoor courts cost $10 per hour during the day, $15 per hour at night; rackets rent for $3 and a set of balls costs $2. Many of the hotels along the Costera have tennis facilities for guests; the best are at the Fairmont Princess, Mayan Palace, and Las Brisas hotels. The **Fairmont Princess** (✆ **744/469-1000**) also allows nonguests to play for $20 per hour.

RIDING & BULLFIGHTS You can go **horseback riding** along the beach. Independent operators stroll the Hotel Zone beachfront offering rides for about $25 to $45 for 1 to 2 hours. Horses are also commonly found on the beach in front of the Acapulco Princess Hotel. There is no phone; you go directly to the beach to make arrangements.

Traditionally called Fiesta Brava, **bullfights** are held during Acapulco's winter season at a ring (called **Plaza de Toros**) up the hill from Caletilla Beach. Tickets purchased through travel agencies cost around $17 to $40 and usually include transportation to and from your hotel. You can also buy a general admission ticket at the stadium for $4.50. Be forewarned that this is a true bullfight—meaning things generally do not fare well for the bull. The festivities begin at 5:30pm each Sunday from late November to late February.

A MUSEUM & A WATER PARK The original **Fuerte de San Diego,** Costera Alemán, east of the *zócalo* (✆ **744/482-3828**), was built in 1616 to protect the town from pirate attacks. At that time, the port reaped considerable income from trade with the Philippine Islands (which, like Mexico, were part of the Spanish Empire). The

Moments Death-Defying Divers

High divers perform at La Quebrada each day at 12:45, 7:30, 8:30, 9:30, and 10:30pm. Admission is 35 pesos for adults, 10 pesos for kids 10 and under. From a spot-lit ledge on the cliffs, divers (holding torches for the final performance) plunge into the roaring surf of an inlet that's just 7m (23 ft.) wide, 4m (13 ft.) deep, and 40m (131 ft.) below—after wisely praying at a small shrine nearby. To the applause of the crowd, divers climb up the rocks and accept congratulations and gifts of money from onlookers. This is the quintessential Acapulco experience. No visit is complete (even for jaded travelers) without watching the cliff divers. To get there from downtown, take the street called La Quebrada from behind the cathedral for 4 blocks. Parking costs 20 pesos.

The public areas have great views, but arrive early, because performances quickly fill up. Another option is to watch from the lobby bar or restaurant terrace of the **Hotel El Mirador.** The bar imposes a $15 cover charge, which includes two drinks. You can get around the cover by having dinner at the hotel's **La Perla restaurant.** Reservations (✆ **744/483-1221,** ext. 802) are recommended during high season.

fort you see today was rebuilt after considerable earthquake damage in 1776 and has undergone a series of renovations since. The structure houses the **Museo Histórico de Acapulco (Acapulco Historical Museum) ★★**, with exhibits that reveal the port's role in the conquest of the Americas, Catholic conversion campaigns in the region, and exotic trade with the Orient. Other exhibits chronicle Acapulco's pre-Hispanic past, the coming of the conquistadors (complete with Spanish armor), and Spanish imperial activity. Temporary exhibits are also on display. Admission to the museum costs about $4, free on Sunday. It's open Tuesday through Sunday from 9am to 6pm. To reach the fort, follow Costera Alemán past Old Acapulco and the *zócalo;* the fort is on a hill on the right.

The **Parque Acuático el CICI ★**, Costera Alemán at Colón (✆ **744/484-8033**), is a sea-life and water park east of the convention center. It offers guests swimming pools with waves, water slides, and water toboggans, and has a cafeteria and restrooms. The park is open daily from 10am to 6pm. General admission is $10 and free for children younger than 2. There are **dolphin shows** (in Spanish) weekdays at 2pm and weekends at 2 and 4pm. There's also a dolphin swim

A House of Art

Of all the exclusive villas and homes in Acapulco, one stands far apart from the others. Though not as elegantly impressive as the villas of Las Brisas, the **home of Dolores Olmedo** in Acapulco's traditional downtown area is a work of art. In 1956, the renowned Mexican artist Diego Rivera covered its outside wall with a mural of colorful mosaic tiles, shells, and stones. The work is unique and one of the last he created. The Olmedo mural, which took him 18 months to complete, features Aztec deities such as Quetzalcoatl and Tepezcuincle, the Aztec dog. Rivera and Olmedo were lifelong friends, and Rivera lived in this house for the last 2 years of his life, during which time he also covered the interior with murals. The home isn't a museum, so you have to settle for a look at the exterior masterpiece. The house is a few blocks behind the Casablanca Hotel, a short cab ride from the central plaza, at Calle Cerro de la Pinzona 6. Have the driver wait while you look around.

program, which includes 30 minutes of introduction and 30 minutes to 1 hour of swim time. The cost for this option is $90 for the half-hour swim, $130 for the hour; both options include total access to the water park and are available by reservation only. Shows are at 10:30am, 12:30, and 4:30pm. Reservations are required; there is a 10-person maximum per show for the dolphin swim option. The minimum age is 4 years.

3 SHOPPING

Acapulco is not among the best places to buy Mexican crafts, but it does have a few interesting shops, and the Costera is lined with places to buy tourist souvenirs, including silver jewelry, Mexico knick-knacks, and the ubiquitous T-shirt.

The shopkeepers aren't pushy, but they'll test your bargaining mettle. The starting price will be steep, and dragging it down may take some time. Before buying silver, examine it carefully and look for ".925" stamped on the back. This supposedly signifies that the silver is 92.5% pure, but the less expensive silver metal called "alpaca" may also bear this stamp. (Alpaca is generally stamped MEXICO or MEX, often in letters so tiny that they are hard to read and look similar to the three-digit ".925".)

P&P Jewelers, located at the Quebrada where the cliff divers perform (✆ **744/482-3428;** www.plazataxco.com.mx), is a large store selling silver and gold pieces, including quality silver from Taxco. It's open Monday through Saturday from 10am to 10pm.

Sanborn's, a good department store and drugstore chain, offers an array of staples, including cosmetics, music, clothing, books, and magazines. It has a number of locations in Acapulco, including downtown at Costera Miguel Alemán 209, across from the boat docks (✆ **744/482-6167**); and Costera Miguel Alemán 1226, at the Condo Estrella Tower, close to the convention center (✆ **744/484-2035**). It's open daily from 7:30am to midnight.

Boutiques selling resort wear crowd the Costera Alemán. These stores carry attractive summer clothing at prices lower than you generally pay in the United States. If there's a sale, you can find incredible bargains. One of the nicest air-conditioned shopping centers on the Costera is **Plaza Bahía,** Costera Alemán 125 (✆ **744/485-6939** or 485-6992), which has four stories of shops, movie theaters, a bowling alley, and small fast-food restaurants. The center is just west of the Costa Club Hotel. The bowling alley, **Aca Bol in Plaza Bahía** (✆ **744/485-0970** or 485-7464), is open daily from noon to midnight (1am on weekends). Another popular shopping strip is the **Plaza Condesa,** adjacent to the Fiesta Americana Condesa; shops include Guess, Izod, and Bronce Swimwear. **Olvido Plaza,** near the restaurant of the same name, has Tommy Hilfiger and Aca Joe.

The top shopping center in Acapulco is **La Isla,** located away from the coast on the road toward the airport. Opened in late 2008 and similar in design to La Isla Cancún, it houses the Mexican department stores Liverpool and Casa Palacio, as well as name-brand stores like Coach, Calvin Klein, DKNY, and Hugo Boss. There's also a cinema and Carlos & Charlie's located here, along with other restaurants and entertainment options.

4 WHERE TO STAY

The listings below begin with the most expensive resorts south of town in Diamante and continue along Costera Alemán to the less expensive, more traditional hotels north of town, in the downtown or "Old Acapulco" part of the city. Hotel prices have tended to fall or stay the same in Acapulco in recent years. Especially in the Expensive category, inquire about promotional rates or check with the airlines for air-hotel packages. During Christmas and Easter weeks, considered the highest season here, some hotels double their normal rates. Low season lasts September through November and April through June; the rest of the year is midseason. The rates below do not include the 17% tax. Private **villas** are available for rent all over the hills south of town; staying in one of these palatial homes is an unforgettable experience. **Acapulco Luxury Villas** (✆ **01-800/030-4444;** www.acapulcoluxuryvillas.com) handles some of the most exclusive villas.

SOUTH OF TOWN

Acapulco's most exclusive and renowned hotels, restaurants, and villas nestle in the steep forested hillsides here, between the naval base and Puerto Marqués. This area is several kilometers from the heart of Acapulco; you'll pay about $20 round-trip taxi fare every time you venture off the property into town.

Very Expensive

Quinta Real ★★★ This exquisite hotel offers the most exclusive accommodations in Acapulco, with just 74 suites perched on a small cliff with uninterrupted views of the Pacific Ocean and Diamante Beach. Part of Mexico's top hotel line, the Quinta Real is defined by understated elegance and attention to detail, designed for relaxing and getting away from it all. (This is not the right place for those looking for entertainment or family-friendly services; for that, I suggest the Fairmont Acapulco Princess.) The suites come in different sizes, with California-style furnishings, still-life paintings, extensive use of marble, and light neutral colors. The larger Governor suites have high ceilings, separate living and dining rooms, and terraces with private plunge pools. All rooms were remodeled in 2009. The inviting hotel pool lies just steps from the beach, where there's also a casual seafood restaurant and beach club. Next to the lobby, the hotel's gourmet restaurant serves delectable Mexican and international cuisine. Service throughout the Quinta Real is impeccable.

Paseo de la Quina 6, Desarrollo Inmobiliario Real Diamante, 39907 Acapulco, Gro. ✆ **744/469-1500.** Fax 744/469-1516. www.quintareal.com. 74 units. $370 and up suite. AE, MC, V. Free valet parking. **Amenities:** 2 restaurants; lobby bar; airport shuttle; babysitting; kids' club; concierge; fitness center; free Wi-Fi in lobby; 2 outdoor pools (1 for children); room service; spa treatments; beach club. *In room:* A/C, TV, hair dryer, minibar.

Expensive

Camino Real Acapulco Diamante ★★ Kids Tucked in an almost hidden location on 32 hectares (79 acres) above Playa Puerto Marqués, this relaxing, self-contained resort is an ideal choice for families or for those who already know Acapulco and want a bit of seclusion. It's one of Acapulco's most enticing hotels because of its

Fun Facts Acapulco, Queen of the Silver Screen

Besides hosting legendary stars of the silver screen, Acapulco has played a few starring roles. More than 250 films were shot here, including *Rambo II* (1985), which used the Pie de la Cuesta lagoon as its backdrop.

family-friendly atmosphere, extensive amenities, and beautiful protected cove ideal for swimming. From Carretera Escénica, a handsome brick road winds down to the resort, but pay close attention to the signs for the reception so you don't end up on one of the residential roads. The hotel lobby features an inviting terrace facing the bay, and the sparkling waterfront pools are the focus of daytime activity. Spacious guest rooms offer balconies or terraces, small sitting areas, marble floors, ceiling fans (in addition to air-conditioning), and bright, colorful decor.

Carretera Escénica Km 14, Baja Catita s/n, Pichilingue, 39867 Acapulco, Gro. ✆ **744/435-1010.** Fax 744/435-1020. www.caminoreal.com/acapulco. 157 units. High season $256 and up double. AE, MC, V. Parking $6. **Amenities:** 2 restaurants; lobby bar; babysitting; kids' club; health club w/aerobics, massage, spa treatments, and complete workout equipment (extra charge); 3 outdoor pools (1 for children); room service; tennis court; watersports equipment rentals. *In room:* A/C, flatscreen TV, hair dryer, minibar.

Casa Yal'ma Ka'an ★★ Finds A romantic hideaway 20 minutes south of Diamante, Casa Yal'ma Ka'an is a small ecological retreat with its own ocean beach. Stone paths with little bridges meander past several lookout towers and over lily ponds with palms and flowers, and the beautiful pool lies just steps from the Pacific. In addition to featuring its own beach club, Casa Yal'ma Ka'an offers a *temazcal,* a Mayan rustic steam bath that will be prepared for you with candles and aromatherapy amenities. Seven individual thatched-roof cottages have king beds, rustic wood furnishings, stone bathrooms, and private sitting decks. Gourmet breakfasts are served under a giant *palapa* overlooking the pool and beach, and private romantic dinners can be arranged on the beach. Service throughout this exclusive hotel is outstanding; children younger than 17 are not allowed.

Carretera hacia Barra Vieja Km 29 L189, 39867 Acapulco, Gro. ✆ **744/444-6389,** 444-6390. www.casayalmakaan.com. 7 units. High season $327 double; low season $300 double. Rates include American breakfast. MC, V. Free parking. **Amenities:** Restaurant; pool bar; outdoor pool; *temazcal* (steam); beach club. *In room:* A/C, TV.

Fairmont Acapulco Princess ★★★ The famous Princess hotel has been fully renovated and again reigns as Acapulco's leading resort, with 192 beachfront hectares (480 acres) of tropical gardens, pools, and golf courses. Guest rooms are housed in three 15-story buildings shaped like Aztec pyramids, with modern Mexican decor and terraces with views of the ocean, gardens, or golf course. Five beautiful free-form pools, including a saltwater lagoon dotted with waterfalls, are surrounded by gardens with 750 plant species and swans, flamingos, and other tropical birds. The wide beach offers many watersports activities, and there's an excellent kids' club. The resort also offers world-class tennis, golf, and spa facilities, and enough dining and entertainment options to obviate your need to leave the facility. In late 2008, the Fairmont "Pearl" opened as a luxury annex to the Princess, targeting hip, urban couples looking for a place to "see and be seen." Chic guest rooms colored in brilliant blues, magentas, and light greens feature plasma TVs, 350-count Egyptian cotton sheets, and beautiful bathrooms with rain showers and Miller Harris amenities. The Pearl Tower features its own lobby, concierge services, and swimming pool, and its guests have access to all the facilities at the Princess and the Pierre Marqués.

Playa Revolcadero s/n, Colonia Granjas del Marques, 39907 Acapulco, Gro. ✆ **800/441-1414** in the U.S., or 744/469-1000. Fax 744/469-1016. www.fairmont.com/acapulco. 710 units. $289 and up double; $444 and up double in the Pearl Tower. AE, MC, V. Free parking. **Amenities:** 5 restaurants; 5 bars; kids' club; concierge; 2 championship golf courses; fitness center; 5 outdoor pools; room service; Willow Stream spa; 8 outdoor lighted tennis courts and 2 indoor tennis courts; watersports activities. *In room:* A/C, TV w/pay movies.

Fairmont Pierre Marqués ★★★ The refined Fairmont Pierre Marqués is both more exclusive and more relaxed than the famous Fairmont Princess next door, to which guests also have access. It once served as a private home for J. Paul Getty and is today one of Acapulco's most prestigious hotels. Together the Pierre Marqués and the Princess offer more activities than you are likely to have time for, with three pools alone at the Pierre Marqués, a beautiful Pacific beach with watersports activities, championship golf, tennis, and a state-of-the-art spa and fitness center. Luxurious guest rooms include villas, bungalows, and low-rise pavilions overlooking the pools, tropical gardens, or beach. Fine dining is available here or at the Princess, with a shuttle regularly connecting the two hotels. Service throughout the hotel is outstanding. The Fairmont lies in Diamante, about a 20-minute drive from the center of Acapulco.

Playa Revolcadero s/n, Colonia Granjas del Marques, 39907 Acapulco, Gro. ✆ **800/441-1414** in the U.S., or 744/435-2600. Fax 744/466-1046. www.fairmont.com/pierremarques. 335 units. $289 and up double. AE, MC, V. Free parking. **Amenities:**

Restaurant; cafe; deli; 2 bars; concierge; championship golf course; health club and spa; 3 outdoor pools; room service; 5 outdoor lighted tennis courts (10 additional courts at Fairmont Princess, including 2 indoor courts). *In room:* A/C, TV w/ pay movies, Wi-Fi, hair dryer.

Las Brisas ★★ Moments This is a local landmark dating from 1957, often considered Acapulco's signature hotel. On a hillside with the best bay views of any hotel in Acapulco, Las Brisas is known for its tiered pink stucco facade, private pools, and 50 pink Jeeps rented exclusively to guests. The retro guest rooms are like separate villas sculpted from a terraced hillside, with panoramic views of Acapulco Bay from a balcony or terrace, as well as a private or semiprivate pool. They have been upgraded and retain the beloved "Las Brisas" style with pink and stone walls, whitewashed wood furnishings, flatscreen TVs and DVD players, and marble bathrooms. Early each morning, continental breakfast arrives in a cubbyhole. The spacious Regency Club rooms, at the apex of the property, offer the best views. In case you tire of your own pool, Las Brisas runs a beach club less than a kilometer (a half-mile) away, on Acapulco Bay; continuous shuttle service departs from the lobby. Mandatory service charges cover the shuttle service and all tips.

Apdo. Carretera Escénica 5255, Las Brisas, 39868 Acapulco, Gro. ✆ **866/427-2779** in the U.S., or 744/469-6900. Fax 744/446-5328. www.brisas.com.mx. 251 units. High season $350 shared pool, $445 private pool, $550 Royal Beach Club; low season $250 shared pool, $334 private pool, $410 Royal Beach Club. $20 per day service charge. Rates include continental breakfast. AE, MC, V. Free parking. **Amenities:** 2 restaurants; deli; concierge; gym; room service; small spa; 4 lighted tennis courts; private beach club w/fresh- and saltwater pools. *In room:* A/C, TV, DVD, hair dryer, minibar.

COSTERA HOTEL ZONE

Moderate

Calinda Beach You'll see this tall cylindrical tower rising at the eastern edge of Condesa Beach. Each room has a view, usually of the bay. Guest rooms have a simple beach feel, with white tile floors, blue and yellow fish-themed bedspreads, and small bathrooms. It affords the most reasonably priced lodgings along the strip of hotels facing popular Condesa Beach. Package prices are available, and the hotel frequently offers promotions, such as rates that include breakfast. The hotel features a narrow pool next to the beach and is popular with Mexican families.

Costera Alemán 1260, 39300 Acapulco, Gro. ✆ **744/435-0600.** Fax 744/484-4676. www.hotelcalindabeach.com. 357 units. High season $190 double; low season $150 double. Ask about promotional specials. AE, DC, MC, V. Parking $5. **Amenities:** 2 restaurants; poolside snacks; lobby bar w/live music; babysitting; small gym; 2 outdoor pools; room service. *In room:* A/C, TV, hair dryer.

Fiesta Americana Villas Acapulco ★ The Fiesta Americana is a long-standing favorite deluxe hotel in the heart of the beach-bar action. The 19-story structure towers above Condesa Beach, just east and up the hill from the Glorieta Diana traffic circle. The studios, suites, and villas have marble floors and can be loud if you're overlooking the pool area. Each has a private terrace or balcony with ocean view. The more expensive rooms feature the best bay views, and all have purified tap water. The hilltop swimming pool affords one of the city's finest views. The location is great for accessing Acapulco's numerous beach activities, shopping, and more casual nightlife.

Costera Alemán 97, 39690 Acapulco, Gro. ✆ **800/343-7821** in the U.S., or 744/435-1600. Fax 744/435-1645. www.fiestamericana.com. 324 units. High season $210 double, $280 suite; low season $80–$130 double, $200 suite. AE, DC, MC, V. Free parking. **Amenities:** 3 restaurants; lobby bar; deli; 2 outdoor pools; room service; spa w/massage service. *In room:* A/C, TV, hair dryer.

Hotel Elcano ★★ (Finds) An Acapulco classic, the Elcano is another personal favorite. It offers exceptional service and a prime location—on a broad stretch of beach (on the bay) in the heart of the hotel zone. The retro-style, turquoise-and-white lobby and beachside pool area are the closest you can get to a South Beach, Miami, atmosphere in Acapulco, and its popular open-air restaurant adds to the lively waterfront scene. Rooms are periodically upgraded, bright, and generally very comfortable. They feature classic navy-and-white tile accents with white wicker furniture. The large junior suites, all on corners, have two queen-size beds and huge closets. Studios are small but adequate, with king-size beds and small sinks outside the bathroom area. In the studios, a small portion of the TV armoire serves as a closet, and there are no balconies—only large sliding windows. All rooms have purified tap water. Avoid the noisy rooms near the ice machines.

Costera Alemán 75, 39690 Acapulco, Gro. ✆ **744/435-1500.** Fax 744/484-2230. www.hotel-elcano.com. 180 units. High season $112 studio, $142 standard double, $150 junior suite, $192 penthouse suite; rates higher during holiday periods. Ask about promotional discounts. AE, MC, V. Free parking. **Amenities:** Restaurant; babysitting; small workout room; beachside pool; room service. *In room:* A/C, TV, hair dryer, minibar.

Inexpensive

Sand's Acapulco (Value) (Kids) A good option for budget-minded families, this unpretentious 1960s-style motel nestles on the inland side, opposite the giant resort hotels and away from the Costera traffic. Guest rooms have basic furnishings with colorful linens, wall-to-wall carpeting, and tile bathrooms with showers only. The bungalows are smaller and less expensive, but more enticing than the motel rooms because they are surrounded by a small garden. Some units have kitchenettes, and all have a terrace or balcony. The family-friendly motel exudes great energy, with a kids' pool and a special play area for youngsters, including minigolf. The rates are reasonable, the accommodations satisfactory, and the location excellent.

Costera Alemán 178, 39670 Acapulco, Gro. ✆ **744/484-2260.** Fax 744/484-1053. www.sands.com.mx. 94 units. High season $150 standard double, $100 bungalow; low season $70 standard double, $50 bungalow. AE, MC, V. Limited free parking. **Amenities:** Babysitting; children's playground w/minigolf; concierge; outdoor pool; children's pool; squash court; volleyball. *In room:* A/C, TV, fridge, Wi-Fi.

DOWNTOWN (ON LA QUEBRADA) & OLD ACAPULCO BEACHES

Numerous budget hotels dot the streets fanning out from the *zócalo.* They're among the best values in town, but be sure to check your room first to see that it meets your needs. Several hotels in this area are close to Caleta and Caletilla beaches, or on the back of the hilly peninsula, at Playa la Angosta.

Moderate

Hotel Mirador Acapulco ★ An Old Acapulco landmark dating from 1934, El Mirador Hotel enjoys an unforgettable view of the famous cove where the cliff divers perform. It has been renovated with tropical landscaping and extensive Mexican tile. The hotel's guest rooms are staggered along the edge of a cliff, with double or queen-size beds and traditional furnishings, small kitchenette areas with minifridge and coffeemaker, and large bathrooms with marble counters. Most have a separate living room, some have a whirlpool tub, and all are accented with colorful Saltillo tile and other Mexican decorative touches. Ask for a room with a balcony or ocean view. Many guests gravitate to the large, breezy lobby bar as day fades into night on the beautiful cove. An a la carte menu ($25 minimum consumption) at La Perla restaurant affords stunning views of the cliff-diving show. Nearby is a protected cove with good snorkeling.

Plazoleta Quebrada 74, 39300 Acapulco, Gro. ✆ **744/483-1221** for reservations. Fax 744/482-4564. www.miradoracapulco.com. 133 units, including 9 junior suites with whirlpools. High season $155–$185 double, $207 junior suite; low season $85 double, $150 junior suite. Add $10 for kitchenette. AE, MC, V. **Amenities:** 2 restaurants; lobby bar; 3 outdoor pools, including 1 rather rundown saltwater pool; room service. *In room:* A/C, TV.

Inexpensive

Hotel Costa Linda (Value) Budget-minded Mexican and American families and couples are drawn to the sunny, well-kept rooms of the Costa Linda, one of the best values in the area. All rooms have individually controlled air-conditioning and a minifridge, and some have a small kitchenette (there's a $10 charge for using the kitchenette).

Closets and bathrooms are ample in size, and mattresses are firm. Cozy as the Costa Linda is, it is adjacent to one of the busier streets in Old Acapulco, so traffic noise can be bothersome. It's just a 1-block walk down to lively Caleta beach, and guests also have free beach access at the nearby Acamar hotel.

Costera Alemán 1008, 39390 Acapulco, Gro. ✆ **744/482-5277** or 482-2549. 44 units. High season $120 double; low season $60 double. Children younger than 8 stay free in parent's room. AE, MC, V. Free parking. **Amenities:** Small outdoor pool. *In room:* A/C, TV, free Wi-Fi.

Hotel Los Flamingos ★ (Finds) Perched on a cliff 150m (492 ft.) above Acapulco Bay, this Acapulco landmark once entertained John Wayne, Cary Grant, Johnny Weissmuller, Errol Flynn, Roy Rogers, and others. The place is a real find in a kitschy, campy sort of way—although the aged rooms are simple and lack modern luxuries, much of the hotel retains the charm of a grand era. Photographs of the old movie stars line the hotel walls, and outdoor passages wind their way along the cliff overlooking the ocean. Most rooms feature dramatic sea views and a large balcony or terrace, although few have air-conditioning and bathrooms are bare-bones. Thursdays at Los Flamingos are especially popular, with a *pozole* party and live music by a Mexican band. Even if you don't stay here, plan to at least come for a margarita or "coco loco" cocktail (invented here) at sunset, and walk along the dramatic lookout point. Prices remain as low as ever.

López Mateos s/n, Fracc. Las Playas, 39300 Acapulco, Gro. ✆ **744/482-0690.** Fax 744/483-9806. www.hotellosflamingos.com. 36 units. High season $65 double, $85 superior double with A/C, $100 junior suite; low season $60 double, $70 superior double, $80 junior suite. AE, MC, V. **Amenities:** Restaurant; bar; outdoor pool; room service. *In room:* A/C (in some), TV.

Hotel Misión Enter this hotel's plant-filled brick courtyard, shaded by two enormous mango trees, and you'll retreat into an earlier, more peaceful Acapulco. This tranquil 19th-century hotel lies 2 blocks inland from the Costera and the *zócalo.* The original L-shaped building is at least a century old. The rooms have simple colonial touches, such as colorful tile and wrought iron, and come simply furnished, with a fan and one or two beds with good mattresses. Four rooms have air-conditioning. Breakfast is served on the patio. This is a good value hotel, but it doesn't offer much in the way of service and it's also located in an area you'd probably not want to walk around at night.

Felipe Valle 12, 39300 Acapulco, Gro. ✆ **744/482-3643.** Fax 744/482-2076. 27 units. High season $50 double; low season $40 double. No credit cards. Parking $5.

5 WHERE TO DINE

Diners in Acapulco enjoy stunning views and fresh seafood. The quintessential setting is a candlelit table with the glittering bay spread out before you. If you're looking for a romantic spot, Acapulco brims with such inviting places; most sit along the southern coast, with views of the bay. If you're looking for simple food or an authentic local dining experience, you're best off in Old Acapulco. Cheap, fresh seafood can also be found at any of the simple restaurants in the local "Barra Vieja" neighborhood near Diamante. Many of Acapulco's fine-dining establishments automatically add a small "cover" charge to your bill (which is ostensibly for the bread served when you sit down), which usually amounts to between $2 and $3 per person.

SOUTH OF TOWN: LAS BRISAS AREA

Very Expensive

Baikal (Overrated) FUSION/FRENCH/ASIAN The exquisite Baikal remains the best-known place in Acapulco for an over-the-top dining experience, although you will be paying top dollar for the view. You enter from the street, then descend a spiral staircase into the stunning bar and restaurant, awash in muted tan and cream colors and natural accents of stone, wood, and water. The restaurant itself is constructed into the cliff, providing sweeping views of Acapulco Bay's glittering lights. The large dining room, with a two-story ceiling, has comfortable seating. The creative menu combines fusion fare and then adds a dash of Mexican flare. Start with the thinly sliced scallops in chipotle vinaigrette or a terrine of foie gras in a port sauce. Notable entrees include the filet of sole and lobster, pork tenderloin in red wine, or medallions of New Zealand lamb in a sweet garlic sauce. There's also an extensive selection of wines. Baikal has a private VIP dining room, wine cellar, and elegant bar, ideal for enjoying a sunset cocktail or after-dinner drink. It's east of town on the scenic highway just before the entrance to the Las Brisas hotel.

Carretera Escénica 16 and 22. © **744/446-6845** or 446-6867. www.baikal.com.mx. Reservations required (reservaciones@baikal.com.mx). Main courses $21–$90. AE, MC, V. Sun–Thurs 7pm–1am; Fri–Sat 7pm–2am. Closed Mon during summer.

Becco ★★ ITALIAN/SEAFOOD Among the city's most exclusive tables, Becco features floor-to-ceiling windows that stretch three floors overlooking the bay. A spiral staircase leads down from the entrance past the cocktail lounge and into the minimalist dining room, which has contemporary cement floors, large white pillars, and refined wood tables and chairs. The multilevel room buzzes with the chatter of Mexico's elite, many on vacation from the capital. The

Moments **Dining with a View**

Restaurants with unparalleled views of Acapulco include **Baikal, Becco, Zibu,** and **Zuntra** in the Las Brisas area; **El Olvido** along the Costera; **Su Casa** on a hill above the convention center; and the appropriately named **Bella Vista Restaurant** at the Las Brisas hotel, which many consider to have the best view of them all.

menu involves a rich selection of *antipasti,* including carpaccios, brochettes, and prosciutto with mozzarella; my favorite starter is seared tuna over a bed of spinach served with fries. The top pastas are homemade taglioli with lobster; spaghetti *allo scoglio* loaded with shrimp, calamari, clams, and crayfish; and seafood risotto. The chefs will prepare the fresh catches any way you like. Becco has an extensive Italian wine and champagne selection—all visible through the glass-enclosed cellar.

Carretera Escénica 14. ✆ **744/446-7402.** www.beccoalmare.com. Reservations required. Main courses $20–$38. AE, MC, V. Sun–Thurs 7pm–midnight; Fri–Sat 7pm–1am.

Zibu ★★★ SEAFOOD/THAI With a gorgeous view over the sea, Zibu blends Mexican and Thai architectural and culinary styles to create a breathtaking dining experience. The open-air venue is furnished with rattan tables and chairs surrounded by warm lighting of candles, tiki torches, and lamps; an infinity pool separates the restaurant patio from the *palapa*-topped lounge. Consider starting with the sea scallop carpaccio or sea bass tartare, and continue with the shrimp medallions with ginger and mango or grilled fish filet with almonds and soy (there are also meat dishes). Although it's not on the menu (just ask for it), the Thai salad with shrimp tempura, mint, cilantro, lettuce, mango, red and green peppers, and soy is out of this world. Finish with a tropical fruit plate and variety of sorbets. The glass-enclosed wine cellar houses a well-balanced though expensive collection. Service is gracious and attentive.

Av. Escénica s/n, Fracc. Glomar. ✆ **744/433-3058** or 433-3069. Reservations recommended. Main courses $18–$46. AE, MC, V. Daily 7pm–midnight.

Zuntra ★★ ASIAN/SEAFOOD One of the hottest tables in Acapulco, Zuntra sits across from Las Brisas hotel and overlooks the spectacular bay. Floor-to-ceiling windows frame the vista, as the fashionably dressed clientele trade knowing glances and spirited conversation. The kitchen focuses on seafood dishes with a pan-Asian flare. I recommend the halibut teriyaki over sushi crab with a chipotle mousse, or seared tuna marinated in a port wine and soy sauce. The cuisine is exquisitely presented and service is top notch. There seem to be as many servers as diners, and when compared to some of Acapulco's trendiest restaurants, Zuntra is also reasonably priced. A sleek bar/lounge sits on the restaurant's upper level.

Carretera Escénica s/n, Marina Brisas (across from Las Brisas hotel). © **744/444-5601.** www.zuntra.com.mx. Reservations required. Main courses $23–$38. AE, MC, V. Tues–Sun 7pm–1am.

COSTERA HOTEL ZONE

Very Expensive

El Olvido ★★ FRENCH/MEXICAN El Olvido gives you all the glittering bayview ambience of the posh Las Brisas restaurants, without the taxi ride. The menu is one of the most sophisticated in the city. It's expensive, but each dish is delightful in presentation and taste. Start with one of the 12 house specialty drinks, such as Olvido, made with tequila, rum, Cointreau, tomato juice, and lime juice. Soups include delicious cold avocado cream, and thick black bean and chorizo. Among the innovative entrees are grilled quails with honey and *pasilla* chiles, thick sea bass with a mild sauce of cilantro and avocado, and lamb chops with chipotle. For dessert, I recommend chocolate fondue or *guanábana* (a tropical fruit) mousse in a rich *zapote negro* (black tropical fruit) sauce. El Olvido sits at the back of the Plaza Marbella shopping center fronting Diana Circle. Although the bay view is lovely, a drawback is that the dance clubs down the shoreline can often be heard after 10pm.

Glorieta Diana traffic circle, Plaza Marbella. © **744/481-0203,** 481-0256, 481-0214. www.elolvido.com.mx. Reservations recommended. Main courses $15–$40. AE, MC, V. Daily 6pm–midnight.

Su Casa/Angel and Shelly's ★★ INTERNATIONAL Relaxed elegance and terrific food at reasonable prices are what you get at Su Casa. Owners Shelly and Angel Herrera created this pleasant, breezy, open-air restaurant on the patio of their hillside home overlooking the city (Angel and Shelly's—previously called La Margarita—is the indoor restaurant below Su Casa that's open during the rainy season). Both Shelly and Angel are experts in the kitchen and are on hand nightly to greet guests on the patio. The menu changes often. Some items are standard, such as shrimp *a la patrona* in herbs and spices, grilled fish, steak, and chicken. The *pasta el padrino,* with fresh shrimp and crème *chipotle,* is a delicious new addition to the menu. Many entrees come with garnishes of cooked banana or pineapple. The margaritas are big and delicious. The banana split or any of the flambées make dessert hard to resist.

V. Anahuac 110. ✆ **744/484-4350** or 484-1261. Fax 744/484-0803. www.sucasa-acapulco.com. Reservations recommended. Main courses $17–$35. Minimum charge of $75 per person 9pm–midnight. MC, V. Daily 5pm–midnight.

Moderate

El Cabrito ★★ NORTHERN MEXICAN With its hacienda-inspired entrance, waitresses in white dresses and *charro*-style neckties, and location in the heart of the Costera, this typical Mexican restaurant targets tourists. But its authentic and delicious food makes it a favorite among Mexicans, too—a comforting stamp of approval. Among the specialties are *cabrito al pastor* (roasted goat), *charro* beans, Oaxaca-style *mole,* and *burritos de machaca* (made with shredded beef). A whole *cabrito* is usually being slowly roasted inside the glass-enclosed *parilla.* Bottles of beer are brought to your table in buckets of ice and then poured in frosty cold mugs. El Cabrito lies on the ocean side of the Costera, south of the convention center.

Costera Alemán 1480. ✆ **744/484-7711.** Main courses $6–$18. AE, MC, V. Daily 2pm–midnight.

Inexpensive

El Zorrito ★★ MEXICAN/TACOS If you're looking for quality, no-nonsense Mexican food, El Zorrito is your place. Plastic tables and chairs, a dozen spinning ceiling fans, and photos of famous diners fill the open-air dining space. Waiters with their names printed on the back of their shirts traverse the restaurant with a smile, making sure customers are well fed and attended to. You can watch as homemade tortillas are prepared hot off the *comal* (the cast-iron plate used to make tortillas), and an expert team of cooks works harmoniously in the open kitchen. The food here is spicy and delicious, and the tacos are among the best you'll find.

Costera Miguel Alemán 212, across from the Costa Club Hotel. ✆ **744/485-7914.** Breakfasts $3–$5; tacos $6.50–$8; other dishes $6.50–$15. AE, MC, V. Open 24 hr.

Ika Tako ★★ Finds SEAFOOD/TACOS These fresh seafood tacos (many served in combinations that include grilled pineapple, fresh spinach, grated cheese, garlic, and bacon) are so tasty that they're addicting. An unusual selection of nine sweet and spicy salsas accompanies them, and there are also excellent burritos, meat and chicken dishes, and vegetarian selections. Unlike most inexpensive places to eat, the setting is also lovely, with a handful of tables overlooking tropical trees and the bay below. The lighting may be bright, the atmosphere occasionally hectic, and the service dependably slow, but the tacos are delectable. Consider the *takabrían,* which comes with shrimp, octopus, calamari, pepper, onion, and cheese. You can also order beer, wine, soft drinks, and dessert here. This restaurant is along the Costera, next to Beto's lobster restaurant. There's another branch across from the Gran Hotel Acapulco.

Costera Alemán 99. ✆ **744/484-9521.** Main courses $5–$16. AE, MC, V. Daily 5pm–3am.

100% Natural ★ Kids BREAKFAST/HEALTH FOOD Healthy, delicious, and inexpensive Mexican food fills the plates at this tropical plant–filled restaurant, on the second level of the shopping center across from the Acapulco Plaza Hotel. (This chain has five other branches in Acapulco, including another one farther east on the Costera.) If you've overindulged the night before, get yourself back on track here with one of the outstanding breakfast selections, served any time of day, such as whole-wheat pancakes with apple and cinnamon, a vegetarian omelet, or any one of nine fresh-fruit plates. Yogurt shakes, steamed vegetables, and cheese enchiladas are alternatives to the yummy sandwiches served on whole-grain breads. Don't miss one of the fruit *licuados,* blended fresh fruit with your choice of yogurt or milk.

Costera Miguel Alemán 200, across from the Costa Club Hotel. ✆ **744/485-3982.** www.100natural.com. Breakfasts $4.50–$5.50; sandwiches $5–$8; other food items $5–$10. AE, MC, V. Open 24 hr.

DOWNTOWN: THE ZOCALO AREA

The old downtown abounds with simple, inexpensive restaurants serving tasty eats. It's easy to pay more elsewhere for food that's not as consistently good as in this part of town. To explore, start at the *zócalo* and stroll west along Juárez. After about 3 blocks, you'll come to Azueta, lined with small seafood cafes and streetside stands.

Inexpensive

El Amigo Miguel ★ Finds MEXICAN/SEAFOOD Locals know that El Amigo Miguel is a standout among downtown seafood restaurants—you can easily pay more elsewhere but not eat better. Impeccably fresh seafood reigns; the large open-air dining room, 3 blocks west of the *zócalo,* is usually brimming with seafood lovers. When it overflows, head to a branch across the street, with the same menu. Try delicious *camarones borrachos* (drunken shrimp), in a sauce made with beer, ketchup, and bits of fresh bacon—it tastes nothing like the individual ingredients. *Filete Miguel* is a fresh fish filet (often red snapper or sea bass) stuffed with seafood and covered in a wonderful chipotle pepper sauce. Grilled shrimp with garlic and *mojo de ajo* (whole red snapper) are served at their classic best. Meat dishes are available as well.

Juárez 31, at Azueta (2nd location across the street, at Juárez 16). ✆ **744/483-6981.** Main courses $6–$15. AE, MC, V. Daily 9:30am–9:30pm.

Moments If There's Pozole, It Must Be Thursday

If you're visiting Acapulco on a Thursday, indulge in the local custom of eating *pozole,* a bowl of white hominy and meat in broth, garnished with sliced radishes, shredded lettuce, onions, oregano, and lime, served with crispy tostadas. The traditional version includes pork, but a newer chicken version has also become a standard. You can also find green *pozole,* which is made by adding a paste of roasted pumpkin seeds to the traditional *pozole* base. Green *pozole* is also traditionally served with a side of sardines. For a singular Acapulco experience, enjoy your Thursday *pozole* at the cliffside restaurant of the Hotel Los Flamingos (see above).

Mariscos Pipo SEAFOOD Check out the photographs of Old Acapulco on the walls while relaxing in this airy dining room decorated with hanging nets, fish, glass buoys, and shell lanterns. The English-language menu lists a wide array of seafood, including ceviche, lobster, octopus, crayfish, clams, baby-shark quesadillas, and fish prepared any way you want. This local favorite is 2 blocks west of the *zócalo* on Breton, just off the Costera.

Almirante Breton 3. ✆ **744/484-0165.** Main courses $5–$25. AE, MC, V. Daily 1–9:30pm.

6 ACAPULCO AFTER DARK

SPECIAL ATTRACTIONS Some major hotels schedule Mexican fiestas and other theme nights that include dinner and entertainment, including the Mayan Palace (✆ **744/469-6000**) on Monday nights at 7pm. Local travel agencies will have information.

NIGHTCLUBS & DANCE CLUBS Acapulco is even more famous for its nightclubs than for its beaches. Because clubs frequently change ownership—and often names—it's difficult to give specific and accurate recommendations. But some general tips will help. Cover charges vary but are almost always higher for men. Drinks can cost anywhere from $5 to $15. Don't even think about going out to one of the hillside dance clubs before 11pm, and don't expect much action until after midnight. But it will keep going until 4 or 5am, and possibly later.

Many dance clubs periodically waive their cover charge or offer some other promotion to attract customers. Look for promotional materials in hotel reception areas, at travel desks or concierge booths, in local publications, and on the beach.

The high-rise hotels have their own bars and sometimes dance clubs. Informal lobby or poolside cocktail bars often offer free live entertainment.

THE BEACH BAR ZONE Prefer a little fresh air with your nightlife? The young, hip crowd favors the growing number of open-air oceanfront dance clubs along Costera Alemán, most of which feature techno or alternative rock. There's a concentration of them between the Fiesta Americana and Continental Plaza hotels. An earlier and more casual option to the glitzy dance clubs, these places include **El Sombrero** (you'll know it when you see it), **Tabú,** and the pirate-themed **Barbaroja.** These mainly charge a cover (around $10) and offer an open bar. Women frequently drink free or with a lesser charge (men may pay more, but then, this is where the beach babes are). Disco Beach is the most popular of the bunch and occasionally—such as during spring break—has live bands on the beachfront stage. Their Friday night foam parties are especially popular. Most of the smaller establishments do not accept credit cards; when they do, MasterCard and Visa are more widely accepted than American Express.

If you are brave enough—or inebriated enough—there's a **bungee jump** in the midst of the beach bar zone at Costera Alemán 101 (**© 744/484-7529**). For $60, you get one jump, plus a T-shirt, diploma, and membership. Additional jumps are $20, and your fourth jump is free. For $90, you can jump as many times as you like from 1pm to 1:30am.

Baby-O ★★★ This longtime Acapulco hot spot is a throwback to the town's heady disco days, although the music is exceptionally contemporary. The mid- to late-20s crowd dances to everything from house to hip-hop and techno to dance. Across from the Days Inn and Hooters, Baby-O has a dance floor surrounded by several tiers of tables and sculpted, cavelike walls, serviced by three bars. Drinks cost $5 to $7. Three-dimensional laser shows and vapor effects keep the dancing going strong. Service is excellent. This is a high-class dance club attracting a beautiful clientele. It opens at 10:30pm, and you'd be wise to make a reservation. Costera Alemán 22. **© 744/484-7474** or 484-1035. www.babyo.com.mx. Cover $20 for women, $60 for men.

Carlos 'n' Charlie's For fun, danceable music and good food, you can't go wrong with this branch of the Carlos Anderson chain. It's always packed. Come early and get a seat on the terrace overlooking the Costera. This is a great place to go for late dinner and a few drinks before moving on to a club. It's east of the Glorieta Diana traffic circle, across the street from the Fiesta Americana Condesa. It's open daily from 1pm to 1am. Costera Alemán 999. **© 744/484-1285** or 484-0039. www.carlosandcharlies.com/acapulco/index.htm.

Classico ★★ One of the newest and hottest clubs in town, Classico is a raging party into the wee hours. A winding mirrored glass entrance leads into this small but trendy *antro* (disco). Digital screens and candlelit tables surround the illuminated dance floor, where music includes house, hip-hop, and reggaeton mixed by top DJs and blasted over a high-tech sound system. The glittery disco and outdoor deck sits just in front of Palladium and attracts a young, trendy crowd. The club is open Friday and Saturday from 11pm to 6am. Carretera Escénica #2, in front of Palladium. ✆ **744/446-6455.** www.classicodelmar.com. Cover $30 for men, free for women.

Mandara ★★ (Moments) Venture into this minimalist chrome-and-neon extravaganza perched on the side of the mountain for a true Acapulco nightlife experience. The plush, dim club has a sunken dance floor and panoramic view of the lights of Acapulco Bay. The after-hours lounge Privado, also in the same building, opens its doors at 4:30am and is most crowded at 6am. Downstairs, there's pumped-in mood smoke, alternating with fresh oxygen to keep you dancing. Tight and slinky is the norm for women; no shorts for men. The club opens nightly at 10:30pm; fireworks rock the usually full house at 3am, which is when a stylized dance performance takes place on weekends, in the style of Euro clubs. Call to find out if you need reservations; this club tends to be busiest on Friday nights. Carretera Escénica, btw. Los Rancheros Restaurant and La Vista Shopping Center. ✆ **744/446-5711** or 446-5712. www.acapulcomandara.com. Cover $30 for women, $40 for men; includes open bar.

Palladium ★★ This cliffside club currently reigns as the top spot in town and is found just down the road from Mandara. Generally, it welcomes a younger, rowdier crowd that enjoys the fabulous views and the dancing platforms set in the 50m-wide (164-ft.) glass windows overlooking the bay. Around 3:30am, Silver Man—complete with an Aztec headdress—performs, followed by a spray of fireworks outside the windows. Palladium consistently books some of the world's finest DJs, and the music seems to rock the earth below. The layout of the club is more open, which makes it conducive to meeting people. Carretera Escénica. ✆ **744/481-0330** or 446-5483. www.palladium.com.mx. Cover $30 for women, $40 for men; includes open bar.

Zuntra ★★★ This chic open-air bar above Zuntra restaurant overlooks Acapulco Bay and is furnished with lounge seating amid tiki torches and candles. The DJ spins lounge beats from the rooftop, and the fashionable crowd tends to arrive late and stay late. Women may wear black cocktail dresses, while men often sport designer button-down shirts. This is my favorite place for an evening cocktail or after-dinner drink in Acapulco. Open daily from 9pm to 4am. Carretera Escénica s/n, across from Las Brisas hotel. ✆ **744/444-5601.** www.zuntra.com.mx. No cover.

3

Northward to Zihuatanejo & Ixtapa

Side-by-side beach resorts, Ixtapa and Zihuatanejo share geography, but they couldn't be more different in character. Ixtapa is a preplanned resort development with modern infrastructure, high-rise hotels, and tourist services, while Zihuatanejo—"Zihua" to the locals—is a charming Mexican beach village that has changed slowly with time. For travelers, this offers the intriguing possibility of visiting two distinct destinations in one vacation. Those looking for a package vacation or all-inclusive resort should opt for Ixtapa (eex-*tah*-pah). You can easily make the quick 6.5km (4-mile) trip into Zihuatanejo for a sampling of the simple life in a *pueblo* by the sea. Those who prefer a more low-key retreat with Mexican personality should settle in Zihuatanejo (see-wah-tah-*neh*-hoh). It's home to some simple beach-close inns as well as ultraluxury boutique hotels.

The area, with the backdrop of the Sierra Madre and foreground of the Pacific Ocean, provides a broad range of outdoor activities and sun-drenched diversions. Scuba diving, deep-sea fishing, bay cruises to remote beaches, and golf are among the favorites. Nightlife in both towns borders on the subdued, although Ixtapa is livelier during holiday periods.

This dual destination is the choice for the traveler looking for a little of everything, from resort-style indulgence to unpretentious simplicity. These two resorts are more welcoming to couples and adults than families, with a number of places that are off-limits to children younger than 16—something of a rarity in Mexico.

1 ESSENTIALS

576km (357 miles) SW of Mexico City; 565km (350 miles) SE of Manzanillo; 253km (157 miles) NW of Acapulco

GETTING THERE & DEPARTING

BY PLANE These destinations tend to be even more seasonal than most resorts in Mexico. Flights are available year-round from U.S.

Tips Motorist Advisory

Motorists planning to follow Hwy. 200 northwest up the coast from Ixtapa or Zihuatanejo toward Lázaro Cárdenas and Manzanillo should be aware of reports of car and bus hijackings on that route, especially around Playa Azul, with bus holdups more common than car holdups. Before heading in that direction, ask locals and the tourism office about the status of the route. Don't drive at night. Police and military patrols of the highway have increased, and the number of incidents has dropped dramatically.

gateways, but they operate less frequently in the summer. See chapter 1, "Planning Your Trip to Southern Pacific Mexico," for information on flying to Ixtapa/Zihuatanejo from the United States and Canada. **AeroMéxico** and **Click Mexicana** fly daily from Mexico City; **InterJet** flies daily from neighboring Toluca (about an hour from Mexico City). Here are the local numbers of some carriers: **AeroMéxico** (✆ 755/554-2018 or 554-2019), **Alaska Airlines** (✆ 755/554-8457), **Continental** (✆ 755/554-4219), **Click Mexicana** (✆ 01-800/112-5425 toll-free in Mexico), **InterJet** (✆ 01-800/011-2345 toll-free in Mexico), and **US Airways** (✆ 755/554-8634). Ask your travel agent about **charter flights** and packages.

The **Ixtapa/Zihuatanejo airport** (✆ **755/554-2070**) is about 11km (6¾ miles) and 15 minutes south of Zihuatanejo. Taxi fares to the Ixtapa hotel zone are $32 and to Zihuatanejo $28. **Transportes Terrestres** (✆ **755/554-3298**) *colectivos* (minivans) transport travelers to hotels in Ixtapa and Zihuatanejo for about $12 and can be purchased just outside the baggage-claim area. Car-rental agencies with booths in the airport include **Hertz** (✆ **800/654-3131** in the U.S., or 755/554-2952) and **Budget** (✆ **800/527-0700** in the U.S., or 755/553-0397).

BY CAR From Mexico City (about 8–9 hrs.), you can take **Hwy. 15** to Toluca, then **Hwy. 130/134** the rest of the way. On the latter road, highway gas stations are few. Another route is the four-lane **Hwy. 95D** to Iguala, then **Hwy. 51** west to **Hwy. 134.** A new toll road, **Hwy. 37** from Morelia to Ixtapa, cuts about an hour off the total trip time.

From Acapulco (3–4 hr.) or Manzanillo (9 hr.), the only choice is the coastal **Hwy. 200.** The ocean views along the winding, mountain-edged drive from Manzanillo can be spectacular, although there are

Zihuatanejo & Ixtapa Area

ACCOMMODATIONS ■
Amuleto 13
Barceló Ixtapa 2
Brisas del Mar 7
Bungalows Ley 5
Casa Kau-Kan 14
La Casa Que Canta 9
La Quinta de Don Andrés 6
Las Brisas Ixtapa 3
NH Krystal Ixtapa 1
Posada Citali 4
The Tides Zihuatanejo 12
Villa Carolina 11
Villa Guadalupe 8
Villas San Sebastián 10

many speed bumps along the way that make for slow going. ***Warning:*** You should not drive this route at night, both because it is dark and curvy and because there are ongoing problems with drug-related crime through the state of Michoacán in particular, where you will encounter numerous military checkpoints.

BY BUS Zihuatanejo has two bus terminals: the **Central de Autobuses Estrella Blanca** (© **755/554-3477**), Paseo Zihuatanejo at Paseo la Boquita, opposite the Pemex station and IMSS Hospital, from which most lines operate; and the **Estrella de Oro** station (© **755/554-2175**), a block away. At the Central de Autobuses, several companies offer daily service to and from Acapulco, Puerto Escondido, Huatulco, Manzanillo, Puerto Vallarta, and other cities. At the other station, first-class Estrella de Oro buses run daily to Acapulco.

The trip from Mexico City to Zihuatanejo (bypassing Acapulco) takes 9 hours; from Acapulco, it's 4 to 5 hours. From Zihuatanejo, it's 9 or 10 hours to Manzanillo, and it's an additional 6 hours to Puerto Vallarta.

ORIENTATION

VISITOR INFORMATION The **Ixtapa/Zihuatanejo Tourism Office** (© **755/554-2001**) sits on the main square at Av. Zihuatanejo Poniente 21; it's open Monday through Friday from 8am to 6pm and provides basic tourist information. The **Convention and Visitor's Bureau** is another source of information; it's in Ixtapa at Paseo de Las Gaviotas 12 (© **755/553-1270**) and open Monday through Friday from 9am to 2pm and 4pm to 7pm. There's also a tourist kiosk in front of the Plaza las Fuentes in Ixtapa, which is open daily from 10am to 6pm.

CITY LAYOUT The fishing village and resort of **Zihuatanejo** spreads out around the beautiful Bay of Zihuatanejo, framed by downtown to the north and a beautiful long beach and the Sierra foothills to the east. The heart of Zihuatanejo is the waterfront walkway **Paseo del Pescador** (also called the *malecón*), bordering the Municipal Beach. Rather than a plaza, as in most Mexican villages, the town centerpiece is a **basketball court,** which fronts the beach. It's a point of reference for directions. The main thoroughfare for cars is **Juan Alvarez,** a block behind the *malecón.* Sections of several of the main streets are designated *zona peatonal* (pedestrian zone).

A cement-and-sand walkway runs from the *malecón* in downtown Zihuatanejo along the water to **Playa Madera.** The walkway is lit at night. Access to Playa La Ropa (Clothing Beach) is by the main road, **Camino a Playa La Ropa.** Playa La Ropa and Playa Las Gatas (Cats Beach) are connected only by boat.

A good highway connects Zihua to **Ixtapa,** 6km (4 miles) northwest. The 18-hole **Ixtapa Golf Club** marks the beginning of the inland side of Ixtapa. Tall hotels line Ixtapa's wide beach, **Playa Palmar,** against a backdrop of lush palm groves and mountains. Access is by the main street, **Bulevar Ixtapa.** On the opposite side of the main boulevard lies a large expanse of small shopping plazas (many with air-conditioned shops) and restaurants. At the far end of Bulevar Ixtapa, **Marina Ixtapa** has excellent restaurants, private yacht slips, and an 18-hole golf course. Condominiums and private homes surround the marina and golf course, and additional exclusive residential areas are rising in the hillsides past the marina on the road to Playa Quieta and Playa Linda. Ixtapa also has a paved bicycle track that begins at the marina and continues around the golf course and on toward Playa Linda.

GETTING AROUND **Taxi** fares are reasonable, but from midnight to 5am, rates increase by 50%. The average fare between Ixtapa and Zihuatanejo is $7. Within Zihua, the fare runs about $3; within Ixtapa, it averages $3 to $5. Radio cabs are available by calling ✆ **755/554-3680** or 554-3311; however, taxis are available from most hotels. A **shuttle bus** (70¢) runs between Zihuatanejo and Ixtapa every 15 or 20 minutes from 5am to 11pm daily but is almost always very crowded with commuting workers. In Zihuatanejo, it stops near the corner of Morelos/Paseo Zihuatanejo and Juárez, about 3 blocks north of the market. In Ixtapa, it makes numerous stops along Bulevar Ixtapa.

Note: The road from Zihuatanejo to Ixtapa is a broad, four-lane highway, which makes driving between the towns easier and faster than ever. Street signs are becoming more common in Zihuatanejo, and good signs lead in and out of both towns. However, both locations have an area called the Zona Hotelera (Hotel Zone), so if you're trying to reach Ixtapa's Hotel Zone, signs in Zihuatanejo pointing to that village's Hotel Zone may be confusing.

Fast Facts Zihuatanejo & Ixtapa

Area Code The telephone area code is **755.**

Banks Ixtapa's banks include **Bancomer,** in the La Puerta Centro shopping center. The most centrally located of Zihuatanejo's banks is **Banamex,** Calle Ejido at Vicente Guerreo. Banks change money during business hours, which are generally Monday through Friday from 9am to 4pm, Saturday from 10am to 1pm. ATMs and currency exchange are available during these and other hours.

Climate Summer is hot and humid, though tempered by sea breezes and brief showers; September is the peak of the tropical rainy season, with showers concentrated in the late afternoons.

Drugstore There's a branch of **Farmacías Coyuca** (✆ **755/554-5390**) at Nicolas Bravo 33 in Zihuatanejo, open from 8am to midnight.

Hospital **Hospital de la Marina Ixtapa** is at Bulevar Ixtapa s/n, in back of the artisans' market (✆ **755/553-0499**). In Zihuatanejo, there's the **Clinica Maciel** (✆ **755/554-2380;** La Palmas 12) or **Hospital Hernández Montejano,** Juan Alvarez s/n (✆ **755/554-5404**). Dial ✆ **065** (Red Cross) from any phone for emergencies.

Internet Access Ixtapa hotels generally have Internet access. Access is cheaper in Zihuatanejo; the most popular is **Zihuatanejo Bar Net,** Agustín Ramírez 2, on the ground floor of the Hotel Zihuatanejo Centro (✆ **755/554-3661**). High-speed access is $1 per hour; it's open 9am to 11pm daily.

Post Office The *correo* is in the SCT building, Edificio SCT, behind El Cacahuate in Zihuatanejo (✆ **755/554-2192**). It's open Monday through Friday from 8am to 6pm, Saturday from 8am to noon.

2 ACTIVITIES ON & OFF THE BEACH

The **Museo de Arqueología de la Costa Grande** (✆ 755/554-7552) traces the history of the area from Acapulco to Ixtapa/Zihuatanejo (the Costa Grande) from pre-Hispanic times, when it was known as Cihuatlán ("the Land of Women" in the Nahuatl language), through the Colonial Era. Most of the museum's pottery and stone artifacts give evidence of extensive trade with far-off cultures and regions, including the Toltec and Teotihuacán near Mexico City, the Olmec on the Pacific and Gulf coasts, and areas known today as the states of Nayarit, Michoacán, and San Luis Potosí. Local indigenous groups gave the Aztec tribute items, including cotton *tilmas* (capes) and *cacao* (chocolate), representations of which can be seen here. This museum, in Zihuatanejo near Vicente Guerrero at the east end of Paseo del Pescador, easily merits the half-hour or less it takes to stroll through; signs are in Spanish and English, and an accompanying brochure is available in English. Admission is $1 (children under 12 are free), and it's open Tuesday through Sunday from 10am to 6pm.

THE BEACHES **In Zihuatanejo** At Zihuatanejo's town beach, **Playa Municipal,** the local fishermen pull their colorful boats up onto the sand, making for a fine photo op. The small shops and restaurants lining the waterfront are great for people-watching and absorbing the flavor of daily village life. **Playa Madera (Wood Beach),** just east of Playa Municipal, is open to the surf but generally peaceful. A number of attractive budget lodgings overlook this area.

All beaches in Zihuatanejo are safe for swimming. Undertow is rarely a problem, and the municipal beach is protected from the main surge of the Pacific. Beaches in Ixtapa are more dangerous for swimming, with frequent undertow problems.

South of Playa Madera is Zihuatanejo's largest and most beautiful beach, **Playa La Ropa ★★**, a long sweep of sand with a great view of the sunset. Some lovely small hotels and restaurants nestle in the hills; palm groves edge the shoreline. Although it's also open to the Pacific, waves are usually gentle. There are a number of beachside restaurants, as well as beach operators renting kayaks, Hobie Cat sailboats, and snorkeling equipment. A taxi from town costs $3. The name Playa La Ropa (Clothing Beach) comes from an old tale of the sinking of a *galeón* during a storm. The silk clothing that it was carrying back from the Philippines washed ashore on this beach—hence the name.

The nicest beach for swimming, and the best for children, is the secluded **Playa Las Gatas (Cats Beach),** across the bay from Playa La Ropa and Zihuatanejo. The small coral reef just offshore is a nice spot for snorkeling and diving, and a little dive shop on the beach rents gear. The waters at Las Gatas are exceptionally clear, without undertow or big waves. Open-air seafood restaurants on the beach make it an appealing lunch spot. The PADI-certified **Carlo Scuba** (**✆ 755/554-6003;** www.carloscuba.com) arranges **scuba-diving** and snorkeling trips from here. Kayaks are also available for rent. Small *pangas* or *lanchas* (boats) with shade run to Las Gatas from the Zihuatanejo town pier, a 10-minute trip; the captains will take you across whenever you wish between 9am and 5pm for $4 round-trip. Usually the last boat back leaves Las Gatas at 6:30pm (5:30pm in low season), but check to be sure.

Playa Larga is a beautiful, uncrowded beach between Zihuatanejo and the airport, with several small *palapa* restaurants, hammocks, and wading pools.

In Ixtapa Ixtapa's main beach, **Playa Palmar,** is a lovely white-sand arc on the edge of the Hotel Zone, with dramatic rock formations silhouetted in the sea. The surf can be rough; use caution, and don't swim when a red flag is posted. Several of the nicest beaches in the area are essentially closed to the public. Although by law all Mexican beaches are open to the public, it is common practice for hotels to create artificial barriers (such as rocks or dunes).

Club Med and Qualton Club have largely claimed **Playa Quieta,** on the mainland across from Isla Ixtapa. The remaining piece of beach was once the launching point for boats to Isla Ixtapa, but it is gradually being taken over by a private development. Isla Ixtapa–bound boats now leave from the jetty on **Playa Linda,** about 13km (8 miles) north of Ixtapa. Inexpensive water taxis ferry passengers to Isla Ixtapa. Playa Linda is the primary out-of-town beach, with watersports equipment and horse rentals available. **Playa las Cuatas,** a pretty beach and cove a few miles north of Ixtapa, and **Playa Majahua,** an isolated beach just west of Zihuatanejo, are both being transformed into resort complexes. Lovely **Playa Vista Hermosa** is framed by striking rock formations and bordered by the Las Brisas hotel high on the hill. All of these are very attractive beaches for sunbathing or a stroll but have heavy surf and strong undertow. Use caution if you swim here.

WATERSPORTS & BOAT TRIPS Probably the most popular boat trip is to **Isla Ixtapa** for snorkeling and lunch at the El Marlin restaurant, one of several on the island. You can book this outing as a tour through local travel agencies, or go on your own from Zihuatanejo by following the directions to Playa Linda above and taking a boat from there. Boats leave for Isla Ixtapa every 10 minutes between 9am and 5pm, so you can depart and return as you like. The round-trip boat ride is $5. Along the way, you'll pass dramatic rock formations and see in the distance **Los Morros de Los Pericos islands,** where a great variety of birds nest on the rocky points jutting out into the blue Pacific. On Isla Ixtapa, you'll find good snorkeling, diving, and other watersports. Gear is available for rent on the island. Be sure to catch the last water taxi back at 5pm, and double-check that time upon arrival on the island.

Local travel agencies can usually arrange day trips to Los Morros de Los Pericos islands for **birding,** though it's less expensive to rent a boat with a guide at Playa Linda. The islands are offshore from Ixtapa's main beach.

Sunset cruises on the sailboat *Picante,* arranged through **Yates del Sol** (✆ **755/554-2694** or 554-8270; www.picantecruises.com), depart from the Zihuatanejo town marina at Puerto Mío. The evening cruises last 2 hours, cost $54 per person, and include an open bar and hors d'oeuvres. There's also a "Sail and Snorkel Adventure" day trip to **Playa Manzanillo** on the very comfortable, rarely crowded sailboat. The 4-hour trip begins at 10am, costs $74 per person, and includes an open bar and lunch (snorkeling gear $7 extra).

You can arrange **fishing trips** with the **boat cooperative** (✆ **755/554-2056**) at the Zihuatanejo town pier. They cost $210 to $450, depending on boat size, number of people, trip length, and so on.

Most trips last about 7 hours. The cooperative accepts only cash; no credit cards. The price includes soft drinks, beer, bait, and fishing gear, but not lunch. You'll pay more for a trip arranged through a local travel agency. The least expensive trips are on small launches called *pangas;* most have shade. Both small-game and deep-sea fishing are offered. The fishing is adequate, though not on par with that of Mazatlán or Baja. Other trips combine fishing with a visit to the near-deserted ocean beaches that extend for miles along the coast. Sam Lushinsky at **Ixtapa Sport-fishing Charters,** 19 Depue Lane, Stroudsburg, PA 18360 (✆ **570/688-9466;** fax 570/688-9554; www.ixtapasportfishing.com), is a noted outfitter. Prices range from $210 to $445 per day, for 8 to 13m (26–43 ft.) custom cruisers, fully equipped. They accept MasterCard and Visa.

Boating and fishing expeditions from the new **Marina Ixtapa,** a bit north of the Ixtapa Hotel Zone, can also be arranged. As a rule, everything available in or through the marina is more expensive and more Americanized.

Sailboats, sailboards, and other **watersports equipment** rentals are usually available at stands on Playa La Ropa, Playa las Gatas, Isla Ixtapa, and the main beach, Playa Palmar, in Ixtapa. There's **parasailing** at La Ropa and Palmar. **Kayaks** are available for rent at hotels in Ixtapa and some watersports operations on Playa La Ropa. **The Tides** has a beach club in front of the hotel on La Ropa with sailboat, sailboard, and kayak rentals open to the public.

The PADI-certified **Carlo Scuba,** on Playa Las Gatas (✆ **755/554-6003;** www.carloscuba.com), arranges **scuba-diving trips.** Fees start at $65 for a one-tank dive, or $85 for two dives, including all equipment and a drink. This shop has been around since 1962 and is very knowledgeable about the area, which has nearly 30 different dive sites, including walls and caves. Diving takes place year-round, though the water is clearest July to August and November to February, when visibility is 30m (98 ft.) or better. The nearest decompression chamber is in Ixtapa Marina. Advance reservations for dives are advised during Christmas and Easter.

Surfing is particularly good at **Petacalco Beach,** north of Ixtapa. **Swimming with dolphins** is possible at **Delfiniti Ixtapa** (www.delfiniti.com), arranged through any of the hotels or travel agents in town.

GOLF, TENNIS & HORSEBACK RIDING In **Ixtapa,** the **Club de Golf Ixtapa Palma Real** (✆ **755/553-1062** or 553-1163), in front of the Barceló Hotel, has an 18-hole course designed by Robert Trent Jones, Jr. The greens fee is $85 for 18 holes, $65 for 9 holes; caddies cost $25 for 18 holes, $20 for 9 holes; electric carts are $35; and clubs are $30. Tee times begin at 7am. The **Marina Ixtapa Golf Course**

(✆ **755/553-1410;** fax 755/553-0825), designed by Robert von Hagge, has 18 challenging holes. The greens fee is $90; carts cost $35; caddies cost $20; and club rental is $35. Discounted rates are available after 1:30pm. The first tee time is 7am. Call for reservations 24 hours in advance. Both courses accept American Express, MasterCard, and Visa. Most hotels offer discounts to the golf courses.

In Ixtapa, the **Club de Golf Ixtapa Palma Real** (✆ **755/553-1062** or 553-1163) has lighted **public tennis courts.** Fees are $8.50 an hour during the day, $14 at night. Call for reservations. In Zihuatanejo, the **Tides** (✆ **755/555-5500**) has lit tennis courts open to $30 an hour; private lessons cost $70 an hour.

For **horseback riding,** the largest local stable is on **Playa Linda** (no phone), offering guided trail rides from the Playa Linda beach (about 13km/8 miles north of Ixtapa). It's just next to the pier where the water taxis debark to Isla Ixtapa. Groups of three or more riders can arrange their own tour, which is especially nice around sunset (though you'll need mosquito repellent). Riders can choose to trace the beach to the mouth of the river and back through coconut plantations, or hug the beach for the entire ride (which usually lasts 1–1½ hr.). The fee is around $40, cash only. Travel agencies in either town can arrange your trip but will charge a bit more for transportation. Reservations are suggested in high season. Another good place to ride is in Playa Larga. There is a ranch on the first exit coming from Zihuatanejo (no phone, but you can't miss it—it is the first corral to the right as you drive toward the beach). The horses are in excellent shape. The fee is about $40 for 1½ hours, and includes transportation to and from your hotel as well as a drink. To arrange riding in advance, call co-owner Ignacio Mendiola on his cellphone at ✆ **755/559-8884.**

3 SHOPPING

ZIHUATANEJO

Zihuatanejo has its quota of T-shirt and souvenir shops, but it has also become a better place to buy crafts, folk art, and jewelry. Shops are generally open Monday through Saturday from 10am to 2pm and 4 to 8pm. Many better shops close Sunday, but some smaller souvenir stands stay open, and hours vary.

The **artisans' market** on Calle Cinco de Mayo is a good place to start shopping before moving on to specialty shops. It's open daily from 8am to 9pm. The **municipal market** on Avenida Benito Juárez sprawls over several blocks (about 5 blocks inland from the waterfront), but

most vendors hawk the same things—*huaraches,* hammocks, and baskets. On the sand next to the pier, there's a daily fish market, and just behind it on Paseo del Pescador there's a small seashell market. Spreading inland from the waterfront some 3 or 4 blocks are numerous small shops well worth exploring.

Besides the places listed below, check out **Alberto's,** Cuauhtémoc 12 and 15 (no phone), for jewelry. Also on Cuauhtémoc, 2 blocks down from the Nueva Zelanda Coffee Shop, is a small shop that looks like a market stand and sells beautiful tablecloths, napkins, and other linens; all are handmade in Aguascalientes.

Casa Marina This small complex extends from the waterfront to Alvarez near Cinco de Mayo and houses five intriguing shops, each specializing in handcrafted wares from all over Mexico. Items include handsome rugs, textiles, masks, colorful woodcarvings, and silver jewelry. Café Marina, the small coffee shop in the complex, sells shelves and shelves of used paperback books in several languages. Open daily from 9am to 9pm during the high season, Monday through Saturday 10am to 2pm and 5 to 9pm the rest of the year. Paseo del Pescador 9. ✆ **755/554-2373.**

El Jumil With small fishing boats pulled up on the sand just in front, this exotic beachside store sells coconut shell masks, exotic figurines, indigenous masks (including those used for ceremonial dances from Guerrero), Oaxacan pottery, and other regional art and crafts. There's a 10% discount on all items paid in cash. Open Monday to Saturday from 10am to 9pm. Casa Marina, Paseo del Pescador 9. ✆ **755/554-6191.**

Fruity Keiko Next to Coconuts restaurant (p. 91), this impressive little shop sells gorgeous gifts from across Mexico. Fruity Keiko carries carefully selected crafts and folk art, including some made by Mexico's best present-day artists. There's also a small selection of regional jewelry, handmade dresses, and Talavera pottery. Prices are higher here than if you were in the towns where these goods are actually made. Open Monday through Saturday from 10am to 9pm and Sunday from noon to 8pm. Vicente Guerrero 5 at Alvarez, opposite the Hotel Citali. ✆ **755/554-6578.**

IXTAPA

Shopping in Ixtapa is not especially memorable, with T-shirts and Mexican crafts the usual wares. **Ferrioni, Bye-Bye, Aca Joe,** and **Navale** sell brand-name sportswear. All of these shops are in the same area on Bulevar Ixtapa, across from the beachside hotels, and most are open daily from 9am to 2pm and 4 to 9pm.

Decoré Ixtapa This small boutique shop at the entr ·ice to the Ixtapa Marina sells fine Mexican furniture and decorations. Among the selections are wood and glass furnishings, onyx lamps, beautiful vases, handbags, and other luxury items. Bulevar Ixtapa. ✆ **755/553-3550.** www.decoreixtapa.com.

La Fuente This terrific shop carries gorgeous Talavera pottery, jaguar-shaped wicker tables, hand-blown glassware, masks, tin mirrors and frames, hand-embroidered clothing from Chiapas, and wood furniture. Open daily from 9am to 10pm during high season, daily from 10am to 9pm in low season. Los Patios Center, Bulevar Ixtapa. ✆ **755/553-0812.**

4 WHERE TO STAY

Larger high-rise hotels and all-inclusive resorts dominate accommodations in Ixtapa and on Playa Madera. Package deals for these are readily available online. There are only a few choices in the budget range. If you're looking for lower-priced rooms, Zihuatanejo offers more selection and better values, although it also has some very expensive (and wonderful) boutique hotels. Lodgings in both towns offer free parking. High season here generally runs from November 15 to April 30, and low season from May 1 to November 14. The rates quoted below do not include the 17% tax.

ZIHUATANEJO

Some of the hotels in Zihuatanejo and its nearby beach communities are more economical than those in Ixtapa, while others are far more expensive and exclusive. The term *bungalow* is used loosely—it may mean an individual unit with a kitchen and bedroom, or just a bedroom. It may also be like a hotel, in a two-story building with multiple units, some of which have kitchens. It may be cozy or rustic, with or without a patio or balcony. Accommodations in town are generally very basic, though clean and comfortable.

Playa Madera and Playa La Ropa, separated by a craggy shoreline, are both accessible by road. Prices tend to be higher here than in town, but the value is much better, and people tend to find that the beautiful, tranquil setting is worth the extra cost. The town is 5 minutes away by taxi and just 10 to 15 minutes by foot.

IN TOWN

Inexpensive

Posada Citlali In this cheerful three-story hotel, small rooms with fans surround a shaded, plant-filled courtyard that holds comfortable rockers and chairs. It's centrally located and a good value for the price, but very basic. Bottled water is in help-yourself containers on the patio. The stairway to the top two floors is narrow and steep.

Vicente Guerrero 3 (near Alvarez), 40880 Zihuatanejo, Gro. ✆ **755/554-2043.** 18 units. $50–$55 double. No credit cards. *In room:* Fan, TV, no phone.

PLAYA MADERA

Madera Beach is a 15-minute walk along the street, a 10-minute walk along the beach pathway, or a cheap taxi ride from Zihuatanejo. Most of the accommodations are on Calle Eva S. de López Mateos, the road overlooking the beach. Many hotels are set against the hill and have steep stairways.

Moderate

Brisas del Mar This simple but enchanted beach hotel has just 30 cheerful suites, all with private terraces overlooking Zihuatanejo Bay. The larger and more expensive units offer separate sitting areas, Jacuzzi tubs, and kitchenettes. Located above Playa Madera, the family-run establishment is known for its friendly service, and maid service includes an artistic presentation of flower petals on the bed. There's direct beach access, a pool, and spa services, including in-room massages upon request. The restaurant and lounge terrace boast a wonderful view of the sea.

Calle Eva S. de López Mateos s/n, Playa Madera, 40880 Zihuatanejo, Gro. ✆ **755/554-2142.** www.hotelbrisasdelmar.com. 30 units. High season $168 and up double; low season $107 and up double. MC, V. **Amenities:** Restaurant; bar; outdoor pool; small spa. *In room:* A/C (in some rooms), TV.

Inexpensive

Bungalows Ley No two suites are the same at this small complex, one of the nicest on Playa Madera. If you're traveling with a group, you may want to book the most expensive suite (Club Madera); it has a rooftop terrace, outdoor bar and grill, and spectacular view. All the units are immaculate; the simplest are studios with one king bed and a kitchen in the same room. Rooms have terraces or balconies just above the beach, and all are decorated in pastel colors. Bathrooms, however, tend to be small and dark, with showers only. The hotel has no pool but leads right to the beach.

Calle Eva S. de López Mateos s/n, Playa Madera (Apdo. Postal 466), 40880 Zihuatanejo, Gro. ✆ **755/554-4087.** Fax 755/554-1365. www.bungalowsley.com. 8 units. $90 double with A/C; $170 2-bedroom suite with kitchen (up to 4 persons). Low-season discounts available after 6-night stay. MC, V. Follow Mateos to the right, up a slight hill; it's on your left. *In room:* A/C, TV, kitchenette.

La Quinta de Don Andrés This inexpensive, family-friendly hotel sits just above Playa Madera and is less than a 10-minute walk from the town center. Seven of the 10 simply decorated rooms are suites, with separate living areas, bedrooms, kitchens, and air-conditioning. Although they're lacking in decor, the regular rooms are perfectly comfortable and some have panoramic views of the bay. There's a small courtyard pool, and the beach is just down the stairs.

Adelita 11, Playa Madera (Apdo. Postal 466), 40880 Zihuatanejo, Gro. ✆ **755/553-8213.** www.laquintadedonandres.com. 10 units. $130 double; $200 suite with kitchen (up to 4 persons). No credit cards. **Amenities:** Pool; direct beach access. *In room:* A/C (in suites only), TV, fridge, free Wi-Fi.

PLAYA LA ROPA

Playa La Ropa is a 20- to 25-minute walk south of town on the east side of the bay, or it's a $5 taxi ride.

Expensive

Amuleto ★★ Perched on a hill high above the bay, this intimate boutique hotel was designed for people who want to relax in luxury and exclusivity. Amuleto, which has only six units, boasts stunning panoramic views of Zihuatanejo Bay that make it seem like you're on top of the world. The *palapa*-covered restaurant serves innovative international food and overlooks a small infinity pool framed by the bay. Each of the bungalow-like units is individually decorated with Mexican and Asian designs using organic textures and earth colors. The *palapa* suite, for example, features meticulous stone, tile, and woodwork; a bed with 1,000-thread-count Egyptian cotton sheets; a separate sitting area with onyx lamps and bamboo chairs; a rooftop terrace with its own hammock surrounded by bougainvillea; and a private plunge pool. Amuleto's open-air restaurant serves wonderful breakfasts and is open to the public for dinner (see p. 92).

Calle Escénica 9, Playa La Ropa, 40880 Zihuatanejo, Gro. ✆ **213/280-1037** in the U.S., or 755/544-6222. Fax 310/496-0286 in the U.S. www.amuleto.net. 6 units. High season $400–$700 double; low season $250–$550 double. $100 extra person. AE, MC, V. **Amenities:** Restaurant; gym; outdoor pool. *In room:* A/C, minibar, free Wi-Fi.

La Casa Que Canta ★★★ (Moments) "The House that Sings" is one of the most romantic accommodations in Mexico and is regularly rated among the top boutique hotels in the world. The striking molded-adobe architecture typifies the rustic-chic style known as Mexican Pacific. Individually decorated rooms named after Mexican songs have handsome natural-tile floors, unusual painted Michoacán furniture, antiques, and stretched-leather *equipale*-style chairs and tables with hand-loomed fabrics throughout. All of the exquisite rooms offer large, beautifully furnished terraces with bay views, and the service includes beautiful flower-petal designs prepared each day atop the beds. Hammocks hang under the thatched-roof terraces, where you could while away an eternity. Most of the spacious units are suites, and 11 of them have private pools. Rooms meander up and down the hillside, and while no staircase is terribly long, there is only one elevator. Two adjacent private villas house four suites, all with private plunge pools. A "well-being" center offers massage, spa services, and yoga. The hotel's service is remarkably gracious, and you'll find La Casa Que Canta pretty close to heaven.

Camino Escénico a Playa La Ropa, 40880 Zihuatanejo, Gro. ✆ **888/523-5050** in the U.S., or 755/555-7000, 555-7026, 555-7030. Fax 755/554-7900. www.lacasaquecanta.com. 25 units. $490–$885 double; 5-night minimum stay required Jan–Apr. AE, MC, V. Children younger than 16 not accepted. **Amenities:** Restaurant (open to outside guests for dinner w/reservation only); bar; fitness center; yoga and stretching; cooking classes; freshwater outdoor pool on main terrace; saltwater outdoor pool on bottom level; room service; spa. *In room:* A/C, hair dryer, minibar.

The Tides ★★ The Tides sits on one of Mexico's most beautiful beaches. Suites feature one or two bedrooms, living areas, large terraces, and private plunge pools. Rooms are decorated with modern Mexican touches and include comfy lounges, excellent reading lights, CD players, and hammocks that beckon at siesta time. There are 11 beachside suites and one presidential suite. Those units that don't overlook the beach surround a fountain-filled lagoon and tropical gardens with enchanted lighting at night. Service remains first rate, though perhaps not as personalized as when this was Villa del Sol. The Tides allows children only in two-bedroom suites and generally has a quiet feel. The meal plan (breakfast and dinner) is mandatory in high season and includes an excellent variety of cuisine. In addition to the exquisite beach area, pools, restaurants, and bars, the Tides offers a full-service spa, tennis courts, and beach club. You can even request a massage on the sand.

Playa la Ropa (Apdo. Postal 84), 40880 Zihuatanejo, Gro. ✆ **866/905-9560** in the U.S., or 755/555-5500. Fax 755/554-2758. www.tideszihuatanejo.com. 70 units. High season $500–$550 double, $875–$1,700 suite; low season $355–$385 double, $570–$1,150 suite. Meal plan $90 per person Dec 17–Mar 31 (mandatory). AE, MC, V. **Amenities:** 2 open-air beachside restaurants; 3 bars; 4 outdoor pools (including 18m/59-ft. lap pool); room service; full-service spa; 2 lighted tennis courts. *In room:* A/C, TV, hair dryer, minibar, free Wi-Fi.

Moderate

Villa Carolina ★★ Finds Located next to the Tides, Villa Carolina is a hidden gem within walking distance of Playa La Ropa. Each of the beautifully designed suites offers privacy, luxury, and enchantment—at far less price than comparable boutique hotels in Zihuatanajo. Garden suites sit on the pool level and have individual patios; the larger master suites are upstairs and have balconies with hammocks and Jacuzzis. With two levels, the "grand house" is the largest suite, with two bedrooms, two bathrooms, and a private pool. All of the suites feature open-air sitting areas under palm-thatched roofs with built-in couches, fully stocked kitchens, and satellite TVs with DVD/CD players. The bedrooms and bathrooms use marble, tile, and stonework extensively, and have muted colors and soft Mexican designs. Service is gracious and unobtrusive, and hosts Tim and Carolina Conti will help with reservations for restaurants and activities.

Camino Escénico Playa La Ropa s/n, 40880 Zihuatanejo, Gro. ✆ **755/554-5612.** Fax 755/554-5615. www.villacarolina.com.mx. 7 units. High season $219 garden suite, $299 master suite, $350–$550 grand house; low season $169 garden suite, $219 master suite, $290–$450 grand house. MC, V. **Amenities:** Breakfast terrace; bar; DVD library; outdoor pool; room service. *In room:* A/C, TV w/DVD/CD player, hair dryer.

Villa Guadalupe ★★ A long wood staircase descends through jungle-like surroundings alongside the tiered villas of Villas Guadalupe, toward the sea. With adobe walls and *palapa* roofs, the villas seem to blend into the landscape, and carefully chosen pieces of Mexican art add to the magical ambience. Each of the individually decorated rooms at this boutique hotel has beach white furnishings and a private terrace with a spectacular view of Zihuatanejo Bay; the largest suite has its own plunge pool. Service is personalized and friendly, and the hotel has a very relaxed, intimate feel. Continental breakfast is served by the small infinity pool, and while there's no restaurant here, a beautiful restaurant looks over the water at the sister Tentaciones Hotel just up the hill.

Camino Escénico a Playa La Ropa, 40880 Zihuatanejo, Gro. ✆ **755/554-3005.** Fax 755/554-6185. www.zihuatanejo.net/villa-guadalupe. 8 units. High season $220–$350 double; low season $165–$250 double. AE, MC, V. Follow the road leading south out of town toward Playa La Ropa, take the 1st right after the traffic circle, and go left on Adelita. **Amenities:** Breakfast terrace; outdoor pool. *In room:* TV, minibar.

Villas San Sebastián On the mountainside above Playa La Ropa, this nine-villa complex offers great views of Zihuatanejo's bay. The one- and two-bedroom villas surround tropical vegetation and a central swimming pool. Each has a kitchenette and a spacious private terrace. The personalized service is one reason these villas come so highly recommended; owner Luis Valle, whose family has lived in this community for decades, is usually available to help guests with any questions or needs.

Bulevar Escénico Playa La Ropa (across from the Dolphins Fountain). ✆ **755/554-4154.** 11 units. High season $145 1-bedroom villa, $255 2-bedroom villa; low season $98 1-bedroom villa, $165 2-bedroom villa. No credit cards. **Amenities:** Outdoor pool. *In room:* A/C, TV, kitchenette, free Wi-Fi.

PLAYA ZIHUATANEJO

Moderate

Casa Kau-Kan ★★ Casa Kau-Kan is an upscale bohemian oasis on the long, secluded beach of Playa Larga. It's located about 20 minutes south of Zihuatanejo on the open Pacific Ocean. The spacious bungalow-like accommodations surrounded by palm trees feature private sitting areas, canopied beds with mosquito nets, and bamboo furnishings; four have private terrace pools. Owned by Ricardo Rodriguez, who also runs Kau-Kan restaurant (p. 93), the hotel serves delicious fresh seafood. There's not much to do in the immediate surroundings except tan, swim, eat, read, and enjoy the quiet lazy days, although horseback riding and kite-surfing are also offered on the beach immediately in front. You should be an experienced swimmer to go in the ocean here, which typically has waves perfect for body-surfing. Hotel service is friendly and extremely attentive2whether it's a coconut or a cocktail you desire, it'll be right up.

Playa Larga s/n, 40880 Zihuatanejo, Gro. ✆ **755/554-8446.** Fax 755/554-5731. www.casakaukan.com. 9 units. High season $120–$235 double; low season $90–$200 double. AE, MC, V. Children younger than 15 not accepted. **Amenities:** Restaurant; pool. *In room:* A/C, fridge.

IXTAPA

Expensive

Barceló Ixtapa ★ (Value) (Kids) An excellent value and a great choice for families, this grand 12-story all-inclusive resort hotel has large, handsomely furnished public areas facing the beach. It's an inviting place to sip a drink and people-watch. Most rooms have balconies with ocean or mountain views. Gardens surround the large pool, with a swim-up bar; daytime activities, including a dive center; and separate section for children. There's a Mexican fiesta night here on Wednesdays.

Bulevar Ixtapa, 40880 Ixtapa, Gro. ✆ **755/555-2000.** Fax 755/553-2438. www.barcelo.com. 340 units. High season $380 double all-inclusive; low season $270 double all-inclusive. AE, DC, MC, V. **Amenities:** 4 restaurants; lobby bar; concierge; fitness room; beachside pool w/activities; room service; spa w/massage treatments; dive center; rooms for those w/limited mobility. *In room:* A/C, TV, minibar, Wi-Fi (for an additional fee)

Las Brisas Ixtapa ★★ Set above the high-rise hotels of Ixtapa on a rocky promontory, Las Brisas is the best of Ixtapa's resorts. Notable for its gorgeous private beach cove and striking stepped architecture, designed by renowned architect Ricardo Legorreta, Las Brisas features large stone and stucco public areas, recently renovated guest rooms with upscale beach decor and oceanview terraces with hammocks, and multitier swimming pools with waterfalls. All rooms face the hotel's gorgeous private beach, which can be accessed by an elevator; although enticing, the water is sometimes rough and can be dangerous for swimming. The six master suites come with private pools. Beach Club rooms offer upgraded amenities, complimentary cocktails, and continental breakfast. The hotel sits in beautiful jungle-like surroundings and has tennis courts on the property. Internet specials are usually available, and guests receive discounts at a nearby golf course.

Bulevar Ixtapa s/n at Playa Vista Hermosa, 40880 Ixtapa, Gro. ✆ **888/559-4329** in the U.S., or 755/553-2121. Fax 755/553-1091. www.brisas.com.mx. 417 units. High season $285 deluxe double, $490 Royal Beach Club; low season $196 deluxe double, $230 Royal Beach Club. AE, MC, V. **Amenities:** 5 restaurants; 3 bars; babysitting; fitness center; 4 outdoor pools (1 just for adults and another just for children); 4 lighted tennis courts w/pro on request; room service; rooms for those w/limited mobility; executive rooms; elevator to secluded beach. *In room:* A/C, TV, hair dryer, minibar.

NH Krystal Ixtapa Kids Krystal hotels are known in Mexico for quality rooms and service. This was the original in the chain and one of the first hotels in Ixtapa, and it upholds its reputation for family-friendly service. Many staff members have been with the NH Krystal for its more than 20 years of operation and are on hand to greet return guests. This large V-shaped hotel has ample grounds and a terrific pool area. Most of the spacious guest rooms feature oceanview balconies and tile bathrooms, while master suites have larger balconies that double as living areas. Club rooms are just $30 more than regular rooms, and some rates include breakfast buffet. The center of Ixtapa nightlife is here, at the hotel's **Christine** dance club.

Bulevar Ixtapa s/n, 40880 Ixtapa, Gro. ✆ **888/726-0528** in the U.S., or 755/555-0510. Fax 755/553-0226. www.nh-hotels.com. 255 units. High season $250 and up double, $350 suite; low season $100 and up double, $350 suite. 2 children younger than 12 stay free in parent's room. Ask about special packages. AE, DC, MC, V. **Amenities:** 4 restaurants; lobby bar; nightclub; kids' club; gym; outdoor pool and kids' pool; room service. *In room:* A/C, TV, minibar.

5 WHERE TO DINE

ZIHUATANEJO

Zihuatanejo's **central market,** on Avenida Benito Juárez, about 5 blocks inland from the waterfront, will whet your appetite for cheap and tasty food. It's best at breakfast and lunch, before the market activity winds down in the afternoon. Look for what's hot and fresh. The market area is one of the coast's best places to shop and people-watch.

Expensive

Coconuts ★★ INTERNATIONAL/SEAFOOD Located in Zihuatanejo's oldest building, Coconuts has long been a Zihua institution serving fresh, innovative cuisine under the direction of chef David Dawson. The historic building, which now has a garden patio, was originally the weigh-in station for Zihua's coconut industry in the late 1800s. For an appetizer, I recommend the roasted pumpkin and ricotta crepes. Among the excellent seafood dishes are grilled red snapper and other locally caught fish prepared any way you like, such as with fresh fruit salsa. The bananas flambé (for two) has earned a loyal following, with good reason. Expect friendly, efficient service here and a large expat clientele.

Augustín Ramírez 1 (at Vicente Guerrero). ✆ **755/554-2518** or 554-7980. Reservations recommended. Main courses $14–$32. AE, MC, V. High season daily 6–10:30pm. Closed July–Sept (rainy season).

Inexpensive

La Sirena Gorda MEXICAN For one of the most popular breakfasts in town, head to the fun and unusual Sirena Gorda. "The Fat Mermaid," as it translates into English, serves a variety of eggs and omelets, hotcakes or French toast, and fruit with granola and yogurt. For lunch, the house specialty is seafood tacos—fish, shrimp, or even lobster in a variety of sauces. Also take a look at the short list of daily specials, such as blackened red snapper, tuna, or steak. The food is excellent, and patrons enjoy the casual sidewalk cafe atmosphere. Passionate illustrations and paintings of colorful fat mermaids decorate the walls, and miniature wood boats hang from the ceiling.

Paseo del Pescador. ✆ **755/554-2687.** Breakfast $4–$6; main courses $6.50–$23. MC, V. Thurs–Tues 8:30am–10:30pm. Closed Wed. From the basketball court, face the water and walk to the right; La Sirena Gorda is on your right just before the town pier.

Nueva Zelanda MEXICAN This open-air snack shop serves rich cappuccino sprinkled with cinnamon, fresh-fruit *licuados* (smoothies mixed with water or milk), and pancakes with real maple syrup. The mainstays are *tortas* and enchiladas, and service is friendly and efficient. There's a second location in Ixtapa, in the back section of the Los Patios shopping center (✆ **755/553-0838**), next to Señor Frog's.

Cuauhtémoc 23 (at Ejido). ✆ **755/554-2340.** *Tortas* $3; enchiladas $6; *licuados* $2.50; cappuccino $2.50. No credit cards. Daily 8am–10pm. From the waterfront, walk 3 blocks inland on Cuauhtémoc; the restaurant is on your right.

PLAYA MADERA & PLAYA LA ROPA

Expensive

Amuleto ★★★ SEAFOOD This intimate restaurant located in the Amuleto boutique hotel feels like it's on top of the world, offering a breathtaking view of the sea and town behind it. Just a handful of candlelit tables sit under the open-air *palapa* next to an infinity pool and tropical vegetation. To start, I recommend the tuna tartare with lime or salmon carpaccio, with fresh citrus fruit. Excellent main dishes include grilled mahimahi with caviar and grapefruit; filet mignon prepared with a rich blue cheese sauce; and lobster and shrimp risotto served with a half-lobster on top. For dessert, the chocolate brownie with vanilla ice cream and Kahlua should top off what promises to be a very special meal. Overseen by Brazilian owners Ricardo Teitelroat and Ticci Tonetto, Amuleto offers outstanding service.

Calle Escénica 9, Playa La Ropa, 40880 Zihuatanejo, Gro. ✆ **755/544-6222.** www.amuleto.net. Main courses $19–$35. AE, MC, V. Daily 6–9pm.

Kau-Kan ★★ MEDITERRANEAN/SEAFOOD Candlelit tables and lamps dot this romantic open-air restaurant with just a handful of tables and an unforgettable view of Zihuatanejo Bay. Head chef Ricardo Rodriguez, who also runs the Casa Kau-Kan, ensures that the fresh dishes are prepared with care and meticulously presented. Among my favorite appetizers are crab and olive tarts and the mahi-mahi carpaccio. For a main dish, consider the baked potato stuffed with lobster, or the shrimp prepared in a basil and garlic sauce. To top off your meal, go for a pecan and chocolate cake served with dark-chocolate sauce, accompanied by one of the aromatic Central American coffees. If you're looking for an enchanted dinner outside your hotel, reserve a candlelit table at Kau-Kan and try to arrive in time for the sunset.

Camino a Playa La Ropa. ✆ **755/554-8446.** Reservations recommended. Main courses $17–$37. AE, MC, V. Daily 5–10:30pm. From downtown on the road to La Ropa, Kau-Kan is on the right side of the road past the 1st curve.

Moderate

La Casa Vieja ★ MEXICAN A casual yet intimate Mexican restaurant at the entrance to Playa Madera, "The Old House" serves delicious fish and traditional dishes, such as *filet a la tampiqueña* (tenderloin steak) and *cochinita pibil* (slow-roasted pork). Among the fresh fish selections prepared any way you like are tuna, red snapper, and mahi-mahi. Tiny white lights, twig lamps, and plants decorate the open-air dining room. Service is friendly and relaxed, and soft music plays in the background. The number of Mexicans dining here testifies to the restaurant's quality. Delicious *pozole* is served on Thursday.

Josefa Ortíz de Domínguez 7. ✆ **755/554-9770.** Main courses $11–$17. MC, V. Mon–Sat noon–10:30pm; Sun 9am–11pm. Restaurant is at the entrance of the road leading into Playa Madera.

Inexpensive

La Perla SEAFOOD Among the many *palapa*-style restaurants on Playa La Ropa, La Perla is the most popular. Somehow the combination of plastic tables plopped on the sand and simple food served unhurriedly makes La Perla a local tradition. The menu is a mix of Mexican and seafood selections, including delectable seafood ceviches, grilled fish filets, and a 1-kilo (2.2-lb.) grilled or broiled lobster for $40. Cold beer and cocktails are available whether or not you eat, as are whole coconuts served with a straw and with or without an added kick of gin. Sports are played throughout the day via satellite TV.

Playa La Ropa. ✆ **755/554-2700.** www.laperlarestaurant.net. Breakfast $3–$7.50; main courses $9–$40. AE, MC, V. Daily 11am–10pm; breakfast 10am–noon. Near the southern end of La Ropa Beach, take the right fork in the road; there's a sign in the parking lot.

IXTAPA

Expensive

Beccofino ★ NORTHERN ITALIAN This restaurant is a standout in Mexico. Owner Angelo Rolly Pavia serves the flavorful northern Italian specialties he grew up knowing and loving. I strongly recommend one of the homemade seafood pastas, which may include calamari, shrimp, clams, mussels, and crayfish. Ravioli, a house specialty, comes stuffed with beef or seafood. The garlic bread is terrific, and there's an extensive wine list. A popular place in a breezy marina location, the restaurant tends to be loud when it's crowded. It's also a popular breakfast spot.

Marina Ixtapa. ✆ **755/553-1770.** Breakfast $7–$18; main courses $18–$28. AE, MC, V. Daily 9am–11:30pm.

Villa de la Selva ★★★ MEXICAN/MEDITERRANEAN Clinging to the edge of a cliff, this elegant restaurant enjoys the most spectacular sea and sunset view in Ixtapa. Beautiful wood terraces surrounded by a palm– and mango tree–filled jungle look directly over the bay, just steps below. Try to come early to get one of the best vistas, especially on the lower terrace. Hidden speakers create music that seems to come from the sea. The cuisine is artfully presented and classically rich. To start, I recommend the coconut shrimp in a mango-and-chile sauce or the tuna carpaccio. For a main course, a wonderful dish is *Filet Villa de la Selva,* red snapper topped with shrimp and hollandaise sauce. Finish with chocolate mousse, and come here with someone looking for romance. It's possible to make reservations online.

Paseo de la Roca. ✆ **755/553-0362.** www.villadelaselva.com. Reservations recommended during high season. Main courses $18–$37. AE, MC, V. Daily 6–11:30pm. Closed Sept.

Moderate

Casa Morelos MEXICAN This is a casual place for tasty Mexican seafood. You can order fresh fish any way you like, such as with lemon and olive oil, mustard, orange, mango, garlic, or chile. You might have the delicious seafood fajitas, tequila and coconut shrimp, or perhaps shrimp enchiladas. The fish tacos *al pastor* are the best in the area. The *mar y tierra* is a succulent shrimp and steak dish, while *mar y mar* is shrimp and lobster. Service is friendly at this casual eatery, which offers indoor and outdoor seating.

Centro Comercial La Puerta. ✆ **755/553-0578.** Main dishes $18–$35. MC, V. Daily 8am–midnight. Located next to Señor Frog's.

Inexpensive

Golden Cookie Shop ★ PASTRIES/DELI This German bakery and deli's freshly baked goods beg for a detour, and the organic coffee menu is the most extensive in town. Come for one of the creative breakfast pancake plates, or for a hot or cold triple-decker sandwich. Nutritional cookies, breads, pastries, and cakes are available, as are vegetarian and low-carb selections. Large sandwiches on fresh soft bread come with a choice of sliced meats. *Bratwurst* and *wienerschnitzel* are also served.

Los Patios Center. ✆ **755/553-0310.** Breakfast $6–$10; sandwiches $6–$9; main courses $8.50–$13. No credit cards. Daily 8am–2pm. Go to the 2nd floor of Los Patios commercial center.

6 ZIHUATANEJO & IXTAPA AFTER DARK

With an exception or two, Zihuatanejo nightlife dies down around 11pm or midnight. For a selection of clubs, dance spots, hotel fiestas, special events, and fun watering holes with live music and dancing, head for Ixtapa. Just keep in mind that the shuttle bus stops at 11pm, and a taxi to Zihuatanejo after midnight costs 50% more than the regular price. During the off season (after Easter and before Christmas), hours vary: Some places open only on weekends, while others close completely. In Zihuatanejo, a lively bar showing satellite TV sports is **Bandido's,** at the corner of Cinco de Mayo and Pedro Ascencio in Zihuatanejo Centro, across from the Artisans' Market (✆ **755/553-8072**). It features live salsa music nightly and is open until 2am. There's no cover, and people often come to dance salsa.

THE CLUB & MUSIC SCENE

Many dance clubs stay open until the last customers leave, so closing hours depend upon revelers. Most dance clubs have a ladies' night at least once a week—admission and drinks are free for women.

Christine This longstanding dance club is best known for its midnight light show, which features classical music played on a mega sound system. A semicircle of tables in tiers overlooks the dance floor. The crowd tends to be in their 20s and 30s. No sneakers, flip-flops, or shorts are allowed, and reservations are recommended during high season. Open Thursday to Saturday at 10:30pm. Off-season hours vary. In the NH Krystal, Bulevar Ixtapa, Ixtapa. ✆ **755/555-0510.** Cover free to $20, depending on the season and night.

Señor Frog's A companion restaurant to Carlos 'n' Charlie's, Señor Frog's has several dining sections and a warehouselike bar with raised dance floors. Large speakers play electronic, rock, and Latin music, sometimes even prompting dinner patrons to shimmy by their tables between courses. The restaurant is open daily from noon to midnight; the bar stays open until 4am. In the La Puerta Center, Bulevar Ixtapa, Ixtapa. ✆ **755/553-2282.** Friday cover (including two drinks) $10.

Zihablue One of Zihuatanejo's few nightlife options, Zihablue opened in late 2007 across from Kau-Kan restaurant. The chic Mediterranean lounge is an open-air oasis with a candlelit bar, small dance floor, canapé beds and sofas, and sand floor. Ambient music fills the air of this small, exclusive retreat, open from 8pm to 2am November through May. Above the lounge is a fine seafood restaurant. Carretera Escenica La Ropa s/n, next to Kau-Kan restaurant. ✆ **755/554-4844.** No cover.

HOTEL FIESTAS & THEME NIGHTS

A number of hotels hold Mexican fiestas and other special events that include dinner, drinks, live music, and entertainment for a fixed price (generally $44 from 7 to 10pm). The **Barceló Ixtapa** (✆ **755/555-2000**) stages a popular Wednesday night fiesta; the **Dorado Pacífico** (✆ **755/553-2025**), in Ixtapa, hosts a Tuesday night fiesta. Only the Barceló Ixtapa offers them in the off season. Call for reservations or visit a travel agency for tickets, and be sure you understand what the price covers, as drinks, tax, and tip are not always included.

visitors, with restaurants, bungalows, surf shops, and hotels, well back from the shoreline. The west side of the bay, to your right, is about 1.5km long (1 mile), with a lighthouse and a long stretch of fine sand. Beaches on this end are not quite as accessible by land, but hotels are overcoming this difficulty by constructing beach clubs reached by steep private roads and jeep shuttles.

The town of Puerto Escondido has roughly an east–west orientation, with the long Zicatela Beach turning sharply southeast. Residential areas behind Zicatela Beach tend to have unpaved streets; the older town, with paved streets, is north of the Carretera Costera (Hwy. 200). The streets are numbered; Avenida Oaxaca divides east *(oriente)* from west *(poniente),* and Avenida Hidalgo divides north *(norte)* from south *(sur).*

South of this is the original **tourist zone,** through which Avenida Pérez Gasga makes a loop. Part of this loop is a paved pedestrian-only zone, known locally as the Adoquín, after the hexagonal bricks used in its paving. Hotels, shops, restaurants, bars, travel agencies, and other services are all here. In the morning, taxis, delivery trucks, and private vehicles may drive here, but at noon it closes to all but foot traffic.

Avenida Pérez Gasga angles down from the highway at the east end; on the west, where the Adoquín terminates, it climbs in a wide northward curve to cross the highway, after which it becomes Avenida Oaxaca.

The beaches—Playa Principal in the center of town and Marineros and Zicatela, southeast of the town center—are connected. It's easy to walk from one to the other, crossing behind the separating rocks. Puerto Angelito, Carrizalillo, and Bacocho beaches are west of town and accessible by road or water. Playa Bacocho is where you'll find the few more expensive hotels.

GETTING AROUND Almost everything is within walking distance of the Adoquín. **Taxis** around town are inexpensive; call ✆ **954/582-0990** for service. It's also easy to hire a boat and possible to walk beside the sea from the Playa Principal to the tiny beach of Puerto Angelito, though it's a bit of a hike.

Fast Facts Puerto Escondido

Area Code The telephone area code is **954.**

Currency Exchange Banamex, Bancomer, Banorte, and HSBC all have branches in town, and all will change money during business hours; hours vary, but you can generally find one of the above open Monday through Saturday from 9am to 3pm. ATMs are also available, as are currency-exchange offices.

Drugstore **Farmacía de Más Ahorro,** Avenida 1 Norte at Avenida 2 Poniente (✆ **954/582-1911**), is open from 7am to 3am.

Hospital **Unidad Médico–Quirúrgica del Sur,** Av. Oaxaca 706 (✆ **954/582-1288**), offers 24-hour emergency services and has an English-speaking staff and doctor.

Internet Access On Zicatela Beach, **Internet Acuario** is a small, extremely busy Internet service at the entrance to the Bungalows & Cabañas Acuario, Calle de Morro s/n (✆ **954/582-1026**). It's open daily from 8am to 10pm and charges just $1.50 per hour.

Post Office The *correo,* on Avenida Oaxaca at the corner of Avenida 7 Norte (✆ **954/582-0959**), is open Monday through Friday from 8am to 4:30pm.

Safety Depending on whom you talk to, you need to be wary of potential beach muggings, primarily at night. Lighting at Playa Principal and Playa Zicatela has caused the crime rate to drop considerably. Local residents say most incidents happen after tourists overindulge and then go for a midnight stroll along the beach. Puerto is so casual that it's an easy place to let your guard down. Don't carry valuables, and use common sense and normal precautions. Also, respect the power of the magnificent waves here. Drownings occur all too often.

Seasons Season designations are somewhat arbitrary, but most consider high season to be from mid-December to January, around and during Easter week, July and August, and other school and business vacations.

Telephones Numerous businesses offer long-distance telephone service. Many are along the Adoquín; several accept credit cards. The best bet remains a prepaid Ladatel phone card.

WHAT TO SEE & DO IN PUERTO ESCONDIDO

BEACHES **Playa Principal,** where small boats are available for fishing and tour services, and **Playa Marineros,** adjacent to the town center on a deep bay, are the best swimming beaches. Beach chairs and sun shades rent for about $5, which may be waived if you order food or drinks from the restaurants that offer them. **Playa Zicatela,** which has lifeguards and is known as the "Mexican Pipeline," adjoins

Playa Marineros and extends southeast for several kilometers. The surfing part of Zicatela, with large curling waves, is about 4km (2½ miles) from the town center. Due to the size and strength of the waves (particularly in summer), it's not a swimming beach, and only experienced surfers should attempt to ride Zicatela's powerful waves. Stadium-style lighting has been installed in both of these areas, in an attempt to crack down on nighttime beach muggings. It has diminished the appeal of the Playa Principal restaurants—patrons now look into the bright lights rather than at the sea. Lifeguard service has recently been added to Playa Zicatela, although the lifeguards are known to go on strike. The best beach for learning how to surf is called **La Punta.**

Barter with one of the fishermen on the main beach for a ride to **Playa Manzanillo** and **Puerto Angelito,** two beaches separated by a rocky outcropping. Here, and at other small coves just west of town, swimming is safe and the overall pace is calmer than in town. You'll also find *palapas,* hammock rentals, and snorkeling equipment. The clear blue water is perfect for snorkeling. Local entrepreneurs cook fresh fish, tamales, and other Mexican dishes right at the beach. Puerto Angelito is also accessible by a road that's a short distance from town, so it tends to be busier. You can also take a cab to the cliff above **Playa Carrizalillo** and descend a hundred stone stairs to a calm and secluded swimming beach. **Playa Bacocho** is on a shallow cove (dangerous for swimming) farther northwest and is best reached by taxi or boat than on foot. It's also the location of the Villa Sol Beach Club. A charge of $4 gives you access to pools, food and beverage service, and facilities.

SURFING **Zicatela Beach,** 2.5km (1½ miles) southeast of Puerto Escondido's town center, is a world-class surf spot. A surfing competition in August and Fiesta Puerto Escondido, held for at least 3 days each November, celebrate Puerto Escondido's renowned waves. There is also a surfing exhibition and competition in February, for Carnaval. The tourism office can supply dates and details. Beginning surfers often start at Playa Marineros before graduating to Zicatela's awesome waves, although you will see intermediate surfers out at **La Punta,** at the southernmost end of Playa Zicatela. The waves and strong currents make Zicatela dangerous for swimming.

NESTING RIDLEY TURTLES The beaches around Puerto Escondido and Puerto Angel are nesting grounds for the endangered Ridley turtle. During the summer, tourists, on lucky occasions, can see the turtles laying eggs or observe the hatchlings trekking to the sea.

Escobilla Beach, near Puerto Escondido, seems to be the favored nesting grounds of the Ridley turtle. In 1991, the Mexican government

Ecotours & Other Adventurous Explorations

An excellent provider of ecologically oriented tour services is **Rutas de Aventura ★**, Hotel Santa Fe (✆ **954/582-0170;** www.rutasdeaventura.com.mx). Gustavo Boltjes speaks fluent English and offers kayak adventures, hiking excursions, and mountain-bike tours. He also leads waterfall hikes, camping trips, and overnight agritourism adventures to learn about local farming and organic coffee production, including trips to a local coffee plantation that has been built upon principles of environmental sustainability. For more, see www.fincalasnieves.com.mx.

Turismo Dimar Travel Agency, on the landward side just inside the Adoquín (✆ **954/582-0737** or 582-2305; fax 954/582-1551; daily 8am–9pm), is another excellent source of information and can arrange all types of tours and travel. Manager Gaudencio Díaz Martinez speaks English and can arrange individualized tours or more organized ones, such as **Michael Malone's Hidden Voyages Ecotours.** Malone, a Canadian ornithologist, leads dawn and sunset trips in high season (winter) to **Manialtepec Lagoon,** a bird-filled mangrove lagoon about 20km (12 miles) northwest of Puerto Escondido. The tour ($40) includes a stop on a secluded beach for a swim. For more, see www.peleewings.ca/ecco.php

One of the most popular all-day tours offered by both companies is to **Chacahua Lagoon National Park,** about 65km (40 miles) west. It costs $45 with Dimar, $52 with

established the Centro Mexicano la Tortuga, known locally as the **Turtle Museum.** On view are examples of all species of marine turtles living in Mexico, plus six species of freshwater turtles and two species of land turtles. The center (✆ **958/584-3376**) lies on **Mazunte Beach ★**, near the town of the same name about an hour and a half from Puerto Escondido. Hours are Tuesday through Saturday 10am to 6:30pm, and Sunday 10am to 4:30pm; suggested donation is $2. If you come between July and September, ask to join an overnight expedition to Escobilla Beach to see mother turtles scuttle to the beach to lay their eggs. The museum is near a unique shop that sells excellent naturally produced soaps, shampoos, bath oils, and other

Michael Malone. These are true ecotours—small groups treading lightly. You visit a beautiful sandy spit of beach and the lagoon, which has incredible bird life and flowers, including black orchids. Crocodiles are sometimes spotted here, too. Locals provide fresh barbecued fish on the beach. If you know Spanish and get information from the tourism office, it's possible to stay overnight under a small *palapa,* but bring insect repellent.

An interesting and slightly out-of-the-ordinary excursion is **Aventura Submarina,** Av. Pérez Gasga 601A, in front of the tourism office (✆ **954/582-2353**). Jorge, who speaks fluent English and is a certified scuba instructor, guides individuals and small groups of qualified divers along the Coco trench just offshore. The price is $60 for a two-tank dive. This outfit offers a refresher scuba course at no extra charge. Jorge also arranges deep-sea fishing, surfing, and trips to lesser-known nearby swimming beaches. **Omar** (✆ **954/559-4406**) runs dolphin-watching tours in high season (winter).

Fishermen keep their colorful *pangas* (small boats) on the beach beside the Adoquín. A **fisherman's tour** around the coastline in a *panga* costs about $35, but a ride to Puerto Angelito beaches is only $5. Most hotels offer or will gladly arrange tours to meet your needs. The waters here are filled with marlin, tuna, and swordfish.

personal-care products. All are packaged by the local community as part of a project to replace lost income from turtle poaching. Buses go to Mazunte from Puerto Angel about every half-hour, and a taxi ride is around $5.50. You can fit this in with a trip to Zipolite Beach (see "A Trip to Puerto Angel: Backpacking Beach Haven," later in this chapter). Buses from Puerto Escondido don't stop in Mazunte; you can cover the 65km (40 miles) in a taxi or rental car.

The tourism cooperative at **Ventanilla** provides another chance to get up close to the turtles. The villagers here have created their own ecological reserve that encompasses a nearby lagoon, inhabited by crocodiles and dozens of species of birds, and a beach where sea turtles lay their eggs. A boat ride to see the crocs costs $4, and nothing on the menu at the restaurant is over $7. Turtles lay their eggs here year round, although summer is the prime season, so there's always a possibility that a nest is about to hatch. Helping the locals release the eggs is free. Ventanilla is a $2 taxi ride from Mazunte or the nearby beaches, but if you're planning to stay past sunset, ask your driver to wait; it's a long walk in the dark to the main highway.

GUIDED WALKING TOURS For local information and guided walking tours, visit the **Oaxaca Tourist Bureau** booth (✆ **954/582-1186;** ginainpuerto@yahoo.com). It's just west of the pedestrian street. Ask for Gina, who speaks excellent English and is incredibly helpful. She provides information with a smile, and many say she knows more about Puerto Escondido than any other person. On her days off, Gina offers walking tours to the market and to little-known nearby ruins. Filled with history and information on native vegetation, a day with Gina promises fun, adventure, and insight into local culture.

A Mixtec ceremonial center was discovered in early 2000, just east of Puerto Escondido, and is considered a major discovery. The site covers many acres with about 10 pyramids and a ball court, with the pyramids appearing as hills covered in vegetation. A number of large carved stones have been found. Situated on a hilltop, it commands a spectacular view of Puerto Escondido and the Pacific coast. The large archaeological site spans several privately owned plots of land and is not open to the public, although Gina has been known to offer a guided walking tour to it.

SHOPPING

During high season, businesses and shops are generally open all day. During low season, many close between 2 and 4pm.

The Adoquín holds a row of tourist shops selling straw hats, postcards, and T-shirts, plus a few excellent shops featuring Guatemalan, Oaxacan, and Balinese clothing and art. You can also get a tattoo or rent surfboards and boogie boards. Interspersed among the shops, hotels, restaurants, and bars are pharmacies and mini-markets. The largest of these is **Oh! Mar,** Av. Pérez Gasga 502. It sells anything you'd need for a day at the beach, plus phone (Ladatel) cards and Cuban cigars.

The first surf shop in Puerto Escondido, **Central Surf** (✆ **954/582-2285;** www.centralsurfshop.com), on Zicatela Beach, Calle del Morro s/n, rents and sells surfboards, offers surf lessons, and sells related gear, including custom-made surf trunks. Board rentals usually go for about $10 to $20 per day, with lessons available for $60 for 2 hours. In front of the Rockaway Resort on Zicatela Beach, there's a 24-hour

minisuper (no phone) that sells the necessities: beer, suntan lotion, and basic food.

Also of interest is **Bazar Santa Fe ★★**, Hotel Santa Fe lobby, Calle del Morro s/n, Zicatela Beach (✆ **954/582-0170**), a small shop that sells antiques, vintage Oaxacan embroidered clothing, jewelry, religious artifacts, and gourmet organic coffee. Right next to Central Surf, **Bikini Brazil,** Playa Zicatela, Calle del Morro s/n (✆ **954/582-2555**), you'll find the hottest bikinis under the sun imported from Brazil, land of the *tanga* (string bikini). The sexy competition lies just south on the beach, **Amazonia do Brazil,** Playa Zicatela, Calle del Morro s/n (✆ **954/100-1315**). Another cool beach shop on Playa Zicatela, Calle del Moro s/n, is **Trapoy y Harapos** (✆ **954/582-0759**), which sells bathing suits, sandals, and surfboards.

To check your email, there are numerous small Internet cafes located along the Adoquin and Zicatela. **Internet Acuario** (✆ **954/582-0788**) is located centrally on Zicatela beach, next to Central Surf, and charges $1 for 30 minutes.

WHERE TO STAY

The rates posted below do not include the 18% tax.

Expensive

Best Western Posada Real Kids On a clifftop overlooking the beach, the expanse of manicured lawn that backs this all-inclusive hotel is one of the most popular places in town for a sunset cocktail. The smallish standard rooms are less enticing than the hotel grounds (six "extra large" rooms are available, and preferable for families). A big plus here is Coco's Beach Club, with a 1km (half-mile) stretch of soft-sand beach, large swimming pool, playground, and bar with occasional live music. This is a great place for families, and it's open to the public (nonguests pay $2.50 to enter). The hotel lies 5 minutes from the airport and about the same from Puerto Escondido's tourist zone, but you'll need a taxi to get to town. Rates include breakfast, lunch, dinner, and unlimited domestic drinks, as well as tips and taxes. Additionally, a new Best Western opened 15 minutes north of Puerto Escondido, offering more moderately priced (and outfitted) accommodations (high season $135 double; low season $95 double). In high season, it may have availability when Puerto Escondido is otherwise fully booked.

Av. Benito Juárez S/N, Fracc. Bacocho, 71980 Puerto Escondido, Oax. ✆ **800/528-1234** in the U.S., or 954/582-0237. Fax 954/582-0192. www.posadareal.com.mx. 100 units. High season $310 double; low season $250 double. AE, MC, V. Free parking. **Amenities:** 2 restaurants; lobby bar; sunset bar; putting green; 2 outdoor pools; wading pool; putting green; tennis court; beach club w/food service. *In room:* A/C, TV, hair dryer, free Wi-Fi.

Moderate

Caracol Plaza This new hotel sits on a small hill overlooking the bay. Guest rooms feature high ceilings, arched French windows, lovely wood furnishings, and small bathrooms. Ask for a room with a bay view. The large white hotel has an adult and children's pool, Mexican restaurant, and *palapa* bar with what may be the best sunset-watching spot in all of Puerto Escondido. The friendly staff will help you with your travel plans. The hotel's one drawback is that it's across the main highway from the beach and is probably a 10-minute walk to the Adoquín. Note that, as of press time, a second wing was being added to the hotel, along with some shops and other additions to the front.

7a. Oriente s/n y 1a. Sur, Col. Marinero, 71980 Puerto Escondido, Oax. ✆ **954/582-3814.** 80 units. High season $165 double; low season $120 double. MC, V. Free parking. **Amenities:** Restaurant; bar; outdoor pool; kids' pool. *In room:* A/C, TV, minibar, Wi-Fi.

Hotel Santa Fe ★★★ Finds If Puerto Escondido is the best beach value in Mexico, then the Santa Fe is, without a doubt, one of the best hotel values in Mexico. It's about 1km (a half-mile) southeast of the town center, off Hwy. 200, at the curve in the road where Marineros and Zicatela beaches join—a prime sunset-watching spot. The three-story hacienda-style buildings have clay-tiled stairs, archways, and blooming bougainvillea. They surround two courtyard swimming pools. The ample but simply styled rooms feature large tile bathrooms, colonial furnishings, hand-woven fabrics, and both air-conditioning and ceiling fans. Most have a balcony or terrace, and the master and presidential suites enjoy ocean views. Bungalows are next to the hotel; each has a living room, kitchen, and bedroom with two double beds. The restaurant (see "Where to Dine," below), one of the best on the southern Pacific coast, is supplied by its own farm.

Calle del Morro (Apdo. Postal 96), 71980 Puerto Escondido, Oax. ✆ **954/582-0170** or 582-0266. Fax 954/582-0260. www.hotelsantafe.com.mx. 61 units, 8 bungalows. High season $173 double, $189 junior suite, $273 suite, $183 bungalow; low season $126 double, $162 junior suite, $263 suite, $136 bungalow. AE, MC, V. Free parking. **Amenities:** Restaurant; bar; babysitting; Internet kiosk; 3 outdoor pools. *In room:* A/C, TV.

Paraíso Escondido ★★ Finds This eclectic inn is hidden away on a shady street a couple of short blocks from the Adoquín and Playa Principal. It's very popular with families and has a small, intimate feel. A curious collection of Mexican folk art, masks, religious art, and paintings makes this an exercise in Mexican magic realism. An inviting pool—surrounded by gardens, Adirondack chairs, and a fountain—affords a commanding view of the bay. The colonial-style rooms each have one double and two twin beds, tile floors, a small bathroom, and a cozy balcony or terrace with French doors. The suites have much plusher decor than the rooms, with recessed lighting, desks set into bay windows, living areas, and large private balconies overlooking the bay. The penthouse suite has a kitchenette, a tile chessboard inlaid in the floor, and murals adorning the walls—it is the owners' former apartment.

Calle Unión 10, 71980 Puerto Escondido, Oax. ✆ **954/582-0444.** Fax 954/582-2767. www.hotelparaisoescondido.net. 25 units. High season $73 double, $93 suite, $120 penthouse suite; low season $63 double, $73 suite, $93 penthouse suite. MC, V. Free parking. **Amenities:** Restaurant; bar; outdoor pool; wading pool. *In room:* A/C, TV.

Inexpensive

Bungalows & Cabañas Acuario Facing Zicatela Beach, this surfer's sanctuary offers cheap accommodations plus an on-site gym, surf shop, and Internet cafe. The two-story hotel and bungalows surround a pool shaded by great palms. Rooms are small and basic; bungalows offer basic kitchen facilities but don't have air-conditioning. The cabañas lack mosquito nets, so you'll need to cover yourself with bug spray from head to toe. There are several rooms with air-conditioning, which offer a far more comfortable night's sleep. The adjoining retail area has public telephones, money exchange, a pharmacy, an Internet cafe, and a vegetarian restaurant. If you're traveling during low season, you can probably negotiate a better deal than the rates listed below once you're there.

Calle del Morro s/n, 71980 Puerto Escondido, Oax. ✆ **954/582-0357.** Fax 954/582-1027. 40 units. High season $60 double, $70 double with A/C, $110 bungalow; 20% less in low season. MC V. Free parking. **Amenities:** Restaurant; well-equipped gym; Internet cafe; Jacuzzi; outdoor pool. *In room:* No phone except in suite and 2 bungalows.

Hotel Arco Iris ★ **Value** Rooms at the Arco Iris occupy a three-story colonial-style house that faces Zicatela Beach. Each is simple yet comfortable, with a spacious terrace or balcony with hangers for hammocks to rent—all have great views, but the upstairs ones are better (12 units include kitchenettes). Beds come with mosquito nets, and bedspreads were made using beautifully worked Oaxacan textiles. The restaurant/bar runs one of the most popular happy hours in town, daily from 5:30 to 7:30pm, with live music during high season.

Calle del Morro s/n, Playa Zicatela, 71980 Puerto Escondido, Oax. ✆ **954/582-2344.** 35 units. High season $75–$90 double, $100 double with kitchen; low season $50–$70 double, $75 double with kitchen. Extra person $4. Rates 10%–20% higher at Easter and Christmas. MC, V. Ample free parking for cars and campers. **Amenities:** Restaurant; bar; outdoor pool; wading pool; TV/game room w/foreign channels. *In room:* No phone.

Hotel Casa Blanca ★ Value If you want to be in the heart of the Adoquín, this is your best bet for excellent value and ample accommodations. The courtyard pool and adjacent *palapa* make great places to hide away and enjoy a margarita or a book from the hotel's exchange rack. The bright, simply furnished rooms offer a choice of bed combinations, but all have at least two beds and a fan. Some rooms have both air-conditioning and a minifridge. The best rooms have a balcony overlooking the action in the street below, but light sleepers should consider a room in the back. Some rooms accommodate up to five. This is an excellent and economical choice for families.

Av. Pérez Gasga 905, 71980 Puerto Escondido, Oax. ✆ **954/582-0168.** www.ptohcasablanca.com. 25 units. High season $52 double, $95 double with A/C; low season $38 double, $85 double with A/C. MC, V. Limited street parking. **Amenities:** Outdoor pool. *In room:* A/C (in some rooms), fan, TV, minifridge (in some rooms), no phone.

Hotel Flor de María Though not right on the beach, the Flor de María offers a welcoming place to stay. This cheery three-story hotel faces the ocean, which you can see from the rooftop. Built around a garden courtyard, each room is colorfully decorated with beautiful *trompe l'oeil* still-lifes and landscapes. Rooms have double beds with orthopedic mattresses, and views that vary between the ocean, courtyard, and exterior. On the roof are a small pool, a shaded hammock terrace, and an open-air bar (noon–8pm during high season) with cable TV. It's a great sunset spot. The hotel lies about .5km (1/4 mile) from the Adoquín, 60m (197 ft.) up a cobblestone road from Marineros Beach on Calle Marinero at the eastern end of the beach.

Playa Marineros, 71980 Puerto Escondido, Oax. ✆ **954/582-0536.** Fax 954/582-2617. 24 units. $40–$65 double. Ask about off-season long-term discounts. MC, V. Limited parking. **Amenities:** Restaurant; bar; small gym; Internet kiosk; small outdoor pool; free Wi-Fi.

Rockaway Facing Playa Zicatela, this surfer's sanctuary offers very clean, cheap accommodations geared for surfers, including newer hotel-style rooms and older cabañas. Every unit is equipped with a private bathroom, as well as ceiling fan and mosquito net. The good-size swimming pool and *palapa* bar form a popular gathering spot. The cabañas in the older section do not have hot water; those in the newer section feature air-conditioning, hot water, and cable TV. The courtyard has a festive and inviting vibe, with music and laughter lasting well into the night. ***Note:*** There's one large cabaña that accommodates up to eight people ($150 in high season).

Calle del Morro s/n, 71980 Puerto Escondido, Oax. ✆ **954/582-0668.** 14 units. High season $60 double room, $40 cabaña; low season $40 double room, $20 cabaña. No credit cards. Free parking. **Amenities:** Bar; outdoor pool. *In room:* A/C (in some), fans, TV (in some), no phone.

WHERE TO DINE

In addition to the places listed below, a Puerto Escondido tradition is the *palapa* restaurants on Zicatela Beach, for early morning surfer breakfasts or casual dining and drinking at night. One of the most popular is **Los Tíos,** offering very reasonable prices and surfer-size portions. After dinner, enjoy homemade Italian ice cream from **Gelateria Giardino.** It has two locations, on Calle del Morro at Zicatela Beach, and Pérez Gasga 609, on the Adoquín (© **954/582-2243**).

Expensive

Pascal ★★ (Finds) FRENCH With an enchanted location on the edge of the bay, Pascal features a beautiful beachside terrace with views of the bobbing boats in front. Opened in 2006, it has quickly become one of the city's top restaurants. All of the French-inspired dishes are prepared by chef-owner Pascal on the outdoor grill using only fresh ingredients. Specials may include breaded goat cheese with tomatoes and pesto on a baguette, Chateaubriand, fish and seafood brochettes, and grilled lobster served in the shape of a tower. The bouillabaisse tastes heavenly. Open only for dinner, Pascal offers candlelit tables amid towering palm trees, a centerpiece fountain, and live music weekends. Service is refined though sometimes slow, and the cuisine matches the quality you would expect from a fine French restaurant. There's an enticing selection of French and international wines as well.

Playa Principal s/n (off the Adoquín). © **954/103-0668.** Reservations recommended. Main courses $6–$25. No credit cards. Daily 6pm–midnight.

Moderate

Cabo Blanco INTERNATIONAL People come to this beachside "rock and blues" bar and grill for a good time and simple beach food, which includes grilled fish, shrimp, steaks, and ribs topped with a variety of flavorful sauces. Favorites are dill–Dijon mustard, wine–fennel, and Thai curry. A bonus is that Cabo Blanco turns into a rowdy Zicatela Beach bar, with special Monday night parties featuring an all-you-can-eat buffet plus dancing, and a Friday night reggae dance that is incredibly fun—but available only in the high season. The late-night food menu includes specials like ribs and barbecue chicken, and snacks all day long. The top-notch team of bartenders keeps the crowd well served, if not always well behaved.

Calle del Morro s/n. © **954/582-0337.** www.geocities.com/oaxiki/cabo_blanco_pe.html. Main courses $7–$15. V. Dec–Apr daily 6pm–2am.

Restaurant Santa Fe ★★★ (Finds) INTERNATIONAL The Hotel Santa Fe's beachside restaurant sits under a welcoming *palapa,* with the gentle waves crashing just in front. The excellent fish and seafood selections include crayfish, red snapper, tuna, octopus, and giant shrimp prepared any way you like. More traditional dishes, such as Oaxacan-style enchiladas with homemade tortillas and *mole,* are also available. The restaurant offers numerous vegetarian and vegan selections, including chiles rellenos with cheese, rice, and beans; and breaded tofu with salad and rice. The food is served on beautiful hand-painted ceramic place settings, and the organic coffee is grown at the hotel's own farm. There's an elaborate breakfast buffet on the weekends for around $13, featuring fresh local specialties. Even if you don't plan to dine, this is an ideal spot to come for a sunset cocktail and perhaps an hors d'oeuvre.

In the Hotel Santa Fe, Calle del Morro s/n. ✆ **954/582-0170.** Breakfast $3–$7; main courses $5.50–$25. AE, MC, V. Daily 7am–10pm.

Inexpensive

Cafecito ★ Value FRENCH PASTRY/MEXICAN Carmen started with a small bakery in Puerto, and when she opened this cafe years ago on Zicatela Beach, with the motto "Big waves, strong coffee!," it quickly eclipsed the bake shop and now is her main business. But not to worry—it still features all the attractions of her early *patisserie,* with the added attraction of serving full meals all day long. This cafe/restaurant sits under a big *palapa* facing the beach. Giant shrimp dinners cost less than $10, and creative daily specials are always a sure bet. An oversize mug of cappuccino is $2.20 and a mango éclair—worth any price—is a steal, at $1.20. Smoothies, natural juices, and a variety of coffee selections are available.

Calle del Morro s/n, Playa Zicatela. ✆ **954/582-0516.** Pastries $1–$2; breakfast $4–$5; main courses $3–$9. No credit cards. Daily 6am–10:30pm.

El Jardín ★★ Value ITALIAN This charming restaurant facing Zicatela Beach is generally packed. It's known for its generous use of fresh, healthy ingredients, including lots of olive oil, tomatoes, and Italian vinaigrette. The service is relaxed, if sometimes extremely slow. The choices are delicious: New York–style pizza, vegetarian sandwiches, crepes, pastas, and large creative salads, such as the *Rey de Reyes,* with spinach, tomato, avocado, pickled eggplant, brown rice, and tofu. Try the Ensalada Caprichosa, with fresh-cut tomatoes, savory pesto, and salty anchovies atop crisp grilled eggplant slices. There's also a selection of fresh fish and seafood. Under a *palapa* roof, El Jardín's extensive menu includes fruit smoothies, Italian and Mexican coffees, herbal teas, and a complete juice bar. The restaurant makes its own tempeh, tofu, pastas, and whole-grain breads. The rich tiramisu is to die for.

Calle del Morro s/n, Playa Zicatela. ✆ **954/110-5408.** Main courses $4.50–$11. No credit cards. Daily 8am–11pm.

Flor de María INTERNATIONAL This open-air dining room near the beach is particularly popular with locals. The menu changes daily but always includes fresh fish, grilled meats, and pastas. The restaurant sits in the Hotel Flor de María, just steps from the center of town and up a cobblestone road from Playa Marinero at the eastern end of the beach.

In Hotel Flor de María, Playa Marinero. ✆ **954/582-0536.** Breakfast $2–$3.50; main courses $5–$14. No credit cards. Daily 8–11am and 6–9pm. Closed May–June and Sept–Oct.

La Galería ★ ITALIAN At the east end of the Adoquín, La Galería offers a satisfying range of eats in a cool, creative setting. Darkwood beams tower above, contemporary works by local artists grace the walls, and jazz music plays. Specialties include homemade pasta and brick-oven pizza (the five-cheese pizza is especially delicious), but burgers and steaks are also available. Or try something light and refreshing, like the crisp grapefruit and shrimp salad, which visitors and locals alike rave about. Cappuccino and espresso, plus desserts such as apple empanadas with vanilla ice cream, finish the meal. Continental and American breakfasts are available in the morning.

Av. Pérez Gasga s/n. ✆ **954/582-2039.** Breakfast $3–$5; main courses $5–$10. No credit cards. Daily 8am–11pm.

Las Margaritas ★ **Value** MEXICAN One of the tastiest Mexican restaurants in town, Las Margaritas lies off a busy street, a short drive from the Adoquín. The casual, open-air terrace offers wood tables and chairs, as well as an open kitchen, bar, and tortilla stand, where you can watch authentic dishes being made. This is Mexican food prepared as though you were in a family's home, featuring such dishes as *empanadas,* quesadillas, fish and seafood brochettes, steaks, and *mole* that explodes with flavor.

8 norte s/n (1 block from the market). ✆ **954/582-0212.** Breakfasts $3–$4.50; main courses $4–$12. MC, V. Daily 8am–6pm.

PUERTO ESCONDIDO AFTER DARK

Sunset-watching is a ritual to plan your days around, and good lookout points abound. At Zicatela, you can watch the sun descend behind the surfers, and at **La Galería,** located on the third floor of the Arco Iris hotel, you can catch up on local gossip while enjoying a sundowner. It has a nightly happy hour (with live music during high season) from 5:30 to 7:30pm. Other great sunset spots are the **Hotel Santa Fe,** at the junction of Zicatela and Marineros beaches, and the rooftop bar of **Hotel Flor de María.** For a more tranquil, romantic setting, take a cab or walk a half-hour or so west to the cliff-top lawn of the **Hotel Posada Real.**

Puerto's nightlife will satisfy anyone dedicated to late nights and good music. Most nightspots are open until 3am or until customers leave; none of them have phones. The Adoquín offers an ample selection of clubs. Favorites include **Wipeout,** a multilevel club that packs in the crowds until 4am, and **Blue Station,** open from 9pm to 1am.

On Zicatela Beach, **Bar Fly** sits upstairs overlooking the beach and features a DJ spinning Latin, retro, and electronic hits. It's open nightly from 9pm to 3am on Calle de Moro s/n. Don't miss **Cabo Blanco's** (see "Where to Dine," above) Monday night dine-and-dance party (all you can eat), or its Friday reggae night. An added draw is the complimentary snacks with drink purchase, in the style of Mexico's cantina tradition. **Casa Babylon,** a few doors down, is a bohemian beach bar with a book exchange and table games. It's open nightly from 7pm until late and has a hip surfer vibe. At the end of Zicatela Beach, **La Piedra de la Iguana** plays electronic, trance, and house music, and has its own iguana nursery. This is a late-night venue, opening at 2am and staying open to 8am in high season.

There's a movie theater on Playa Zicatela called **Cinemar.** It's a pretty simple setup consisting of a small bookstore, a large screen, and some beach chairs. It serves up popcorn and movies nightly, and also rents surfboards during the day.

2 A TRIP TO PUERTO ANGEL: BACKPACKING BEACH HAVEN

Seventy-four kilometers (46 miles) southeast of Puerto Escondido and 50km (31 miles) northwest of the Bays of Huatulco lies the tiny fishing port of **Puerto Angel** (*pwer*-toh *ahn*-hehl). With its beautiful beaches, unpaved streets, and budget hotels, Puerto Angel is popular with the international backpacking set and those seeking an inexpensive and restful vacation. Repeated hurricane damage and the 1999 earthquake took its toll on the village, driving the best accommodations out of business, but Puerto Angel continues to attract visitors. Its small bay and several inlets offer peaceful swimming and good snorkeling. The village's way of life is slow and simple: Fishermen leave very early in the morning and return with their catch before noon. Taxis make up most of the traffic, and the bus from Pochutla passes every half-hour or so.

ESSENTIALS

GETTING THERE & DEPARTING **By Car** North or south from **Hwy. 200,** take coastal **Hwy. 175** inland to Puerto Angel. The road

Warning! Important Travel Note

Although car and bus hijackings along Hwy. 200 north to Acapulco have greatly decreased (thanks to improved security measures and police patrols), you're still wise to travel this road only during the day. There are numerous military checkpoints, and the road at points is dirt-only and pothole ridden.

is well marked with signs to Puerto Angel. From Huatulco or Puerto Escondido, the trip should take about an hour.

By Taxi Taxis are readily available to take you to Puerto Angel or Zipolite Beach for a reasonable price (about $3.50 to or from either destination), or to the Huatulco airport or Puerto Escondido (about $50).

By Bus There are no direct buses from Puerto Escondido or Huatulco to Puerto Angel; however, numerous buses leave Puerto Escondido and Huatulco for Pochutla, 11km (6¾ miles) north of Puerto Angel. Take the bus to Pochutla, and then switch to a bus going to Puerto Angel. If you arrive in Pochutla from Huatulco or Puerto Escondido, you may be dropped at one of several bus stations that line the main street; walk 1 or 2 blocks toward the large sign reading POSADA DON JOSE. The buses to Puerto Angel are in the lot just before the sign.

ORIENTATION The town center is only about 4 blocks long, oriented more or less east–west. There are few signs in the village, and off the main street, much of Puerto Angel is a narrow sand-and-dirt path. The navy base is toward the west end of town, just before the creek crossing toward Playa Panteón (Cemetery Beach).

Puerto Angel has several public (Ladatel) telephones that use widely available prepaid phone cards. The closest bank is **Bancomer** in Pochutla, which changes money Monday through Friday from 9am to 6pm, Saturday from 9am to 1pm.

BEACHES, WATERSPORTS & BOAT TRIPS

The golden sands and peaceful village life of Puerto Angel and the nearby towns are all the reasons you'll need to visit. Playa Principal, the main beach, lies between the Mexican navy base and the pier that's home to the local fishing fleet. Near the pier, fishermen pull their colorful boats onto the beach and unload their catch in the late morning while trucks wait to haul it off to processing plants in Veracruz. The rest of the beach seems light-years from the world of work and commitments. Except on Mexican holidays, it's relatively deserted. It's important to note that Pacific coast currents deposit trash on Puerto Angel beaches. The locals do a fairly good job of keeping it picked up, but the currents are constant.

Playa Panteón is the main swimming and snorkeling beach. Cemetery Beach, ominous as that sounds, is about a 15-minute walk from the center, straight through town on the main street that skirts the beach. The *panteón* (cemetery), on the right, is worth a visit, with its brightly colored tombstones and bougainvillea.

In Playa Panteón, some of the *palapa* restaurants and a few of the hotels rent snorkeling and scuba gear and can arrange boat trips, but they tend to be expensive. Check the quality and condition of gear—particularly scuba gear—that you're renting.

Playa Zipolite (see-poh-*lee*-teh) and its village are 6km (3¾ miles) down a paved road from Puerto Angel and about an hour and a half from Puerto Escondido. Taxis charge about $3 from Puerto Angel. You can catch a *colectivo* on the main street in the town center and share the cost.

Zipolite is well known as a good surf break and as a nude beach, although there's more nudity these days at nearby Chambala beach. Although public nudity (including topless sunbathing) is technically illegal, it's allowed here—this is one of only a handful of beaches in Mexico that permits it. This sort of open-mindedness has attracted an increasing number of young European travelers. Most sunbathers concentrate beyond a large rock outcropping at the far end of the beach. Police will occasionally patrol the area, but they are much more intent on drug users than on sunbathers. The ocean and currents are strong (that's why the surf is so good), and a number of drownings have occurred over the years—so know your limits. There are places to tie up a hammock and a few *palapa* restaurants for a lunch and a cold beer.

Hotels in Playa Zipolite are basic and rustic; most have rugged walls and *palapa* roofs. Prices range from $10 to $50 a night.

Traveling north on Hwy. 175, you'll come to another hot surf break and a beach of spectacular beauty: **Playa San Agustinillo.** If you want to stay in San Agustinillo, there are no formal accommodations, but you'll see numerous signs for local guesthouses, which rent rooms for an average of $10 to $20 a night, often with a home-cooked meal included. One of the pleasures of a stay in Puerto Angel is discovering the many hidden beaches nearby and spending the day. Local boatmen and hotels can give details and quote rates for this service.

You can stay in Puerto Angel near Playa Principal in the tiny town, or at Playa Panteón. Most accommodations are basic, older, cement-block style hotels, not meriting a full-blown description. Between Playa Panteón and town are several bungalow and guesthouse setups with budget accommodations.

3 BAHÍAS DE HUATULCO

64km (40 miles) SE of Puerto Angel; 680km (422 miles) SE of Acapulco

Huatulco has the same unspoiled nature and laid-back attitude as its neighbors to the north, Puerto Angel and Puerto Escondido, but with a difference. Amid the natural splendor, you'll also encounter indulgent hotels and modern roads and facilities.

Pristine beaches and jungle landscapes can make for an idyllic retreat from the stress of daily life—and when viewed from a luxury hotel balcony, even better. Huatulco is for those who want to enjoy the beauty of nature during the day and then retreat to well-appointed comfort by night.

Undeveloped stretches of pure white sand and isolated coves await the promised growth of Huatulco, which lags far behind Cancún, the previous resort planned by FONATUR, Mexico's Tourism Development arm. FONATUR development of the Bahías de Huatulco is an ambitious project that aims to cover 21,000 hectares (51,870 acres) of land, with over 16,000 hectares (39,520 acres) to remain ecological preserves. The small local communities have been transplanted from the coast into Crucecita. The area consists of three sections: **Santa Cruz, Crucecita,** and **Tangolunda Bay** (see "City Layout," below).

Though Huatulco has increasingly become known for its ecotourism attractions—including river rafting, rappelling, and hiking jungle trails—it has yet to develop a true personality. There's little shopping, nightlife, or even dining outside of the hotels, and what is available is expensive for the quality. However, the service in the area is generally very good.

A cruise-ship dock in Santa Cruz Bay has given the sleepy resort an important business boost. The dock handles up to two 3,000-passenger cruise ships at a time (passengers are currently ferried to shore aboard tenders). Still being refined is the relatively new 20,000-hectare (49,400-acre) "eco-archaeological" park, **El Botazoo,** at Punta Celeste, where there is a recently discovered archeological site. Hiking, rappelling, and bird-watching are popular activities there. This new development is all being handled with ecological sensitivity in mind.

If you're drawn to snorkeling, diving, boat cruises, and simple relaxation, Huatulco nicely fits the bill. Nine bays encompass 36 beaches and countless inlets and coves. Huatulco's main problem has been securing enough incoming flights. It relies heavily on charter service from the United States and Canada.

ESSENTIALS

Getting There & Departing

BY PLANE **Click Mexicana** flights (© **01-800/112-5425** toll-free in Mexico; www.click.com.mx) connect Huatulco with Mexico City. Prices start at about $150 each way.

From Huatulco's international airport (airport code: HUX; © **958/ 581-9007** or 581-9008), about 20km (12 miles) northwest of the Bahías de Huatulco, private **taxis** charge $44 to Crucecita, $46 to Santa Cruz, and $51 to Tangolunda. **Transportes Terrestres** (© **958/ 581-9014** or 581-9024) *colectivos* fares are about $10 per person. When returning, make sure to ask for a taxi, unless you have a lot of luggage. Taxis to the airport run $42, but unless specifically requested, you'll get a Suburban, which costs $56.

Hertz (© **958/581-9092**), **Europe Car** (© **958/581-9094**), and **Thrifty** (© **958/581-9000**) all offer car rentals at the airport, and Hertz also has an in-town location (© **958/581-0588**), as does Europe Car (© **958/583-4067**). Because Huatulco is spread out and has excellent roads, you may want to consider a rental car, at least for 1 or 2 days, to explore the area.

BY CAR Coastal **Hwy. 200** leads to Huatulco (via Pochutla) from the north and is generally in good condition. The drive from Puerto Escondido takes just over 2½ hours. The road is well maintained, but it's filled with curves and potholes and doesn't have lights, so avoid travel after sunset. Allow at least 6 hours for the trip from Oaxaca City on mountainous **Hwy. 175.**

BY BUS There are three bus stations in Crucecita, all within a few blocks, but none in Santa Cruz or Tangolunda. The **Gacela** and **Estrella Blanca** station, at the corner of Gardenia and Palma Real, handles service to Acapulco, Mexico City, Puerto Escondido, and Pochutla. The **Cristóbal Colón** station (© **958/587-0261**) is at Avenida Riscalillo, Sector T. It serves destinations throughout Mexico, including Oaxaca, Puerto Escondido, and Pochutla. The **Estrella del Valle** station, on Jasmin between Sabali and Carrizal, serves Oaxaca.

Orientation

VISITOR INFORMATION The **State Tourism Office,** or Oficina del Turismo (© **958/581-0176;** www.baysofhuatulco.com.mx), has an information booth in Tangolunda Bay, near the Grand Pacific hotel. It's open Monday to Friday from 8am to 5pm.

CITY LAYOUT The overall resort area is called **Bahías de Huatulco** and includes nine bays. The town of Santa María de Huatulco,

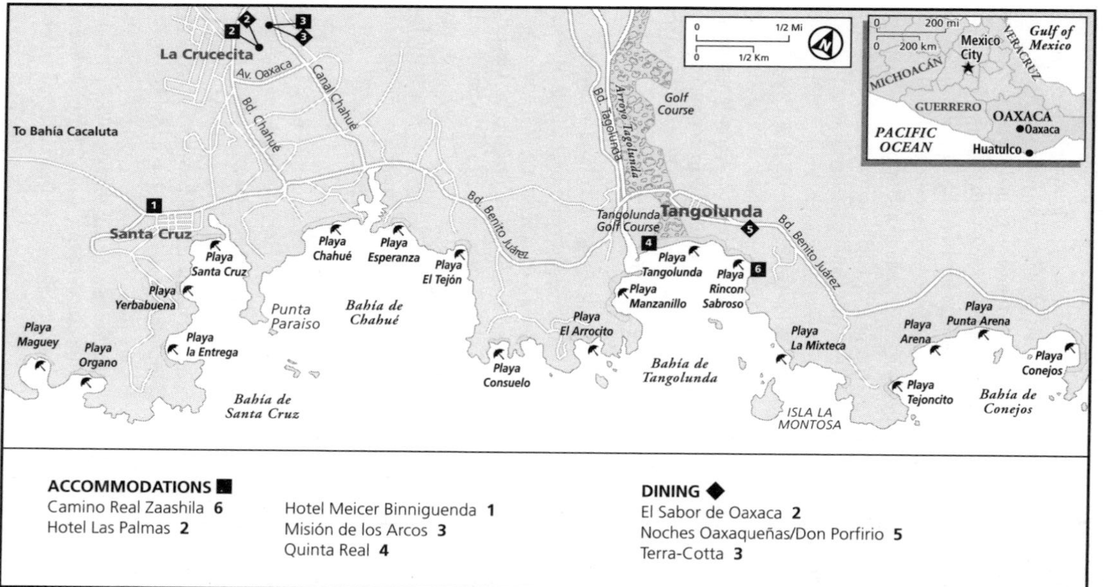
La Crucecita
Av. Oaxaca
Canal Chahué
Bd. Chahué
To Bahía Cacaluta
Santa Cruz
Playa Santa Cruz
Playa Yerbabuena
Playa Maguey
Playa Organo
Playa la Entrega
Bahía de Santa Cruz
Punta Paraiso
Playa Chahué
Playa Esperanza
Bahía de Chahué
Playa El Tejón
Bd. Benito Juárez
Playa Consuelo
Playa El Arrocito
Bd. Tagolunda
Arroyo Tagolunda
Golf Course
Tangolunda Golf Course
Tangolunda
Playa Tangolunda
Playa Manzanillo
Playa Rincon Sabroso
Bahía de Tangolunda
Playa La Mixteca
ISLA LA MONTOSA
Playa Arena
Playa Punta Arena
Playa Tejoncito
Bahía de Conejos
Playa Conejos
0 1/2 Mi
0 1/2 Km
0 200 mi
0 200 km
Mexico City
MICHOACÁN
VERACRUZ
Gulf of Mexico
GUERRERO
OAXACA
Oaxaca
PACIFIC OCEAN
Huatulco
ACCOMMODATIONS ■
Camino Real Zaashila 6
Hotel Las Palmas 2
Hotel Meicer Binniguenda 1
Misión de los Arcos 3
Quinta Real 4
DINING ◆
El Sabor de Oaxaca 2
Noches Oaxaqueñas/Don Porfirio 5
Terra-Cotta 3

the original settlement in this area, is 27km (17 miles) inland. **Santa Cruz Huatulco,** usually called Santa Cruz, was the first developed area on the coast. It has a central plaza with a bandstand kiosk, which has been converted into a cafe that serves regionally grown coffee. It also has an artisans' market on the edge of the plaza that borders the main road, a few hotels and restaurants, and a marina where bay tours and fishing trips set sail. **Juárez** is Santa Cruz's 4-block-long main street, anchored at one end by the Hotel Castillo Huatulco and at the other by the Meigas Binniguenda hotel. Opposite the Hotel Castillo is the marina, and beyond it are restaurants in new colonial-style buildings facing the beach. The area's banks are on Juárez. It's impossible to get lost, and you can take in almost everything at a glance. This bay is the site of Huatulco's cruise-ship dock.

About 3km (1³/₄ miles) inland from Santa Cruz is **Crucecita,** a planned city that sprang up in 1985. It centers on a lovely grassy plaza. This is the residential area for the resorts, with neighborhoods of new stucco homes mixed with small apartment complexes. Crucecita has evolved into a lovely, traditional town where you'll find the area's best and most reasonably priced restaurants, plus some shopping and several less expensive hotels.

Until other bays are developed, **Tangolunda Bay,** 5km (3 miles) east, is the focal point of development. Over time, half the bays will have resorts. For now, Tangolunda has an 18-hole golf course, as well as the Las Brisas, Quinta Real, Barceló Huatulco, Royal, Casa del Mar, and Camino Real Zaashila hotels, among others. Small strip centers with a few restaurants occupy each end of Tangolunda Bay. **Chahué Bay,** between Tangolunda and Santa Cruz, is a small bay with a beach club and other facilities under construction along with houses and a few small hotels.

GETTING AROUND Crucecita, Santa Cruz, and Tangolunda are too far apart to walk, but **taxis** are inexpensive and readily available. Crucecita has taxi stands opposite the Hotel Grifer and on the Plaza Principal. Taxis are readily available through hotels in Santa Cruz and Tangolunda. The fare between Santa Cruz and Tangolunda is roughly $3.50; between Santa Cruz and Crucecita, $2; between Crucecita and Tangolunda, $2.50. To explore the area, you can hire a taxi by the hour (about $15) or for the day.

There is **minibus service** between towns; the fare is 50¢. In Santa Cruz, catch the bus across the street from Castillo Huatulco; in Tangolunda, in front of the Grand Pacific; and in Crucecita, cater-corner from the Hotel Grifer.

Fast Facts Bahías de Huatulco

Area Code The area code is **958.**

Banks All three areas have banks with ATMs, including the main Mexican banks, Banamex and Bancomer, and HSBC. They change money during business hours, Monday through Friday from 9am to 4pm. Banks line Calle Juárez in Santa Cruz and surround the central plaza in Crucecita.

Drugstores **Farmacía El Centro,** just off the central plaza in Crucecita (✆ **958/587-0232**), is one of the largest drugstores in town. It's open Monday through Saturday from 8am to 10pm and Sunday from 8am to noon. **Farmacía La Clínica** (✆ **958/587-0591**), Sabalí 1602, Crucecita, offers 24-hour service and delivery.

Emergencies **Police emergency** (✆ **060**); **federal police** (✆ **958/587-0815**); **transit police** (✆ **958/587-0186**); and **Cruz Roja (Red Cross),** Bulevar Chahué 110 (✆ **958/587-1188**).

Information **Oficina del Turismo,** the State Tourism Office (✆ **958/581-0176** or 581-0177; sedetur6@oaxaca.gob.mx), has an information module in Tangolunda Bay, near the Campo de Golf. It's open weekdays 8am to 5pm.

Internet Access Several Internet cafes are in Crucecita. One is at the Terra-Cotta cafe in the Misión de los Arcos, Av. Gardenia 902 (✆ **958/587-0165**), which, in addition to paid service, is a free wireless hot spot. Another lies on the ground-floor level of the **Hotel Plaza Conejo,** Av. Guamúchil 208, across from the main plaza (✆ **958/587-0054**). It's about $1 per hour.

Medical Care **Clínica Médico Quirúrgica,** Jabali 403 (✆ **958/587-0687** or 587-0600), is a medical clinic with emergency care run by Dr. Ricardo Carrillo, who speaks English.

Post Office The *correo,* at Bulevar Chahué 100, Sector R, Crucecita (✆ **958/587-0551**), is open Monday through Saturday from 8am to 4:30pm.

BEACHES, WATERSPORTS & OTHER THINGS TO DO

Attractions around Huatulco concentrate on the nine bays and their watersports. The number of ecotours and interesting side trips into the surrounding mountains is growing. Though it isn't a traditional Mexican town, the community of Crucecita is worth visiting. Just off the central plaza is the **Iglesia de Guadalupe,** with a large mural of Mexico's patron saint gracing the entire ceiling of the chapel. The image of the Virgin is set against a deep blue night sky and includes 52 stars—a modern interpretation of Juan Diego's cloak.

You can dine in Crucecita for a fraction of the price in Tangolunda Bay, with the added benefit of some local color. Considering that shopping in Huatulco is generally poor, you'll find the best choices here, in the shops around the central plaza. They tend to stay open late, and offer a good selection of regional goods and typical tourist take-homes, including *artesanía,* silver jewelry, Cuban cigars, and tequila. A small free trolley train takes visitors on a short tour of the town.

BEACHES A section of the beach at Santa Cruz (away from the small boats) is an inviting sunning spot. Beach clubs for guests at non-oceanfront hotels are here. In addition, several restaurants are on the beach, and *palapa* umbrellas run down to the water's edge. For about $15 one-way, *pangas* from the marina in Santa Cruz will ferry you to **La Entrega Beach,** also in Santa Cruz Bay. There you'll find a row of *palapa* restaurants, all with beach chairs out front. Find an empty one, and use that restaurant for your refreshment needs. A snorkeling equipment rental booth is about midway down the beach, and there's some fairly good snorkeling on the end away from where the boats arrive.

Between Santa Cruz and Tangolunda bays is **Chahué Bay.** The beach club has *palapas,* beach volleyball, and refreshments for an entrance fee of about $3.50. However, a strong undertow makes this a dangerous place for swimming.

Tangolunda Bay beach, fronting the best hotels, is wide and beautiful. Theoretically, all beaches in Mexico are public; however, nonguests at Tangolunda hotels may have difficulty entering the hotels to get to the beach.

BAY CRUISES & TOURS Huatulco's major attraction is its coastline—a magnificent stretch of pristine bays bordered by an odd blend of cactus and jungle vegetation right at the water's edge. The only way to really grasp its beauty is to take a cruise of the bays, stopping at **Organo** or **Maguey Bay** for a dip in the crystal-clear water and a fish lunch at a *palapa* restaurant on the beach.

One way to arrange a bay tour is to go to the **boat-owners' cooperative** (✆ **958/587-0081**), located in the red-and-yellow tin shack at the entrance to the marina. Prices are posted, and you can buy tickets for sightseeing, snorkeling, or fishing. Beaches other than La Entrega, including Maguey and San Agustín, are noted for offshore snorkeling. They also have *palapa* restaurants and other facilities.

Several of these beaches, however, are completely undeveloped, so you will need to bring your own provisions. Boatmen at the cooperative will arrange return pickup at an appointed time. Prices run about $25 for 1 to 10 persons to La Entrega, and $50 for a trip to Maguey and Organo bays. The farthest bay is San Agustín; that all-day trip will run $100 in a private *panga.*

Another option is to join an organized daylong bay cruise. Any travel agency can easily make arrangements. Cruises are about $35 per person, plus $5 for snorkeling equipment rental and lunch. One excursion is on the *Tequila,* complete with guide, drinks, and onboard entertainment. Another, more romantic option is the *Luna Azul,* a 13m (43-ft.) sailboat that runs bay tours and sunset sails.

Ecotours are growing in popularity and number throughout the Bays of Huatulco. The mountain areas surrounding the Copalita River are also home to other natural treasures worth exploring, including the **Copalitilla Cascades.** Thirty kilometers (19 miles) north of Tangolunda, at 395m (1,296 ft.) above sea level, this group of waterfalls—averaging 20 to 25m (66–82 ft.) in height—form natural whirlpools and clear pools for swimming. The area is also popular for horseback riding and rappelling.

An all-day **shopping tour** takes you around the area, including a small village called La Crucecita, to peruse quality hand-made arts and crafts, and experience authentic Oaxacan cuisine. Contact **Paraíso Tours** (http://paraisohuatulco.com) for reservations.

Guided **horseback riding** through the jungles and to Conejos and Magueyito beach makes for a wonderful way to see the natural beauty of the area. The ride lasts 3 hours, with departures at 9:45am and 1:45pm, and costs $35 to $45. Contact **Caballo del Mar Ranch** (**© 958/589-9387**).

Another recommended guide for both **hiking** and **bird-watching** is Laura Gonzalez, of **Nature Tours Huatulco** (**© 958/583-4047**; lauriycky@hotmail.com). Ms. Gonzalez leads a hike around Punta Celeste with views of the river, open sea, and forest, for sightings of terrestrial and aquatic birds. The 3½-hour tour can be made in the early morning or late afternoon and costs $45. An 8-hour excursion to the Ventanilla Lagoons takes you by boat through a mangrove to view birds, iguanas, and crocodiles. The cost is $80, including lunch. Tours include transportation, binoculars, specialized bird guide, and beverages.

GOLF & TENNIS The 18-hole, par-72 **Tangolunda Golf Course** (**© 958/581-0037**) is adjacent to Tangolunda Bay. It has tennis courts as well, for $11 per hour. The greens fee is $80 for 18 holes and $6 for 9 holes; carts cost $34. Tennis courts are also available at the **Barceló** hotel (**© 958/581-0055**) for $10 per person per hour.

 SHOPPING Shopping in the area is limited and unmemorable. It concentrates in the **Santa Cruz Market,** by the marina in Santa Cruz, and in the **Crucecita Market,** on Guamúchil, a half-block from the plaza. Both are open daily from 10am to 8pm (no phones). Among the prototypical souvenirs, you may want to search out regional specialties, which include Oaxacan embroidered blouses and dresses, and *barro negro,* pottery made from dark clay exclusively found in the Oaxaca region. Also in Crucecita is the Plaza Oaxaca, adjacent to the central plaza. Its clothing shops include **Poco Loco Club/Coconut's Boutique** (✆ **958/587-0279**), for casual sportswear; and **Mic Mac** (✆ **958/587-0565**), for beachwear and souvenirs. **Coconuts** (✆ **958/587-0057**) has English-language magazines, books, and music.

WHERE TO STAY

Moderate- and budget-priced hotels in Santa Cruz and Crucecita are generally more expensive than similar hotels in other Mexican beach resorts. The luxury hotels have comparable rates, especially when they're part of a package that includes airfare. The trend here is toward all-inclusive resorts, which in Huatulco are an especially good option, given the lack of memorable dining and nightlife options. Hotels that are not oceanfront generally have an arrangement with a beach club at Santa Cruz or Chahué Bay, and offer shuttle service. Low-season rates apply August through November only. Parking is free at these hotels; the 18% tax is not included in the rack rates listed below.

Expensive

Camino Real Zaashila ★★ Kids One of the original hotels in Tangolunda Bay, the Camino Real Zaashila sits on a wide stretch of sandy beach secluded from other beaches by small rock outcroppings. It has been renovated with a newly designed *palapa* bar with sit-down check-in. The calm water, perfect for swimming and snorkeling, makes it ideal for families. The white stucco building is Mediterranean in style and washed in colors on the ocean side. The boldly decorated rooms are large and have an oceanview balcony or terrace and a large bathroom with an Italian marble tub/shower. Each of the 41 club rooms on the lower levels has its own private plunge pool and includes buffet breakfast and evening cocktails. The main pool is a free-form design that spans 150m (500 ft.) of beach, with chaises built into the shallow edges. Well-manicured tropical gardens surround it and the guest rooms.

Bulevar Benito Juárez 5, Bahía de Tangolunda, 70989 Huatulco, Oax. ✆ **800/722-6466** in the U.S., or 958/581-0460. Fax 958/581-0468. www.camino-zaashila.com 120 units. High season $160 and up double; low season $130 and up double, AE, DC, MC, V. **Amenities:** 3 restaurants (1 Oaxacan); lobby bar w/live music; kids' club;

2 large outdoor pools; outdoor whirlpool; room service; lighted tennis court; beachside watersports center. *In room:* A/C, TV, minibar, free Wi-Fi.

Quinta Real ★★★ Double Moorish domes mark this romantic, relaxed hotel, known for its richly appointed cream-and-white decor and complete attention to detail. From the welcoming reception area to the luxurious beach club below, the staff emphasizes excellence in service. The small groupings of suites are built into the sloping hill to Tangolunda Bay and offer spectacular views of the ocean and golf course. Suites on the eastern edge of the resort sit above the highway, which generates some traffic noise. Interiors are elegant and comfortable, with stylish Mexican furniture, original art, wood-beamed ceilings, and marble tub/showers with whirlpool tubs. Balconies have overstuffed seating areas and stone-inlay floors. Eight Grand Class Suites and the Presidential Suite have private pools. The most luxurious hotel in Huatulco and the top Mexican hotel chain, the Quinta Real is perfect for weddings, honeymoons, or small corporate retreats.

Bulevar Benito Juárez Lt. 2, Bahía de Tangolunda, 70989 Huatulco, Oax. ✆ **888/561-2817** in the U.S., or 958/581-0428, 581-0430. Fax 958/581-0429. www.quintareal.com. 28 units. $300 and up suites. AE, MC, V. **Amenities:** Restaurant (breakfast, dinner); poolside restaurant (lunch); bar w/stunning view; concierge; room service.; tennis court; beach club w/2 outdoor pools (1 for children). *In room:* A/C, TV, hair dryer, minibar.

Moderate

Hotel Meicer Binniguenda ★ Huatulco's first hotel retains the charm and comfort that originally made it memorable. Rooms have Mexican-tile floors, foot-loomed bedspreads, and colonial-style furniture; French doors open onto tiny wrought-iron balconies overlooking Juárez or the pool and gardens. There's a section with newer rooms that have modern teak furnishings. A nice shady area surrounds the small pool in back of the lobby. The hotel is away from the marina at the far end of Juárez, only a few blocks from the water. It offers free transportation every hour to the beach club at Chahué.

Bulevar Santa Cruz 201, 70989 Santa Cruz de Huatulco, Oax. ✆ **958/587-0129.** www.meicerhotels.com. 165 units. $100–$160 double. Children younger than 7 stay free in parent's room. MC, V. **Amenities:** Large *palapa*-topped restaurant and bar; shuttle to beach; small outdoor pool. *In room:* A/C, TV.

Inexpensive

Hotel Las Palmas The central location and accommodating staff add to the appeal of the bright, cheerful rooms at Las Palmas. Located a half-block from the main plaza, it's connected to the popular El Sabor de Oaxaca restaurant (see "Where to Dine," below), which offers room service to guests. The accommodations have tile floors, cotton textured bedspreads, tile showers, and cable TV; most also have balconies. This hotel is partnered with another inexpensive and reliable choice in case this one sells out, featuring similarly comfortable rooms with a bright, open courtyard overlooking El Sabor restaurant.

Av. Guamúchil 206, 70989 Bahías de Huatulco, Oax. ✆ **958/587-0060.** Fax 958/587-0057. 10 units. High season $60 double; low season $40 double. AE, MC, V. *In room:* A/C, TV.

Misión de los Arcos ★★ Finds This exceptional hotel, just a block from the central plaza, is similar in style to the elegant Quinta Real—but at a fraction of the cost. The hotel is mostly white, accented with abundant greenery, giving it a fresh, inviting feel. The simple rooms—many of which were in the process of being remodeled at press time—continue the theme, washed in white, with cream and beige bed coverings and upholstery. At the entrance level, an excellent cafe offers high-speed Internet access, Huatulco's regionally grown coffee, tea, pastries, and ice cream. It's open from 7:30am to 11:30pm. The adjacent Terra-Cotta restaurant (see below) serves breakfast, lunch, and dinner, and is equally stylish and budget friendly. Although there's no pool, for $3 guests can use the Castillo Beach Club, at Chahué bay, open daily from 9am to 7pm. The hotel is close to all the shops and restaurants.

Gardenia 902, La Crucecita, 70989 Huatulco, Oax. ✆ **958/587-0165.** Fax 958/587-1903. www.misiondelosarcos.com. 16 units. High season $80 double, $85–$105 suite; low season $50 double, $55–$65 suite. Rates increase over Christmas and Easter holiday periods. AE, MC, V. Street parking. **Amenities:** Restaurant; nearby beach club. *In room:* A/C, TV, free Wi-Fi.

WHERE TO DINE

El Sabor de Oaxaca ★★★ OAXACAN This is the best place in the area to enjoy authentic, richly flavorful Oaxacan food, among the best of traditional Mexican cuisine. This colorful restaurant is a local favorite that also meets the quality standards of tourists. A popular item is the mixed grill for two, with an Oaxacan beef filet, tender pork tenderloin, and chorizo (zesty Mexican sausage). If you're feeling adventurous, try the salty grilled *chapulines* (grasshoppers, an Oaxacan specialty). Generous breakfasts include hearty Oaxacan favorites such as *emoladas,* tortillas generously stuffed with meat fillings and soaked in the zesty traditional *mole* sauce.

Av. Guamúchil 206, Crucecita. ✆ **958/587-0060.** Fax 958/587-0057. Breakfast $5–$7; main courses $7.50–$15. AE, MC, V. Daily 7am–11pm.

Noches Oaxaqueñas/Don Porfirio ★ SEAFOOD/OAXACAN This dinner show presents the colorful, traditional folkloric dances of

Oaxaca in an open-air courtyard reminiscent of an old hacienda (but in a modern strip mall). The dancers perform traditional ballet under the direction of owner Celicia Flores Ramírez, wife of Don Willo Porfirio. House specialties include grilled lobster, shrimp with *mescal* flambéed at the table, and spaghetti marinara with seafood, along with a fountain of seafood that includes shrimp, octopus, and snails, all cooked on hot grills right in front of your table. Meat lovers will enjoy American-style cuts or a juicy *arrachera* (skirt steak). The *Guelaguetza Show* showcases an important annual cultural celebration in Oaxaca. There are two-for-one specials for children, and the show normally takes place nightly at 8pm during high season, and Tuesday, Thursday, and Saturday nights at 8pm in low season. You should confirm showtimes before making a reservation, since timings are somewhat sporadic.

Bulevar Benito Juárez s/n (across from Royal Maeva), Tangolunda Bay. ✆ **958/581-0001.** Main courses $10–$20. AE, MC, V. Daily noon–11pm. Show $12 extra.

Terra-Cotta ★ (Finds) INTERNATIONAL/MEXICAN Located inside the Hotel Misión de los Arcos, this stylish yet casual restaurant is best known for breakfast, and it's just as tasty at lunch and dinner. Start the day in this white-washed, Mediterranean setting with gourmet coffee, fruit salad, and an array of morning favorites, including specials such as French toast stuffed with cream cheese and orange marmalade. Lunch and dinner share the same menu, which offers fajitas, baby back ribs, gourmet tacos, and six different sandwich options. Scrumptious desserts such as caramelized pineapple with coconut ice cream offer a sweet finish.

Gardenia 902, at the Hotel Misión de los Arcos, in front of La Crucecita's central plaza. ✆ **958/587-0165.** Breakfast $8.90–$14; lunch and dinner main courses $6.50–$20. AE, MC, V. Daily 8am–11pm.

HUATULCO AFTER DARK

There's a very limited selection of dance clubs around Huatulco—meaning that's where everyone goes. Huatulco seems to have the least consistent nightlife of any resort in Mexico, and clubs seem to change ownership—and names—almost annually. Check with your hotel concierge to see if any new places have opened; none of the places listed below have phones. The current hot spot is **Bar La Crema,** in Crucecita (about 4 blocks south of the *zócalo,* at the corner of Bugambilia and La Ceiba), with a lounge atmosphere and a mix of tunes. Nearby is **Café Dublin,** Carrizal 504 (1 block east and a half-block south from the *zócalo*), an Irish pub with a book exchange. Both bars open in the evening during high season and stay open as long as the management sees fit; hours are sporadic in low season. On the east side of the *zócalo* lies **The Tipsy Blowfish,** which plays rock music and features televised sports. The bar is open daily from noon to 4am during high season, with limited hours in low season.

La Papaya, on Bulevar Chahué, is a popular dance club, open Thursday through Saturday into the wee hours. Each Wednesday, the Barceló Resort hosts its **Fiesta Mexicana** from 7 to 11pm, featuring folkloric dances, mariachi music, and a buffet of Mexican food and drinks.

5

Inland to Old Mexico: Taxco, Cuernavaca & Tepoztlán

It may seem as though the small towns in this region are trying to capitalize on recent trends in travel toward spas and self-exploration, but in reality, they've helped define them. From the restorative properties of thermal waters and earth-based spa treatments to the mystical and spiritual properties of gemstones and herbs, the treasures and knowledge in these towns have existed for years—and, in some cases, for centuries.

This is only a sampling of towns south and west of Mexico City. They are fascinating in their diversity, history, and mystery, and make for a unique travel experience, either on their own or combined. They vary in character from mystical villages to sophisticated spa towns, with archaeological and colonial-era attractions in the mix. And with their proximity to Mexico City, all are within easy reach by private car or taxi—or by inexpensive bus—in under a few hours.

The legendary silver city of **Taxco,** on the road between Acapulco and Mexico City, is renowned for its museums, picturesque hillside colonial-era charm, and, of course, its silver shops. North of Taxco and southwest of Mexico City, over the mountains, are the venerable thermal spas at **Ixtapan de la Sal,** as well as their more modern counterparts in **Valle de Bravo.** Verdant **Cuernavaca,** known as the land of eternal spring, has gained a reputation for its exceptional spa facilities and its wealth of cultural and historic attractions. Finally, **Tepoztlán,** with its enigmatic charms and legendary pyramid, captivates the few travelers who find their way there.

I found that the region as a whole is the perfect place for solo travel. I spent 3 days in **Taxco** and never felt alone because the locals were so friendly and the whole city is bursting with tiny details. **Tepoztlán** is a place of reflection as its spirituality oozes from every rock and new age shop, and in **Cuernavaca** you'll find plenty of out-of-town Chilangos to keep you company.

1 TAXCO: COBBLESTONES & SILVER ★★

178km (110 miles) SW of Mexico City; 80km (50 miles) SW of Cuernavaca; 296km (184 miles) NE of Acapulco

In Mexico and around the world, the town of Taxco de Alarcón—most commonly known simply as Taxco (*tahs*-koh)—is synonymous with silver. The town's geography and architecture are equally precious: Taxco sits at nearly 1,515m (4,969 ft.) on a hill among hills, and almost any point in the city offers fantastic views.

Hernán Cortez discovered Taxco as he combed the area for treasure, but its rich caches of silver weren't fully exploited for another 2 centuries. In 1751, the French prospector Joseph de la Borda—who came to be known locally as José—commissioned the baroque Santa Prisca Church that dominates Taxco's *zócalo* (Plaza Borda) as a way of giving something back to the town. In the mid-1700s, Borda was considered the richest man in New Spain.

The fact that Taxco has become Mexico's most renowned center for silver design, even though it now mines only a small amount of silver, is the work of an American, William Spratling. Spratling arrived in the late 1920s with the intention of writing a book. He soon noticed the skill of the local craftsmen and opened a workshop to produce handmade silver jewelry and tableware based on pre-Hispanic art, which he exported to the U.S. in bulk. The workshops flourished, and Taxco's reputation grew.

Today most of the residents of this town are involved in the silver industry in some way. Taxco is home to hundreds (some say up to 900) of silver shops and outlets, ranging from sleek galleries to small stands in front of stucco homes. You'll find silver in all of its forms here—the jewelry basics, tea sets, silverware, candelabras, picture frames, and napkin holders.

The tiny one-man factories that line the winding cobbled streets all the way up into the hills supply most of Taxco's silverwork. "Bargains" are relative, but nowhere else will you find this combination of diversity, quality, and rock-bottom prices. Generally speaking, the larger shops that most obviously cater to the tourist trade will have the highest prices—but they may be the only ones to offer "that special something" you're looking for. For classic designs in jewelry or other silver items, shop around, and wander the back streets and smaller venues.

You can get an idea of what Taxco is like by spending an afternoon, but there's much more to this picturesque town than just the Plaza Borda and the shops surrounding it. Stay overnight, wander its steep

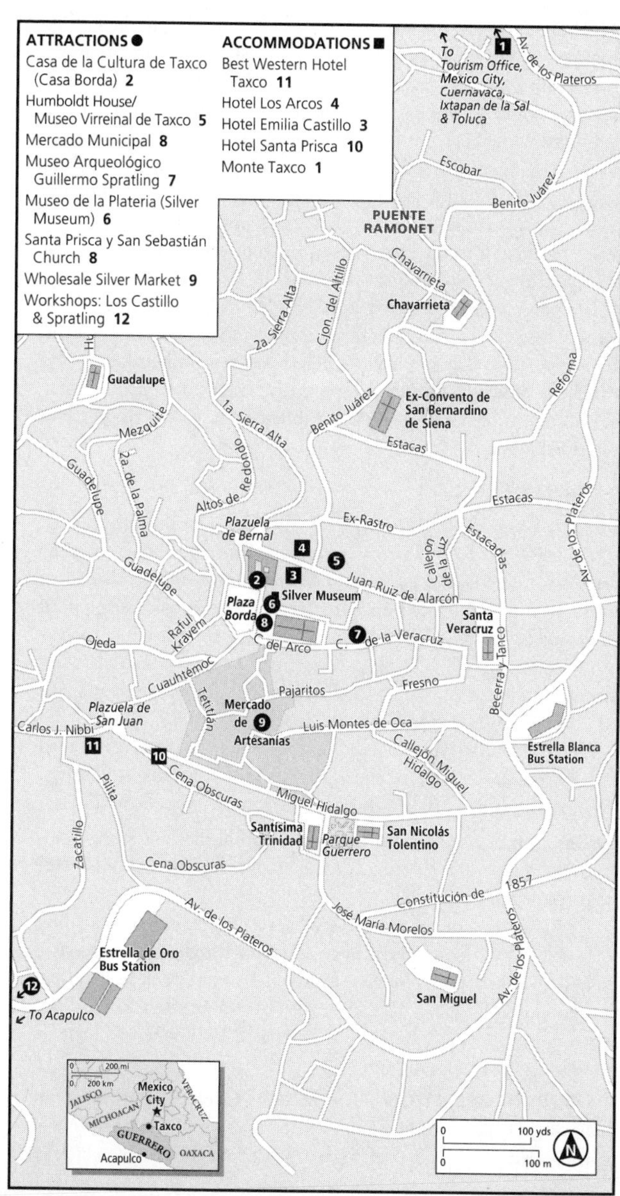
ATTRACTIONS
Casa de la Cultura de Taxco (Casa Borda) 2
Humboldt House/ Museo Virreinal de Taxco 5
Mercado Municipal 8
Museo Arqueológico Guillermo Spratling 7
Museo de la Plateria (Silver Museum) 6
Santa Prisca y San Sebastián Church 8
Wholesale Silver Market 9
Workshops: Los Castillo & Spratling 12
ACCOMMODATIONS
Best Western Hotel Taxco 11
Hotel Los Arcos 4
Hotel Emilia Castillo 3
Hotel Santa Prisca 10
Monte Taxco 1
To Tourism Office, Mexico City, Cuernavaca, Ixtapan de la Sal & Toluca
Av. de los Plateros
Escobar
Benito Juárez
PUENTE RAMONET
Chavarrieta
Chavarrieta
Cjon. del Altillo
2a. Sierra Alta
Guadalupe
Reforma
Ex-Convento de San Bernardino de Siena
1a. Sierra Alta
Benito Juárez
Estacas
Mezquite
Redondo
Guadelupe
2a. de la Palma
Altos de
Plazuela de Bernal
Ex-Rastro
Estacas
Estacadas
Callejon de la Luz
Av. de los Plateros
Guadelupe
Juan Ruiz de Alarcón
Silver Museum
Plaza Borda
Raful Krayem
Santa Veracruz
Ojeda
C. del Arco
C. de la Veracruz
Becerra y Tanco
Cuauhtémoc
Tetitlán
Pajaritos
Fresno
Plazuela de San Juan
Mercado de Artesanías
Carlos J. Nibbi
Luis Montes de Oca
Callejón Miguel Hidalgo
Estrella Blanca Bus Station
Cena Obscuras
Pilita
Miguel Hidalgo
Santísima Trinidad
Parque Guerrero
San Nicolás Tolentino
Zacatillo
Cena Obscuras
Constitución de 1857
Av. de los Plateros
José María Morelos
Estrella de Oro Bus Station
Av. de los Plateros
San Miguel
To Acapulco
200 mi
200 km
Mexico City
JALISCO
MICHOACAN
VERACRUZ
Taxco
GUERRERO
OAXACA
Acapulco
100 yds
100 m
N

cobblestone streets, and you'll discover little plazas, fine churches, and, of course, an abundance of silversmiths' shops.

The main part of town is relatively flat. It stretches up the hillside from the highway, and it's a steep but brief walk up. White VW minibuses, called *combis,* make the circuit through and around town, picking up and dropping off passengers along the route, from about 7am until 9pm. These taxis are inexpensive (about 50 pesos from the bus station to most hotels), and you should use them even if you arrive by car, because parking is practically impossible. Also, the streets are so narrow and steep that most visitors find them nerve-wracking. Find a secured parking lot for your car, or leave it at your hotel and forget about it until you leave.

Warning: Self-appointed guides will likely approach you in the *zócalo* (Plaza Borda) and offer their services—they get a cut of all you buy in the shops they take you to. Before hiring a guide, ask to see his SECTUR (Tourism Secretary) credentials. The Department of Tourism office on the highway at the north end of town can recommend a licensed guide.

ESSENTIALS

GETTING THERE & DEPARTING **By Car** From Mexico City, take Paseo de la Reforma to Chapultepec Park and merge with the Periférico, which will take you to Hwy. 95D on the south end of town. From the Periférico, take the Insurgentes exit and merge until you come to the sign for CUERNAVACA/TLALPAN. Choose either *cuernavaca cuota* (toll) or *cuernavaca libre* (free). Continue south around Cuernavaca to the Amacuzac interchange, and proceed straight ahead for Taxco. The drive from Mexico City takes about 3½ hours.

From Acapulco, you have two options: Hwy. 95D is the toll road through Iguala to Taxco, or you can take the old two-lane road (Hwy. 95) that winds more slowly through villages; it's in good condition.

By Bus From Mexico City, buses depart from the Central de Autobuses del Sur station (Metro: Taxqueña) and take 2 to 3 hours, with frequent departures.

Taxco has two bus stations. Estrella de Oro buses arrive at their own station on the southern edge of town. Estrella Blanca service, including Futura executive-class buses, and Flecha Roja buses arrive at the station on the northeastern edge of town on Avenida Los Plateros ("Avenue of the Silversmiths," formerly Av. Kennedy). Taxis to the *zócalo* cost around 20 pesos.

VISITOR INFORMATION The **State of Guerrero Dirección de Turismo** (✆/fax **762/622-2274**) has offices at the arches on the main highway at the north end of town (Av. de los Plateros 1), which is useful if you're driving into town. The office is open Monday through Saturday from 9am to 8pm, and Sunday from 9am to 6pm. To get there from the Plaza Borda, take a ZOCALO-ARCOS *combi* and get off at the arch over the highway. As you face the arches, the tourism office is on your right.

CITY LAYOUT The center of town is the tiny **Plaza Borda,** shaded by perfectly manicured Indian laurel trees. On one side is the imposing twin-towered, pink-stone **Santa Prisca Church;** whitewashed, red-tile buildings housing the famous silver shops and a restaurant or two line the other sides. Beside the church, deep in a crevice of the mountain, is the **wholesale silver market**—the best place to begin your silver shopping, to get an idea of prices for more standard designs. It's open daily from 9am to 7pm. You'll be amazed at the low prices. Buying just one piece is perfectly acceptable, and buying in bulk can lower the per-piece price. One of the beauties of Taxco is that its brick and cobblestone streets are completely asymmetrical, zigzagging up and down the hillsides. The plaza buzzes with vendors of everything from hammocks and cotton candy to bark paintings and balloons.

FAST FACTS The telephone area code is **762.** The main post office, Benito Juárez 6, at the City Hall building (✆ **762/622-8596**), is open Monday through Saturday from 8:30am to 3:30pm. The older

Spanish Lessons & Art Classes in Taxco

The Taxco campus of the **Universidad Nacional Autónoma de México (UNAM; ✆ 762/622-3410;** www.cepetaxco.unam.mx) houses the Center of Instruction for Foreign Students on the grounds of the Hacienda del Chorrillo, formerly part of the Cortez land grant. Here, students can learn silversmithing, Spanish, drawing, composition, and history under the supervision of UNAM instructors. Classes are small, and courses generally last 3 months. The school provides a list of accommodations that consist primarily of hotels. More reasonable accommodations for a lengthy stay are available but are best arranged once you're there. At many locations all over town, you'll find notices of furnished apartments or rooms for rent. For information about the school, either contact the Dirección de Turismo (tourist office) in Taxco (see "Visitor Information," above) or write the school directly, at Hacienda del Chorrillo, 40200 Taxco, Gro.

branch of the post office (✆ **762/622-0501**), open Monday through Friday from 8:30am to 2:30pm, is on the outskirts, on the highway to Acapulco. It's in a row of shops with a black-and-white CORREO sign.

EXPLORING TAXCO

Shopping for jewelry and other items is the major pastime for tourists. Prices for silver jewelry at Taxco's shops are about the best in the world, and everything is available, from 10-peso trinkets to artistic pieces that cost hundreds of dollars. In addition to the workshops listed below, there are several standout shops in town, including **TeGo,** Benito Juarez 46 (✆ **762/622-0615**), which features the unique jewelry of designer Teresa Gonzalez.

In addition, Taxco is the home of some of Mexico's finest stone sculptors and is a good place to buy masks. However, beware of so-called "antiques"—there are virtually no real ones for sale.

If you purchase a large item during your stay and need help with packaging and/or mailing it, visit the folks at **Empaques San David,** Miguel Hidalgo 15 (✆ **762/622-2036**).

SPECIAL EVENTS & FESTIVALS **January 18** marks the annual celebration in honor of Santa Prisca, with public festivities and fireworks displays. **Holy Week ★★** in Taxco is one of the most poignant in the country, beginning the Friday a week before Easter with processions daily and nightly. The most riveting, on Thursday evening, lasts almost 4 hours. Villagers from the surrounding area carry statues of saints, followed by hooded members of a society of self-flagellating penitents, chained at the ankles and carrying huge wooden crosses and bundles of thorny branches. On Saturday morning, the Plaza Borda fills for the **Procession of Three Falls,** reenacting the three times Christ stumbled and fell while carrying the cross.

Taxco's **Silver Fair** starts the last week in November and continues through the first week in December. It includes a competition for silver works and sculptures among the top silversmiths. In late April to early May, **Jornadas Alarconianas** features plays and literary events in honor of Juan Ruiz de Alarcón (1572–1639), a world-famous dramatist who was born in Taxco—and for whom Taxco de Alarcón is named. Art exhibits, street fairs, and other festivities are part of the dual celebration.

Sights in Town

Casa de la Cultura de Taxco (Casa Borda) Diagonally across from the Santa Prisca Church and facing Plaza Borda is the home José de la Borda built for his son around 1759. Now the Guerrero State Cultural Center, it houses a bookstore, library, classrooms, and exhibit halls where period clothing, engravings, paintings, and crafts are on display. The center also books traveling art exhibits, theatrical performances, music concerts, and dance events.

Plaza Borda 1. © **762/622-6617.** Fax 762/662-6634. Free admission. Tues–Fri 9am–4pm; Sat-Sun 10am–5pm.

Humboldt House/Museo Virreinal de Taxco Stroll along Ruiz de Alarcón (the street behind the Casa Borda) and look for the richly decorated facade of the Humboldt House, where the renowned German scientist and explorer Baron Alexander von Humboldt (1769–1859) spent a night in 1803. The museum houses 18th-century memorabilia pertinent to Taxco, most of which came from a secret room discovered during a recent restoration of the Santa Prisca Church. Signs with detailed information are in Spanish and English. As you enter, to the right are very rare *túmulos funerios* (painted funerary altars). The bottom two were painted for Charles III of Spain; the top one, with a carved phoenix, was reputedly painted for the funeral of José de la Borda.

Another section presents historical information about Don Miguel Cabrera, Mexico's foremost 18th-century artist. Fine examples of clerical garments decorated with gold and silver thread hang in glass cases, and on the bottom level there's an impressive 17th-century carved wood altar of Dolores. Next to it, a small room is devoted to Humboldt and his sojourns through South America and Mexico.

Calle Juan Ruiz de Alarcón 12. © **762/622-5501.** Admission 20 pesos adults, 15 pesos students and teachers w/ID. Tues–Sat 10am–6pm; Sun 10am–4pm.

Mercado Municipal Located to the right of the Santa Prisca Church, behind and below Berta's, Taxco's central market meanders deep inside the mountain. Take the stairs off the street. In addition to a collection of wholesale silver shops, you'll find numerous food stands, always the best place for a cheap meal.

Plaza Borda. Shops daily 10am–8pm; food stands daily 7am–6pm.

Museo Arqueológico Guillermo Spratling A plaque in Spanish explains that most of the collection of pre-Columbian art displayed here, as well as the funds for the museum, came from William Spratling (1900–67). You'd expect this to be a silver museum, but it's not—for Spratling silver, go to the Spratling Ranch Workshop (see "Nearby Attractions," below). The entrance floor and the one above display a good collection of pre-Columbian statues and implements in clay, stone, and jade. The upper floor holds changing exhibits.

Calle Porfirio A. Delgado 1. © **762/622-1660.** Admission 31 pesos adults, free for children younger than 13; free to all Sun. Tues–Sat 9am–5pm; Sun 9am–3pm. Leaving Santa Prisca Church, turn right and right again at the corner; continue down the street, veer right, then immediately left. The museum will be facing you.

Museo de la Plateria The silver museum holds a small collection of exquisite silver pieces, the most interesting of which is *La Conquista de Anahuac,* in which copper Aztec warriors and silver Spanish conquistadors face off on a chess board made with black wood and oyster shell. The owner, Antonio Pineda, declined a $1-million offer to sell it. This museum represents his private collection and includes silver pieces from throughout the last century, such as coins, sculptures, jewelry, and crowns. A mural created by a local artist represents the history of Mexico's silver industry.

Plaza Borda 1. ✆ **762/622-0658.** Admission 10 pesos. Tues–Sun 10am–6pm. The museum is located downstairs in the Patio de las Artesanias.

Santa Prisca y San Sebastián Church ★★ This is Taxco's centerpiece parish church; it faces the pleasant Plaza Borda. José de la Borda, a French miner who struck it rich in Taxco's silver mines, funded the construction. Completed in 1758, it's one of Mexico's most impressive baroque churches. The ultracarved facade is eclipsed by the interior, with breathtakingly intricate gold-leafed saints and cherubic angels. The paintings by Miguel Cabrera, one of Mexico's most famous colonial-era artists, are the pride of Taxco. The sacristy (behind the high altar) contains more Cabrera paintings.

Guides, both children and adults, will approach you outside the church offering to give a tour. Make sure the guide's English is passable, and establish whether the price is per person or per tour. Note that flash photos are not allowed.

Plaza Borda. ✆ **762/622-0184.** Free admission. Daily 6:30am–8pm.

Nearby Attractions

The impressive **Grutas de Cacahuamilpa ★**, known as the Cacahuamilpa Caves or Grottoes, lie less than a half-hour north of Taxco. Hourly guided tours run daily at the caverns, which house fascinating stalactite and stalagmite formations. To see them, you can join a tour from Taxco (see "Exploring Taxco," above) or take a *combi* from the Flecha Roja terminal in Taxco; one-way is 50 pesos, and admission to the caves is 50 pesos. For more information, see "Sights Near Tepoztlán," later in this chapter.

Rancho Emilia Castillo Don Antonio Castillo was one of hundreds of young men to whom William Spratling taught silversmithing in the 1930s. He was also one of the first to branch out with his own shops and line of designs, which over the years have earned him a fine reputation. Castillo has shops in several Mexican cities. Now his daughter Emilia creates her own noteworthy designs, including decorative pieces with silver fused onto porcelain. After roaming the steep streets of Taxco, a visit to the sprawling hacienda is the perfect way to have the beauty of Guerrero spread out in front of you. The grounds are lush, with a waterfall feeding a stream that runs through the whole property. A tour includes a visit to a workshop where skilled artisans create everything from silver housewares to ceramic figures. Emilia's work is for sale on the ground floor of the Posada de los Castillo, just below the Plazuela Bernal.

8km (5 miles) south of town on the Acapulco Hwy. Also at Plazuela Bernal, Taxco. ✆ **762/622-6901.** If you take a taxi tell them to drop you off near the crocodile sculpture. Free admission. Workshop Mon–Sat 10am–3pm and 4–7pm; open to groups at other hours by appointment only.

Spratling Ranch Workshop William Spratling's hacienda-style home and workshop on the outskirts of Taxco still bustles with busy hands reproducing unique designs. A trip here will show you what distinctive Spratling work was all about, for the designs crafted today

Silversmiths and Wordsmiths

Imagine you're walking through a cavernous marketplace, carved into the Guerrero mountainside. The sights, smells, and sounds are unfamiliar, and all of a sudden you look up and see a Herman Hesse quote neatly written on a chalkboard among the pipes, screws, and water heater parts of an old-fashioned hardware store. It says in Spanish, "Not being loved is only a question of luck; the true tragedy is not being able to love at all." The store's owner, Miguel Angel Aviles, was hoping to make you think just a little. Aviles has been putting up intriguing phrases in front of his locale for more than 20 years and says that people often pass by just to read them. One of the biggest attention getters was this one by former Mexican President Alvaro Obregon: "Certainly bad luck exists, but god only distributes it among fools." One Uruguayan visitor liked that one so much that he turned it into his Christmas card—one of the recipients came to complain to Aviles that he'd been looking at the phrase on his refrigerator all year.

If you'd like to read Aviles's latest phrase, enter the market from the stairway on Real de Cuauhtémoc, just in front of the pharmacy. Make a quick right at the bottom of the stairs, and the hardware store will be on your immediate right.

show the same fine work. Although the prices are higher than at other outlets, the designs are unusual and considered collectible. There's no store in Taxco, and most of the display cases hold only samples. With the exception of a few jewelry pieces, most items are by order only. Ask about U.S. outlets.

10km (6¼ miles) south of town on the Acapulco Hwy. **762/622-0026.** Free admission. Call in advance for hours, which vary. The *combi* to Iguala stops at the ranch; fare is 18 pesos.

WHERE TO STAY

Moderate

Best Western Hotel Taxco ★★ This is the newest and most modern hotel in the town center, with professional service and an international clientele. Rooms are small but very comfortable, with white tiles and bedspreads and Mexican architectural touches. Some have windows (interior rooms do not), and the junior suite has a terrace with views of the surrounding hills. Near the Santa Prisca church, this hotel has a quality Mexican restaurant and access to a nearby pool. The friendly staff will arrange in-room massages upon request. They offer a 10% discount on cash payments.

Carlos J. Nibbi 2, Plazuela de San Juan, 40200 Taxco, Gro. ✆ **762/627-6194.** Fax 762/622-3416. www.bestwesterntaxco.com. 23 units. 1,100 pesos double; 1,500 pesos junior suite. AE, MC, V. Free parking. **Amenities:** Restaurant; access to outdoor pool. *In room:* AC, TV, Wi-Fi.

Monte Taxco (Overrated) This resort and country club sits atop a hill near the entrance to Taxco coming from Mexico City. A longtime landmark of the city, it offers golf and tennis, spa services, and access to the mountain's cable car, which operates daily from 8am to 7pm. Colonial-style rooms are a bit dated but comfortable. Open weekends for dinner only, Toni's boasts the best city views of any restaurant in Taxco, and you can finish the night at the flashy dance club next door. You'll need to drive or take a taxi to reach the city center.

Fracc. Lomas de Taxco s/n, 40210 Taxco, Gro. ✆ **762/622-1300.** Fax 762/622-1428. www.montetaxcohotel.com. 156 units. 2,150 pesos and up double. AE, MC, V. Free parking. **Amenities:** 2 restaurants (1 w/spectacular city view; see "Where to Dine," below); bar; dance club; 9-hole golf course; gym; heated outdoor pool; room service; spa services; 3 tennis courts. *In room:* A/C, TV.

Inexpensive

Hotel Emilia Castillo (Value) Each room in this delightful small hotel is simply but handsomely appointed with carved doors and furniture; the small tile bathrooms have showers only. Ask for an interior room, which are much quieter than those facing the street. A high-quality silver shop lies next to the colorful lobby. The hotel does not have parking but contracts with a local parking garage.

Juan Ruiz de Alarcón 7, 40200 Taxco, Gro. ✆/fax **762/622-1396.** www.hotelemiliacastillo.com. 14 units. 500 pesos double; 550 pesos triple with TV. MC, V. From the Plaza Borda, go downhill a short block to the Plazuela Bernal and make an immediate right; the hotel is a block farther on the right, opposite the Hotel los Arcos (see below). **Amenities:** Internet. *In room:* TV.

Hotel los Arcos ★ Los Arcos occupies a converted 1620 monastery. The handsome inner patio is bedecked with Puebla pottery and rustic furnishings surrounding a central fountain. Guest rooms are nicely but sparsely appointed, with natural tile floors and colonial-style furniture; the spacious junior suite has two levels. You'll feel immersed in colonial charm and blissful quiet. To find the hotel from the Plaza Borda, follow the hill down (with Hotel Agua Escondida on your left) and make an immediate right at the Plazuela Bernal.

Juan Ruiz de Alarcón 4, 40200 Taxco, Gro. ✆ **762/622-1836.** Fax 762/622-7982. www.hotellosarcos.net. 21 units. 500 pesos and up. No credit cards. **Amenities:** Internet. *In room:* TV, fan.

Hotel Santa Prisca (Value) The Santa Prisca, 1 block from the Plaza Borda on the Plazuela San Juan, is one of the oldest and best-located hotels in town. Rooms are small but comfortable ("superior doubles" are slightly larger), with standard bathrooms (showers only), tile floors, wood beams, and a colonial atmosphere. For longer stays, ask for a room in the adjacent new addition, where the rooms are sunnier, quieter, and more spacious. There is a reading area in an upstairs salon overlooking Taxco, as well as a garden patio with fountains.

Cenaobscuras 1, 40200 Taxco, Gro. ✆ **762/622-0080,** 622-0980. Fax 762/622-2938. 34 units. 500 pesos double; 600 pesos superior double; 700 pesos junior suite. AE, MC, V. Limited free parking. **Amenities:** Breakfast cafe and bar; room service. *In room:* No phone.

WHERE TO DINE

Taxco gets a lot of day-trippers, most of whom choose to dine close to the Plaza Borda. Prices in this area are high for what you get. Just a few streets back, you'll find some excellent, simple *fondas* (taverns) or restaurants.

Very Expensive

Toni's ★ STEAKS/SEAFOOD High on a mountaintop, Toni's is an intimate, classic restaurant enclosed in a huge, cone-shaped *palapa* with a panoramic view of the city. Eleven candlelit tables sparkle with crystal and crisp linen, and piano music accompanies dinner. The menu, mainly shrimp or beef, is limited, but the food is quite good. Try tender, juicy prime roast beef carved at your table, which comes with creamed spinach and baked potato. To reach Toni's, it's best to take a taxi. Note that it's open for dinner on weekends only.

In the Hotel Monte Taxco. ✆ **762/622-1300.** Reservations recommended. Main courses 90–260 pesos. AE, MC, V. Fri–Sun 7pm–1am.

Moderate

Cafe Sasha ★★ INTERNATIONAL/VEGETARIAN One of the cutest places to dine in town, Cafe Sasha is very popular with locals and offers a great array of vegetarian options—such as falafel with tabouleh and vegetarian crepes, as well as Mexican and international classics. Try their Thai chicken curry or a hearty burrito. Open for breakfast, lunch, and dinner, it's also a great place for a cappuccino and pastry, or an evening cocktail. The music is hip, and the atmosphere is inviting and chic. The friendly owners, Javier and Sasha, are world travelers who delight in hearing their customers' tales.

Calle Juan Ruiz de Alarcón 1, just down from Plazuela de Berna. No phone. www.cafesasha.com. Breakfast 20–70 pesos; main courses 50–80 pesos. No credit cards. Daily 8am–midnight.

El Adobe ★ MEXICAN This charming restaurant is an eclectic Mexican mix of adobe, brick, and wood with decor that includes regional art, old black-and-white photos of Mexican and American entertainers, and some kitsch memorabilia. There are a number of romantic balcony tables lit with candles and lamps after dark. The hearty fare includes *cecina taxqueña* (thin strip steak served with guacamole), *pollo Guerrero* (chicken cooked with paprika, onion, small potatoes, and guacamole), and enchiladas prepared any way you want. A guitar player/singer performs weekend nights, and brunch is offered on Sunday.

Plazuela de San Juan 13. ✆ **762/622-1416.** Breakfast 30–50 pesos; main courses 55–140 pesos. MC, V. Daily 8:30am–11pm.

El Rincon del Toril LATIN This festive restaurant combines Mexican, Spanish, Italian, and Argentine cuisines. Delicious steaks are served sizzling hot on the skillet at your table. For a meat-eating extravaganza, order the *parrillada El Toril* for two, which includes *arrachera* beef, ribs, chorizo, and an American steak. Apart from the steaks, the menu offers an enticing selection of fish, chicken, and pasta dishes. The casual and often crowded dining room is brightly decorated with mementos from Mexican bullfights. It leads to an outdoor terrace next to the Plaza Borda. Traditional Mexican music plays cheerfully in the background.

Plaza Borda 3. ✆ **762/627-6207.** Main courses 70–180 pesos. MC, V. Daily 8am–10pm.

La Terraza Café-Bar INTERNATIONAL One of two restaurants at the Hotel Agua Escondida (on the *zócalo*), the rooftop La Terraza is a scenic spot for a meal or a drink, with tasty food and a great view of the church, town, and surrounding mountains. The diverse menu includes dishes such as breaded veal, grilled pork chops, chicken fajitas, and mole enchiladas. Even if you're normally not into desserts, you should seriously think about ordering a delicious crepe or flan here. Frosty margaritas and rich cappuccinos are also on order. During the day, cafe umbrellas shade the sun, and you can stargaze here at night.

Plaza Borda 4. ✆ **762/622-1166.** Main courses 40–100 pesos. MC, V. Daily noon–10:30pm.

Sotavento Restaurant Bar Galería ★★ ITALIAN/INTERNATIONAL Vibrant Mexican paintings decorate the walls of this stylish restaurant, which offers tables inside, on the balcony, or in the garden patio. The extensive menu features Italian and Mexican dishes—for starters, try the delicious fresh spinach salad with goat cheese and bacon, followed by a large pepper steak. For vegetarians, I recommend the Spaghetti Barbara with poblano peppers, onions, avocado, and cream. Savory crepes are also available.

Benito Juárez 12, next to City Hall. ✆ **762/627-1217.** Main courses 45–150 pesos. MC, V. Tues–Sun 9am–11pm. From the Plaza Borda, walk downhill beside the Hotel Agua Escondida, then follow the street as it bears left on Agustin de Tulsa (don't go right on Juan Ruiz de Alarcón) about 1 block; the restaurant is on the left just after the street bends left.

Inexpensive

Punto del Cielo INTERNATIONAL Normally, I'd hesitate to point anyone in the direction of a chain, but I'll make an exception for Punto del Cielo. The coffee shop is Mexican owned and uses coffee beans from Oaxaca, Chiapas, and Veracruz at a good price. Also, you can't beat the view from the Taxco location in Plaza Borda. Several tables are set up on a small patio that overlooks the bustling plaza and the Santa Prisca Church. The rest of the tables are spread throughout the spacious cafe, which is decorated with black-and-white photographs and has a supply of local newspapers and magazines on hand. After being served your coffee, you're invited to personalize it at a fully stocked flavor bar. Choices include amaretto, guava, mango, and hazelnut. They also offer croissants and paninis, which are perfect if you've already had your share of tacos.

Plaza Borda 4. Below Hotel Agua Escondida. ✆ **762/627-2722.** www.puntodelcielo.com.mx. Coffee 17–45 pesos; baguettes and snacks 45–70 pesos. MC, V. If you're leaving the Santa Prisa Church, it will be on your right side after you pass the Casa Borda.

TAXCO AFTER DARK

Located upstairs at Plaza Borda 12, **Acerto** (✆ **762/622-0064**) is an enticing all-purpose hangout overlooking the square. It serves as an

Internet cafe, sports bar, and restaurant. Taxco's popular, modern dance club, **Windows,** sits high up the mountain in the **Hotel Monte Taxco** (© **762/622-1300**). The entire city is on view, and music runs the gamut from Latin pop to '80s hits. For 50 pesos cover, you can dance away Friday or Saturday night from 9pm to 3am. The club seldom gets crowded.

Completely different in tone is **Bar Berta's** (© **762/622-0172**), next to the Santa Prisca Church at Plaza Borda 9. Opened in 1930 by a lady named Berta, who made her fame on a drink of the same name (tequila, soda, lime, and honey), it's the traditional gathering place of the local gentry and more than a few tourists. Spurs and old swords decorate the walls. Grab a seat on the balcony overlooking the plaza and church. A Berta (the drink, of course) costs about 50 pesos; rum, the same. It's open daily from 11am to 8pm.

La Concha Nostra (© **762/622-7944**), has a local, edgy feel and features live rock music Saturday nights for a 25 pesos cover. It's located upstairs inside the Hotel Casa Grande at Plazuela de San Juan 7, and is open nightly until 1am. If you're looking to get down on the dance floor, **Ibiza Night Club** (© **762/627-1664**) is the place to go. Located on Avenida de los Plateros 137, it hosts local disc jockeys and theme nights; check their website, www.ibizataxco.com, for upcoming events.

2 CUERNAVACA: LAND OF ETERNAL SPRING ★★★

102km (63 miles) S of Mexico City; 80km (50 miles) N of Taxco

Often called the "land of eternal spring," Cuernavaca is known these days as much for its rejuvenating spas and spiritual sites as for its perfect climate and flowering landscapes. Spa services are easy to find. More important, Cuernavaca exudes a deep sense of connection with its historical and spiritual heritage. Its palaces, walled villas, and elaborate haciendas are home to museums, spas, and extraordinary guesthouses.

Wander the traditional markets and you'll see crystals, quartz, onyx, and tiger's eye amid the trinkets. These stones come from the Tepozteco Mountains—for centuries considered an energy source—which cradle Cuernavaca to the north and east. Mexico begins to narrow here, and several mountain ranges converge. East and southeast of Cuernavaca are two volcanoes, also potent symbols of earth energy: **Ixtaccihuatl** (the Sleeping Woman) and the recently active **Popocatépetl** (the Smoking Mountain).

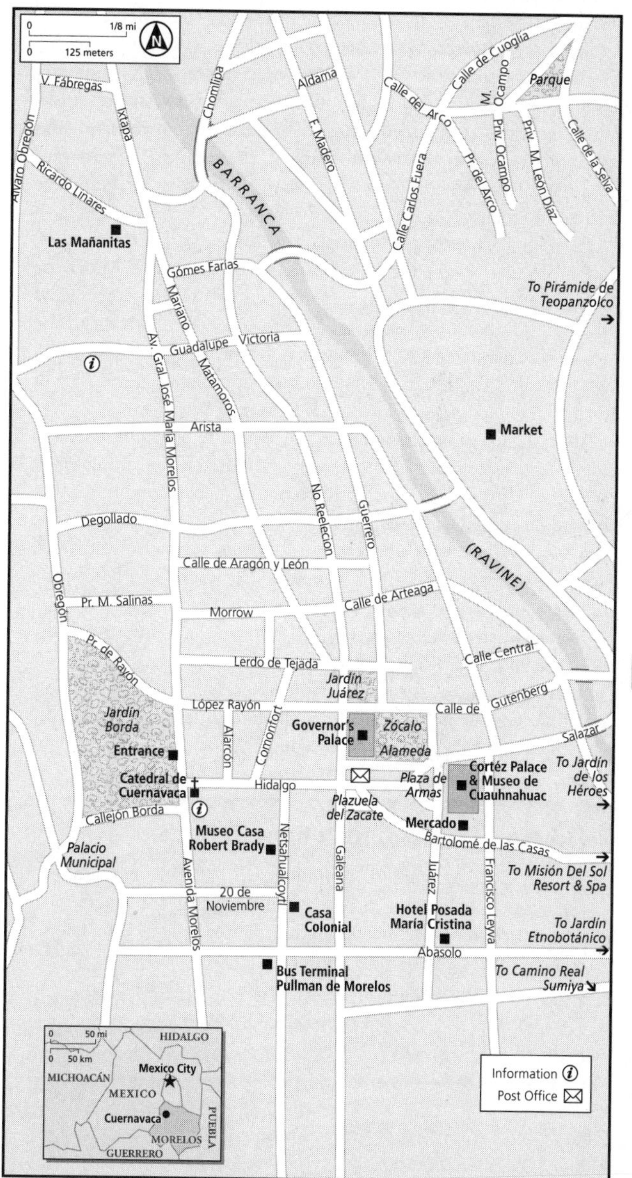
0
1/8 mi
0
125 meters
N
V. Fábregas
Ixtapa
Álvaro Obregón
Ricardo Linares
Las Mañanitas
Chomilpa
Aldama
F. Madero
BARRANCA
Calle del Arco
Calle de Cuoglia
M. Ocampo
Parque
Priv. Ocampo
Priv. M. León Díaz
Calle de la Selva
Pr. del Arco
Calle Carlos Fuera
Gómes Farías
Mariano
To Pirámide de Teopanzolco
Guadalupe
Victoria
Matamoros
Av. Gral. José María Morelos
Arista
Market
No Reelección
Guerrero
Degollado
(RAVINE)
Calle de Aragón y León
Obregón
Pr. M. Salinas
Morrow
Calle de Arteaga
Pr. de Rayón
Calle Central
Lerdo de Tejada
Jardín Juárez
López Rayón
Calle de Gutenberg
Jardín Borda
Alarcón
Comonfort
Governor's Palace
Zócalo
Alameda
Salazar
Entrance
Catedral de Cuernavaca
Hidalgo
Plaza de Armas
Cortéz Palace & Museo de Cuauhnahuac
To Jardín de los Héroes
Callejón Borda
Plazuela del Zacate
Mercado
Museo Casa Robert Brady
Netsahualcoyotl
Galeana
Bartolomé de las Casas
Palacio Municipal
Avenida Morelos
Juárez
Francisco Leyva
To Misión Del Sol Resort & Spa
20 de Noviembre
Casa Colonial
Hotel Posada María Cristina
To Jardín Etnobotánico
Abasolo
Bus Terminal Pullman de Morelos
To Camino Real Sumiya
0
50 mi
0
50 km
HIDALGO
MICHOACÁN
Mexico City
MEXICO
Cuernavaca
PUEBLA
MORELOS
GUERRERO
Information
Post Office

Cuernavaca, capital of the state of Morelos, is also a cultural treasure, with a past that closely follows the history of Mexico. So divine are the landscape and climate that both the Aztec ruler Moctezuma II and French Emperor Maximilian built private retreats here. Today Cuernavaca remains the most popular weekend getaway for moneyed residents of Mexico City. As a result, the roads between the capital and Cuernavaca are jammed almost every weekend, but you can avoid some of the crowds by traveling early in the morning. Cuernavaca even has a large American colony, plus many students attending the numerous language and cultural institutes.

Emperor Charles V gave Cuernavaca to Hernán Cortez as a fief, and in 1532 the conquistador built a palace (now the Museo de Cuauhnáhuac), where he lived on and off for half a dozen years before returning to Spain. Cortez introduced sugar-cane cultivation to the area, and African slaves were brought in to work in the cane fields, by way of Spain's Caribbean colonies. His sugar hacienda at the edge of town is now the impressive Hotel de Cortez.

After Mexico gained independence from Spain, powerful landowners from Mexico City gradually dispossessed the remaining small landholders, imposing virtual serfdom on them. This condition led to the rise of Emiliano Zapata, the great champion of agrarian reform, who battled the forces of wealth and power, defending the small farmer with the cry of "*¡Tierra y libertad!*" (Land and liberty!) during the Mexican Revolution of 1910.

Today Cuernavaca's popularity has brought an influx of wealthy foreigners and industrial capital. With this commercial growth, the city has also acquired the less desirable by-products of increased traffic, noise, and air pollution—although still far, far less than nearby Mexico City, which you may be escaping.

Fun Facts **You Wouldn't Know It But...**

The city of Cuernavaca has nothing to do with bull's horns, as the direct translation of its name would suggest. The Aztecs were much more succinct when they named their favorite leisurely retreat Cuauhnáhuac (pronounced *kwow-nah-wak*), or place of the trees. Cortés and his men had trouble getting their tongues around that word, so they just named it after something that sounded similar.

ESSENTIALS

GETTING THERE & DEPARTING **By Car** From Mexico City, take Insurgentes or Periférico south, which will take you to Hwy. 95D, the toll road on the far south of town that goes to Cuernavaca. From the Periférico, take the Insurgentes exit and continue until you come to signs for Cuernavaca/Tlalpan. Choose either the *cuernavaca cuota* (toll) or *cuernavaca libre* (free) road on the right. The free road is slower and very windy, but more scenic. The toll road costs about 90 pesos.

By Bus ***Important note:*** Buses to Cuernavaca depart directly from the Mexico City airport. (See "Getting There," in chapter 3, for details.) The trip takes an hour. The Mexico City Central de Autobuses del Sur exists primarily to serve the Mexico City–Cuernavaca–Taxco–Acapulco–Zihuatanejo route. Pullman de Morelos has two stations in Cuernavaca: downtown, at the corner of Abasolo and Netzahualcóyotl (✆ **777/318-0907** or 312-6063), 4 blocks south of the center of town; and Casino de la Selva (✆ **777/312-9473**), less conveniently located at Plan de Ayala 14, near the railroad station.

Autobuses Estrella Blanca (✆ **777/312-2626;** www.estrellablanca.com.mx) depart from the Central del Sur, with four buses daily from Mexico City. They arrive in Cuernavaca at Av. Morelos Sur 329, between Arista and Victoria, 6 blocks north of the town center. Here you'll find frequent buses to Toluca, Chalma, Ixtapan de la Sal, Taxco, Acapulco, the Cacahuamilpa Caves, Querétaro, and Nuevo Laredo.

Estrella de Oro (✆ **777/312-3055;** www.estrelladeoro.com.mx), Morelos 900, serves Iguala, Chilpancingo, Acapulco, and Taxco.

Estrella Roja (✆ **777/318-5934;** www.estrellaroja.com.mx), a second-class station at Galeana and Cuauhtemotzin in Cuernavaca, about 8 blocks south of the town center, serves Cuautla, Yautepec, Oaxtepec, and Izúcar de Matamoros.

VISITOR INFORMATION Cuernavaca's **Municipal Tourist Office** is at Calle Hidalgo 5, next to the Jardin Morelos (Morelos Garden; ✆ **777/314-3920;** www.cuernavaca.gob.mx). It's open daily from 9am to 6pm. The **Morelos State Tourism Office** is located on Av. Morelos Sur 187 (✆ **777/314-3881;** www.morelostravel.com). It's open Monday through Friday from 9am to 5pm. There's also a **City Tourism kiosk** (✆ **777/329-4404**) at Morelos Sur 278, beside the El Calvario Church, open daily from 9am to 5pm.

CITY LAYOUT In the center of the city are two contiguous plazas. The smaller and more formal, across from the post office, has a Victorian gazebo (designed by Gustave Eiffel, of Eiffel Tower fame) at its center. This is the **Alameda.** The larger, rectangular plaza with trees, shrubs, and benches is the **Plaza de Armas.** These two plazas are known collectively as the *zócalo* and form the hub for strolling vendors selling balloons, baskets, bracelets, and other crafts from surrounding villages. It's all easy-going, and one of the great pleasures of the town is hanging out at a park bench or table in a nearby restaurant. On Sunday afternoons, orchestras play in the gazebo. At the eastern end of the Alameda is the **Cortez Palace,** the conquistador's residence, now the Museo de Cuauhnáhuac.

Note: The city's street-numbering system is extremely confusing. It appears that the city fathers, during the past century or so, imposed a new numbering system every 10 or 20 years. An address given as "no. 5" may be in a building that bears the number "506," or perhaps *"Antes no. 5"* (former no. 5).

Fast Facts Cuernavaca

American Express The local representative is **Viajes Marín,** Pericón 116 (✆ **777/372-1000**). It's open Monday to Friday from 9am to 7pm and Saturday from 10am to 2pm.

Area Code The telephone area code is **777.**

Banks Bank tellers (9am–4pm, depending on the bank), ATMs, and *casas de cambio* change money. The closest bank to the *zócalo* is **Bancomer,** Matamoros and Lerdo de Tejada, catercorner to Jardín Juárez (across López Rayón from the Alameda).

Drugstore **Farmacias del Ahorro** (✆ **777/322-2277**) offers hotel delivery service, but you must ask the front desk of your hotel to place the order, because the pharmacy requires the name of a hotel employee. It has 12 locations around the city, but the individual pharmacies have no phone. Some are open 24 hours a day, while others are open daily from 7am to 10pm.

Elevation Cuernavaca sits at 1,533m (5,028 ft.).

Hospital **Hospital Inovamed** is located at Calle Cuauhtémoc 305, Col. Lomas de la Selva (✆ **777/311-2482,** -2483, -2484).

Internet Access **GAP,** Hidalgo 7 (✆ **777/318-2288**), offers high-speed access for less than a dollar per hour.

Population Cuernavaca has 400,000 residents.

Post Office The *correo* (✆ **777/312-4379**) is on the Plaza de Armas, next door to Café los Arcos. It's open Monday through Friday from 8am to 6pm, Saturday from 10am to 2pm.

Spanish Lessons Cuernavaca is known for its Spanish-language schools. Generally, the schools will help students find lodging with a family or provide a list of places to stay. Rather than make a long-term commitment in a family living situation, try it for a week, then decide. Contact the **Universidad Internacional,** San Jerónimo 304 (Apdo. Postal 1520), 62000 Cuernavaca, Morelos (✆ **800/574-1583** in the U.S., or 777/317-1087; www.spanish.com.mx); **Instituto de Idioma y Cultura en Cuernavaca** (✆ **777/317-8947;** fax 777/317-0455); or **Universal Center for Language and Social Communication: Innovative Spanish,** J. H. Preciado 171 (Apdo. Postal 1-1826, 62000 Cuernavaca, Morelos; ✆ **777/318-2904** or 312-4902; www.universal-spanish.com). Note that the entire experience, from classes to lodging, can be quite expensive; the school may accept credit cards for the class portion.

EXPLORING CUERNAVACA

On weekends, the whole city (including roads, hotels, and restaurants) fills with people from Mexico City. This makes weekends more hectic, but also more fun. You can spend 1 or 2 days sightseeing pleasantly enough. If you've come on a day trip, you may not have time to make all the excursions listed below, but you'll have enough time to see the sights in town. The traditional ***mercado* (public market)** adjacent to the Cortez Palace is open daily from 10am to 10pm. The colorful rows of stands are a lively place to test your bargaining skills as you purchase pottery, silver jewelry, crystals, and other trinkets. Note that the Cuauhnáhuac museum is closed on Monday.

Catedral de Cuernavaca ★ (Moments) As you enter the church precincts and pass down the walk, try to imagine what life in Mexico was like in the old days. Construction on the church, also known as the *Catedral de Asunción de María,* began in 1529, a mere 8 years after Cortez conquered Tenochtitlán (Mexico City) from the Aztec, and was completed in 1552. The churchmen could hardly trust their safety to the tenuous allegiance of their new converts, so they built a fortress as a church. The skull and crossbones above the main door are a symbol of the Franciscan order, which had its monastery here. The monastery is open to the public, on the northwest corner of the church property. Also visible on the exterior walls of the main church are inlaid rocks, placed there in memory of the men who lost their lives during its construction.

Once inside, wander through the sanctuaries and the courtyard, and pay special attention to the impressive frescoes painted on the walls, in various states of restoration. The frescoes date from the 1500s and have a distinct Asian style.

The main sanctuary is stark, even severe, with an incongruous modern feeling (it was refurbished in the 1960s). Frescoes on these walls, discovered during the refurbishing, depict the persecution and martyrdom of St. Felipe de Jesús and his companions in Japan. No one is certain who painted them. In the churchyard, you'll see gravestones marking the tombs of the most devout (or wealthiest) parishioners. Being buried on the church grounds was believed to be the most direct route to heaven.

At the corner of Hidalgo and Morelos (3 blocks southwest of the Plaza de Armas). ✆ **777/318-4590.** Free admission. Daily 8am–2pm and 4–7pm.

Jardín Borda Across Morelos Street from the cathedral lies the Jardín Borda (Borda Gardens). José de la Borda, the Taxco silver magnate, ordered a sumptuous vacation house built here in the late 1700s. When he died in 1778, his son Manuel inherited the land and transformed it into a botanical garden. The large enclosed garden next to the house was a huge private park, laid out in Andalusian style, with kiosks and an artificial pond. Maximilian took it over as his private summer house in 1865. He and Empress Carlota entertained lavishly in the gardens and held concerts by the lake.

The gardens were completely restored and reopened in 1987 as the Jardín Borda Centro de Artes. In the gateway buildings, several galleries hold changing exhibits and large paintings showing scenes from the life of Maximilian and from the history of the Borda Gardens. One portrays the initial meeting between Maximilian and La India Bonita, a local maiden who became his lover.

On your stroll through the gardens, you'll see the little man-made lake on which Austrian, French, and Mexican nobility rowed small boats in the moonlight. Ducks have taken the place of dukes, however. There are rowboats for rent. The lake is now artfully adapted as an outdoor theater (see website for performance information), with seats for the audience on one side and the stage on the other. Music concerts are often held on Sunday evenings. A cafe serves refreshments and light meals, and a weekend market inside the *jardín* sells arts and crafts.

Av. Morelos Sur 271, at Hidalgo. ✆ **777/318-1044.** www.arte-cultura-morelos.gob.mx. Admission 30 pesos adults, 15 pesos children. Tues–Sun 10am–5:30pm.

Jardín Etnobotánico y Museo de Medicina Tradicional y Herbolaria ★★ This serene museum of traditional herbal medicine, in the south Cuernavaca suburb of Acapantzingo, occupies a former resort residence built by Maximilian, the Casa del Olvido. During his brief reign, the Austrian-born emperor came here for trysts with La India Bonita, his Cuernavacan lover. The building was restored in 1960, and the house and gardens now preserve the local wisdom of folk medicine. The shady gardens are lovely to wander through, and you shouldn't miss the hundreds of orchids growing near the rear of the property.

Matamoros 14, Acapantzingo. ✆ **777/312-5955,** 312-3108, or 314-4046. www.inah.gob.mx. Free admission. Daily 9am–4:30pm. Take a taxi, or catch *combi* no. 6 at the mercado on Degollado. Ask to be dropped off at Matamoros near the museum; turn right on Matamoros and walk 1½ blocks; the museum will be on your right.

Museo Casa Robert Brady ★★ This private home and garden–turned–museum houses an eclectic collection of religious, folk, and ethnic art, including pre-Hispanic and colonial pieces; oil paintings by Frida Kahlo and Rufino Tamayo; popular Mexican art; and handicrafts from America, Africa, Asia, and India. Robert Brady, an Iowa native with a degree in fine arts from the Art Institute of Chicago, assembled the collections. The brightly decorated house (tiled with hand-painted Talavera throughout) is a work of art in its own right. Brady lived in Venice for 5 years before settling in Cuernavaca in 1960. The wildly colorful rooms remain exactly as Brady left them when he died here in 1986. Admission includes a guide in Spanish; English and French guides are available if requested in advance. A small cafe in the main patio serves refreshments.

Calle Netzahualcóyotl 4 (btw. Hidalgo and Abasolo). ✆ **777/318-8554.** www.bradymuseum.org. Admission 30 pesos. Tues–Sun 10am–6pm.

Museo Regional Cuauhnáhuac ★ The Palacio Cortez, once home to Mexico's most famous conquistador, is now the Museo de Cuauhnahuac, devoted to the history of Morelos state. It's also home to a stunning Diego Rivera mural, *The History of Cuernavaca & Morelos,* an unflinching illustrated history of the brutality and treachery of the Spanish Conquest. In one panel, a Spanish soldier holds a hot poker, poised to brand an Aztec prisoner on the neck; behind him, men in armor pour gold pieces into a large trunk while a priest blesses the transaction. True to Rivera's communist faith in the power of the Mexican people, the largest images in the gallery are full-length portraits of Emiliano Zapata, the revolutionary who fought for agrarian reform with the cry, "*¡Tierra y libertad!*" ("Land and liberty!"), and Father José Maria Morelos, a hero of the War of Independence.

On the lower level, the excellent bookstore is open daily from 11am to 8pm. Tour guides in front of the palace offer their services in the museum, and for other sights in Cuernavaca, for about 100 pesos per hour. Make sure you see official SECTUR (Tourism Secretary) credentials before hiring one of these guides. This is also a central point for taxis in the downtown area.

In the Cortez Palace, Leyva 100. © **777/312-8171.** www.morelostravel.com. Admission 37 pesos; free Sun. Tues–Sun 10am–5pm.

ACTIVITIES & EXCURSIONS

GOLF With its perpetually springlike climate, Cuernavaca is an ideal place for golf. The **Tabachines Golf Club and Restaurant,** Km 93.5 Carr. Mexico-Acapulco (© **777/314-3999**), the city's most popular course, is open for public play. Percy Clifford designed this 18-hole course, surrounded by beautifully manicured gardens blooming with bougainvillea, gardenias, and other flowers. The elegant restaurant is a popular place for breakfast, lunch, and especially Sunday brunch. Greens fees are 750 pesos during the week and 2,000 pesos on weekends, with fees reduced by half after 1:30pm. American Express, Visa, and MasterCard are accepted. It's open Tuesday through Sunday from 7am to 6pm; tee times are available from 7am to 2pm.

Also in Cuernavaca is the **Club de Golf Hacienda San Gaspar,** Avenida Emiliano Zapata, Col. Cliserio Alanis (© **777/319-4424;** www.sangaspar.com), an 18-hole golf course designed by Joe Finger. It's surrounded by more than 3,000 trees and has two artificial lagoons, plus beautiful panoramic views of Cuernavaca, the Popocatépetl and Ixtaccihuatl volcanoes, and the Tepozteco Mountains. Greens fees are 800 pesos on weekdays, 1,400 pesos on weekends (discounted after 2pm); carts cost an additional 450 pesos for 18 holes, and a caddy is 200 pesos plus tip. American Express, Visa, and MasterCard are accepted. Additional facilities include a gym with whirlpool and sauna, pool, four tennis courts, and a restaurant and snack bar. It's open Wednesday through Monday from 7am to 7pm.

LAS ESTACAS Either a side trip from Cuernavaca or a destination on its own, Las Estacas, Km 6.5 Carretera Tlaltizapán–Cuautla, Morelos (© **777/312-4412,** 312-7610 in Cuernavaca, or 734/345-0350; www.lasestacas.com), is a natural water park. Its clear spring waters reputedly have healing properties. In addition to the crystal-clear rivers with aquatic ropes, water swings, diving platforms, and hanging bridges, Las Estacas has two pools, wading pools for children, horseback riding, an 18-hole minigolf course, and a diving school. Several restaurants serve such simple food as quesadillas, fruit with yogurt, sandwiches, and *tortas.* Admission is 235 pesos for adults, 144 pesos for children under 1.2m (4 ft.) tall. A small, basic hotel charges 1,200 to 1,500 pesos for a double room; rates include the entrance fee to the *balneario* and breakfast. Cheaper lodging options include a trailer and camping park; you can rent an adobe or straw hut with two bunk beds for 340 pesos. Visit the website for more information. MasterCard and Visa are accepted. On weekends, the place fills with families. Las Estacas is 36km (22 miles) east of Cuernavaca. To get there, take Hwy. 138 to Yautepec, then turn right at the first exit past Yautepec.

PYRAMIDS OF XOCHICALCO ★ This pre-Columbian ceremonial center provides clues to the history of the whole region. Artifacts and inscriptions link the site to the mysterious cultures that built Teotihuacán and Tula, and some of the objects found here would indicate that residents were also in contact with the Mixtec, Aztec, Maya, and Zapotec. The most impressive building in Xochicalco is the Pirámide de la Serpiente Emplumada (Pyramid of the Plumed Serpent), with its magnificent reliefs of plumed serpents twisting around seated priests. Underneath the pyramid is a series of tunnels and chambers with murals on the walls. At the observatory, from April 30 to August 15, you can follow the sun's trajectory as it shines through a hexagonal opening. The pyramids (✆ **777/314-3920** for information) are 36km (22 miles) southwest of Cuernavaca, open daily from 9am to 6pm. Admission is 51 pesos.

WHERE TO STAY

Expensive

Camino Real Sumiya ★★ About 11km (6³/₄ miles) south of Cuernavaca, this unusual resort, whose name means "the place of peace, tranquility, and longevity," was once the home of Woolworth heiress Barbara Hutton. Using materials and craftsmen from Japan, she constructed the estate in 1959 for $3.2 million on 12 wooded hectares (30 acres). The main house, a series of large connected rooms and decks, overlooks the grounds and contains restaurants and the lobby. Sumiya's charm rests in its relaxing atmosphere, which is best midweek (escapees from Mexico City tend to fill it on weekends). Guest rooms cluster in three-story buildings bordering manicured lawns. They're simple compared to the main house's striking Japanese architecture. Rooms have subtle Japanese accents, with austere but comfortable furnishings and scrolled wood doors. Hutton built a

Kabuki-style theater and exquisite Zen meditation garden, which are now used only for special events. The theater contains vividly colored silk curtains and gold-plated temple paintings protected by folding cedar and mahogany screens. Strategically placed rocks in the garden represent the chakras, or energy points of the human body. Some regulars, who have been coming to the hotel for years, have complained that service has become less personalized under new management.

Interior Fracc. Sumiya s/n, Col. José Parres, 62550 Jiutepec, Mor. ✆ **01-800/901-2300** in Mexico, or 777/329-9888. Fax 777/329-9889. www.caminoreal.com/sumiya. 163 units. 2,132 pesos double; 3,600 pesos suite. Low-season packages and discounts available. AE, DC, MC, V. Free parking. From the freeway, take the Atlacomulco exit and follow signs to Sumiya. Ask directions in Cuernavaca if you're coming from there, as the route is complicated. **Amenities:** 2 restaurants; lobby bar; poolside snack bar; concierge; golf privileges nearby; outdoor pool; room service; tennis club; convention facilities with translation equipment. *In room:* A/C, ceiling fan, TV, hair dryer, minibar, Wi-Fi.

Las Mañanitas This hotel and garden has been Cuernavaca's most renowned luxury lodging for years. It's also a popular weekend dining spot for affluent visitors from Mexico City. Guest rooms are formal in style, with gleaming polished molding and brass accents, large bathrooms, and rich fabrics. Rooms in the original mansion, called terrace suites, overlook the restaurant and inner lawn; the large rooms in the patio section each have a secluded patio; and those in the luxurious, expensive garden section each have a patio overlooking the pool and emerald lawns. Sixteen rooms have fireplaces, and the hotel also has a heated pool in the private garden of exotic birds, flowers, and trees. Las Mañanitas is one of the only hotels in Mexico associated with the prestigious Relais & Châteaux chain. The restaurant overlooking the peacock-filled gardens is one of the country's premier dining places (see "Where to Dine," below). It's open to nonguests for all meals.

Ricardo Linares 107 (5½ long blocks north of the Jardín Borda), 62000 Cuernavaca, Mor. ✆ **777/362-0000.** Fax 777/318-3672. www.lasmananitas.com.mx. 32 units. Weekdays 2,260–2,976 pesos double; weekends 2,623–3,230 pesos double. Rates include breakfast. AE, MC, V. Free valet parking. **Amenities:** Restaurant; airport transfers (fee); babysitting; concierge; outdoor pool; room service *In room:* TV, hair dryer.

Misión Del Sol Resort & Spa ★★★ Finds This adults-only hotel and spa is an exceptional value, offering an experience that rivals any in North America or Europe. You feel a sense of peace from the moment you enter the resort, which draws on the mystical wisdom of the ancient cultures of Mexico, Tibet, Egypt, and Asia. Guests and visitors are encouraged to wear light-hued clothes to contribute to the harmonious flow of energy.

Architecturally stunning adobe buildings house the guest rooms, villas, and common areas. Group activities, such as reading discussions, a chess club, and painting workshops, take place in the salon. Spacious rooms are designed according to feng shui principles; each looks onto its own garden or stream and has three channels of ambient music. Bathrooms are large, with sunken tubs, and the dual-headed showers have river rocks set into the floor, as a type of reflexology treatment. Beds contain magnets for restoring proper energy flow. Villas feature two separate bedrooms, plus a living/dining area and a meditation room. Spa services include facials, body treatments, and massages, with an emphasis on water-based treatments. Elegant relaxation areas are interspersed among the treatment rooms and whirlpool.

Av. General Diego Díaz González 31, Col. Parres, 62550 Cuernavaca, Mor. ✆ **01-800/999-9100** toll-free inside Mexico, or 777/321-0999. Fax 777/320-7981. www.misiondelsol.com. 42 units, plus 12 villas. 2,540 pesos deluxe double; 5,260 pesos 2-bedroom villa (up to 4 persons); 6,220 pesos 3-bedroom villa (up to 6 persons). Special spa and meal packages available. AE, MC, V. Free parking. No children 12 and under. **Amenities:** Restaurant; well-equipped gym; basketball; volleyball; daily meditation, yoga, and Tai Chi classes; extensive spa services; 2 tennis courts. *In room:* A/C.

Moderate

Casa Colonial ★★ Finds This splendid inn consists of only 18 guest rooms, individually decorated in a warm colonial style with dark-wood antique furnishings. The rooms surround an idyllic courtyard filled with palms, bamboo, and ficus plants, as well as a shimmering pool. An inviting breakfast patio looks upon the courtyard, which is an intimate setting for weddings and other special events. During the day, the sound of classical music fills the air. The grounds were originally part of the cathedral property, which took up much of the neighborhood. Casa Colonial lies 1 block from the central square and within easy walking distance of all sights in the historic center.

Nezahualcóyotl 37 (at Abasolo), Col. Centro, 62000 Cuernavaca, Mor. ✆ **777/312-7033.** Fax 777/310-0395. www.casacolonial.com. 18 units. 1,495 pesos and up double. AE, MC, V. Limited free parking. **Amenities:** Restaurant; bar; outdoor pool. *In room:* Ceiling fan, TV, minibar.

Hotel Posada María Cristina ★★ The María Cristina's high walls conceal many delights: a small swimming pool, lush gardens with fountains, a good restaurant, and patios. Guest rooms vary in size; all are exceptionally clean and comfortable, with firm beds and colonial-style furnishings. Bathrooms have inlaid Talavera tiles and skylights. Suites are only slightly larger than normal rooms; junior suites have Jacuzzis. La Calandria, the handsome little restaurant, overlooks the gardens and serves excellent meals based on Mexican and international recipes. Even if you don't stay here, consider having a meal. The popular Sunday brunch (160 pesos per person) features live classical music. The hotel is a half-block from the Palacio de Cortez.

Bulevar Juárez 300 (at Abasolo), Col. Centro (Apdo. Postal 203), 62000 Cuernavaca, Mor. ✆ **777/318-2981.** Fax 777/312-9126 or 777/318-2981. www.maria-cristina.com.mx. 20 units. 1,114 pesos and up double. AE, MC, V. Free parking. **Amenities:** Restaurant; bar; outdoor pool. *In room:* Ceiling fan, TV, hair dryer, minibar.

WHERE TO DINE

Very Expensive

Restaurant Las Mañanitas MEXICAN/INTERNATIONAL Las Mañanitas has set the standard for sumptuous, leisurely dining in Cuernavaca, filling with wealthy families from Mexico City on weekends and holidays. The setting of this hotel garden and restaurant is exquisite, the service superb, and the food better than average. Tables stand on a shaded terrace with a view of gardens, strolling peacocks, and softly playing violinists or a trio playing romantic boleros. Diners have the option of ordering drinks and making their menu selections from chairs in the garden, waiting to take their seats at their tables when their meals are served. The Mexican cuisine with an international flair draws on seasonal produce. They also serve a full selection of fresh seafood, certified Angus beef, lamb chops, baby back ribs, and free-range chicken, in standard preparations. Try the zucchini flower soup, filet of red snapper in curry sauce, and black-bottom pie, the house specialty. A tasting menu is also available.

In Las Mañanitas hotel, Ricardo Linares 107 (5½ long blocks north of the Jardín Borda). ✆ **777/362-0000,** ext. 240. www.lasmananitas.com.mx. Reservations recommended. Main courses 190–400 pesos. AE, MC, V. Daily breakfast 8am–noon, lunch 1–6pm, and dinner 6–11pm.

Moderate

Casa Hidalgo ★★ GOURMET MEXICAN/INTERNATIONAL Casa Hidalgo lies in a beautifully restored colonial building across from the Palacio de Cortez. The food is more sophisticated and innovative than that at most places in town. Specialties include chilled mango and tequila soup, smoked rainbow trout, and the exquisite Spanish-inspired filet Hidalgo—breaded and stuffed with serrano ham and *manchego* cheese. There are always daily specials, and bread is baked on the premises. Tables on the balcony afford a view of the action in the plaza below. The restaurant is accessible by wheelchair.

Jardin de los Héroes 6. ✆ **777/312-2749.** www.casahidalgo.com. Reservations recommended on weekends. Main courses 140–200 pesos. AE, MC, V. Mon–Thurs 1:30–11pm; Fri–Sat 1:30pm–midnight; Sun 1:30–10pm.

Gaia INTERNATIONAL The dining area at Gaia overlooks a classic Cuernavacan scene: a fantastically tiled swimming pool and trees and shrubs laced with twinkling lights. The food, however, is far from the usual. I ate every last morsel of the house raviolis, which are prepared with a rich tomato sauce and garnished with sun-dried tomatoes. My dining companion had the tamarind shrimp and left a similarly empty plate. The extensive wine menu includes selections from Baja California, and the knowledgeable waitstaff can suggest the perfect compliment to your meal. If you're looking to impress a date, top off your meal with an Irish coffee, which is prepared tableside and lit on fire. If you're a fan of black-and-white Mexican movies, you'll dig Gaia even more, as it occupies the former home of Mario Moreno, aka Cantinflas, the Mexican equivalent of Charlie Chaplin.

Benito Juarez 102, Col Centro. ✆ **777/312-3656.** www.gaiarest.com. Main courses 80–300 pesos. AE, MC, V. Mon–Thurs 1–11pm; Fri–Sat 1pm–midnight; Sun 1–6pm.

Restaurant La India Bonita ★★ MEXICAN Cuernavaca's oldest restaurant is housed among the interior patios and portals of the restored home—known as Casa Mañana—of former U.S. Ambassador Dwight Morrow. The beautiful setting features patio tables amid trickling fountains, palms, and flowers. Specialties include *mole poblano* (chicken with a sauce of bitter chocolate and fiery chiles) and the signature *La India Bonita* plate with steak, enchiladas, rice, and beans. There are also several daily specials. A breakfast mainstay is *desayuno Maximiliano,* a gigantic platter of chicken enchiladas with an assortment of sauces. A Mexican folkloric dance show fills the restaurant with colorful energy on Saturday nights from 8 to 9pm.

Morrow 15 (btw. Morelos and Matamoros), Col. Centro, 2 blocks north of the Jardín Juárez. ✆ **777/312-5021.** Breakfast 40–90 pesos; main courses 70–160 pesos. AE, MC, V. Tues–Thurs 8am–10pm; Fri 8am–10:30pm; Sat 9am–11pm; Sun–Mon 9am–5pm.

Inexpensive

La Universal ★★ (Value) MEXICAN/PASTRIES This is a busy place, partly because of its great location (overlooking both the Alameda and Plaza de Armas), partly because of its traditional Mexican specialties, and partly because of its reasonable prices. It's open to the street and has many outdoor tables, usually filled with older men discussing the day's events or playing chess. These tables are perfect for watching the parade of street vendors and park life. The specialty is a Mexican grilled sampler plate, including *carne asada,* enchilada, pork cutlet, green onions, beans, and tortillas, for 120 pesos. A full breakfast special (110 pesos) for two is served Monday through Friday from 9:30am to 12:30pm. Live music is played weekdays from 3 to 5pm and again from 8 to 10pm.

Guerrero 2. ✆ **777/318-6732.** Breakfast 500–800 pesos; main courses 90–140 pesos; *comida corrida* 890 pesos. MC, V. Daily 9am–midnight.

CUERNAVACA AFTER DARK

Cuernavaca has a number of cafes right off the Jardín Juárez where people gather to sip coffee or drinks till the wee hours—check out La Universal (above). Band concerts are held in the Jardín Juárez on Thursday and Sunday evenings. **La Plazuela,** a pedestrian-only stretch across from the Cortez Palace, features cafes, kitsch stores, and live-music bars. It's geared toward a 20-something, university crowd.

3 TEPOZTLÁN ★★

72km (45 miles) S of Mexico City; 45km (28 miles) NE of Cuernavaca

Tepoztlán is one of the strangest and most beautiful towns in Mexico. Largely undiscovered by foreign tourists, it occupies the floor of a broad, lush valley whose walls were formed by bizarrely shaped mountains that look like the work of some abstract expressionist giant. The mountains are visible from almost everywhere in town; even the municipal parking lot boasts a spectacular view.

Tepoztlán remains small and steeped in legend and mystery—it lies adjacent to the alleged birthplace of Quetzalcoatl, the Aztec serpent god—and comes about as close as you're going to get to an unspoiled, magical mountain hideaway. Eight chapels, each with its own cultural festival, dot this traditional Mexican village. Though the town stays tranquil during the week, escapees from Mexico City descend in droves on the weekends, especially Sunday. Most Tepoztlán residents, whether foreigners or Mexicans, tend to be mystically or artistically oriented—although some also appear to be just plain disoriented. The village wears its New Age heart on its sleeve—homeopathic pharmacies and health-food stores coexist happily alongside Internet cafes, tortilla stands, and satellite-dish companies.

The town is famous throughout Mexico as a symbol of fierce civic pride and independence. In 1994, a multinational firm secretly negotiated a deal to build a Jack Nicklaus golf course and residential development on communally held lands; part of the plan involved construction of a heliport and a funicular to the top of Tepozteco pyramid. When the project came to light, townspeople joined forces, ran the city government out of town (hanging them in effigy), and occupied the *Ayuntamiento* (town hall), sealing off the city limits and repelling state military forces until the developers backed out of the project.

Aside from soaking up the ambience, two things you must do are climb up to the Tepozteco pyramid and hit the weekend folkloric market. In addition, Tepoztlán offers a variety of treatments, cures, diets, massages, and sweat lodges. Some of these are available at hotels; for some, you have to ask around. Many locals swear that the valley possesses mystical curative powers.

If you have a car, Tepoztlán provides a great starting point for traveling this region of Mexico. Within 90 minutes are Las Estacas, Taxco, las Grutas de Cacahuamilpa, and Xochicalco (some of the prettiest ruins in Mexico). Tepoztlán lies 20 minutes from Cuernavaca and only an hour south of Mexico City (that is, an hour once you're able to get out of Mexico City), which—given its lost-in-time feel—seems hard to believe.

ESSENTIALS

GETTING THERE & DEPARTING **By Car** From Mexico City, the quickest route is Hwy. 95 (the toll road) to Cuernavaca; just before the Cuernavaca city limits, you'll see the clearly marked turnoff to Tepoztlán on 95D and Hwy. 115. The slower, free federal Hwy. 95D, direct from Mexico City, is also an option and may be preferable if you're departing from the western part of the city. Take 95D south to Km 71, where the exit to Tepoztlán on Hwy. 115 is clearly indicated.

By Bus From Mexico City, buses to Tepoztlán run regularly from the Terminal de Sur and the Terminal Poniente. The trip takes an hour.

You can book round-trip transportation to the Mexico City airport through **Marquez Sightseeing Tours** (marqueztours@hotmail.com; www.tourbymexico.com/marqueztours) and some hotels. The round-trip is about 2,000 pesos.

EXPLORING TEPOZTLÁN

Tepoztlán's **weekend folkloric market** is one of the best in central Mexico. More crafts are available on Saturdays and Sundays, but the market also opens on Wednesdays. Vendors sell all kinds of ceramics, from simple fired-clay works resembling those made with pre-Hispanic techniques, to the more commercial versions of majolica and pseudo-Talavera. There are also puppets, carved-wood figures, and some textiles, especially thick wool Mexican sweaters and jackets made out of *jerga* (a coarse cloth). Very popular currently is the "hippie"-style jewelry that earned Tepoztlán its fame in the '60s and '70s. The market is also remarkable for its variety of food stands selling fruits and vegetables, spices, fresh tortillas, and indigenous Mexican delicacies.

Cooking Classes in Tepoztlán

An engaging cooking school called **Cocinar Mexicano** offers weeklong programs in Mexican cuisine. The founder, Magda Bogin, conducts class from her large, sunny outdoor kitchen, tiled in blue-and-white Talavera. Participants study recipes typical of the festival that coincides with their visit. During the Day of the Dead workshop, for example, students learn to make tamales, the traditional dish that families bring to the gravesites of deceased loved ones. For other festivals, the focus is *mole,* a typical fiesta food often made with chocolate and chiles that's arguably the most complex dish in Mexican cuisine. All the programs include a range of contemporary dishes, and participants spend a day of fine dining in Mexico City, where they meet with the country's top chefs. Prices range from $150 for a 1-day class to $2,895 for a 5-day workshop, which includes round-trip transportation from Mexico City and most meals, but not airfare or accommodations. Frommer's readers receive a $100 discount. For more information, visit **www.cocinarmexicano.com**.

A hike to the **Tepozteco pyramid** is probably one of the most rewarding experiences you will have on your journey in Mexico. The climb is steep and fairly strenuous, especially toward the end, although it is perfectly doable in a few hours and is not dangerous. I forgot to bring along hiking shoes and bought a pair of plastic *huarachis* at the market, and I managed just fine. That being said, I'm sure it would have been even more enjoyable had I been wearing sneakers. Dense vegetation shades the trail (actually a long natural staircase), which is beautiful from bottom to top. Once you arrive at the pyramid, you are treated to remarkable views and, if you are lucky, a great show by a family of *coatis* (tropical raccoons), who visit the pyramid most mornings to beg for food; they especially love bananas. The pyramid is a *Tlahuica* construction that predates the *Náhuatl* (Aztec) domination of the area. It was the site of important celebrations in the 12th and 13th centuries. The main street in Tepoztlán, Avenida 5 de Mayo, takes you to the path that leads you to the top of the Tepozteco. The 2km (1.2 mile) winding rock trail begins where the name of Avenida 5 de Mayo changes to Camino del Tepozteco. The hike takes about an hour each way, but if you stop and take in the scenery and really enjoy the trail, it can take up to 2 hours each way. Water and drinks are available at the top. The trail is open daily from 9am to 5:30pm and, while the hike is free, the pyramid costs 30 pesos to enter.

Also worth visiting is the former convent **Dominico de la Navidad.** The entrance to the Dominican convent lies through the religious-themed "Gate of Tepoztlán," constructed with beads and seeds, just east of the main plaza. Built between 1560 and 1588, the convent is now a museum, open Tuesday through Sunday from 10am to 6pm; it costs 10 pesos to enter.

SIGHTS NEAR TEPOZTLÁN

Many nearby places are easily accessible by car. One good tour service is **Marquez Sightseeing Tours,** located in Cuernavaca (marqueztours@hotmail.com; www.tourbymexico.com/marqueztours). Marquez has four- and seven-passenger vehicles, very reasonable prices, and a large variety of set tours. The dependable owner, Arturo Marquez Diaz, speaks better-than-passable English and will allow you to design your own tour, including to archeological sites and museums. He also offers transportation to and from Mexico City airport for approximately 2,000 pesos.

Two tiny, charming villages, **Santo Domingo Xocotitlán** and **Amatlán,** are only a 20-minute drive from Tepoztlán and can be reached by minibuses, which depart regularly from the center of town. There is nothing much to do in these places except wander around absorbing the marvelous views of the Tepozteco Mountains and drinking in the magical ambience.

Las Grutas de Cacahuamilpa ★, the Cacahuamilpa Caves or Grottoes, are an unforgettable system of caverns with a wooden illuminated walkway for easy access. As you pass from chamber to chamber, you'll see spectacular illuminated rock formations, including stalactites, stalagmites, and twisted rock formations with names like Dante's Head, the Champagne Bottle, the Tortillas, and Madonna with Child. Admission for 2 hours is 50 pesos. A guide for groups, which can be assembled on the hour, costs about 100 pesos. The caverns are open daily from 10am to 7pm (last tickets sold at 5pm), and are located 90 minutes from Tepoztlán and 30 minutes from Taxco.

About 50 minutes southeast of Tepoztlán is **Las Estacas,** an ecological resort with a cold-water spring that is said to have curative powers (p. 150). The ruins of **Xochicalco** (see "Cuernavaca," earlier in this chapter) and the colonial town of **Taxco** (earlier in this chapter) are easily accessible from Tepoztlán.

WHERE TO STAY

The town gets very busy on the weekends, so if your stay will include Friday or Saturday night, make reservations well in advance. In addition to the choices noted below, consider two other excellent options just outside of town. **Casa Bugambilia ★★★**, Callejón de Tepopula 007, Valle de Atongo (✆ **739/395-0158;** www.casabugambilia.com), is a nine-room hotel property 3km (1¾ miles) outside Tepoztlán. Don't confuse this hotel with Posada Bugambilia, a modest hotel in town. The spacious rooms are elegantly furnished with high-end, carved Mexican furniture, and every room has a fireplace. Doubles average 250 pesos, including breakfast. **Las Golondrinas ★★★**, Callejón de Términas 4 (✆ **739/395-0649;** http://homepage.mac.com/marisolfernandez/LasGolondrinas), is a three-bedroom B&B in the area behind Ixcatepec church; it's so far off the beaten track that even cab drivers have trouble finding the place. But owner Marisol Fernández has imbued the house with her tranquil, down-to-earth charm; the guest rooms open onto a wraparound terrace that overlooks the garden, a small pool, and the Tepozteco Mountains beyond. Doubles cost 1,850 pesos, including breakfast.

Hotel Nilayam Formerly Hotel Tepoztlán, this holistic-oriented retreat lies in a colonial building, but the decor has been brightened up considerably. The gracious, helpful staff offers complete detox programs and a full array of services, including body and facial treatments, reflexology, hot stone and shiatsu massages, yoga, Tai Chi, and meditation. The hotel has a great view of the mountain, and the restaurant features a creative menu of vegetarian cuisine. Spa packages are available.

Industrias 6, 62520 Tepoztlán, Mor. ✆ **739/395-0522.** Fax 739/395-0522. www.nilayam.net. 34 units. 1,200 pesos double. AE, MC, V. Free parking. **Amenities:** Restaurant; outdoor pool; spa services; private *temazcal* (pre-Hispanic sweat lodge). *In room:* TV.

Posada del Tepozteco ★★ This inviting inn has magnificent views overlooking the town and down the length of the spectacular valley. Rooms are tastefully furnished in colonial style. All but the least expensive feature terraces with superb views, and the suites have small whirlpool tubs. The intimate restaurant focuses on healthy and vegetarian dishes. The grounds are exquisitely landscaped, and the atmosphere is intimate and romantic. When you check in, look for the picture of Angelina Jolie behind the reception desk; she stayed here for 3 weeks while filming *Original Sin* in 2001. The hotel reception will arrange in-room massages, and the hotel has a traditional *temazcal* with herbal healing properties. Most rates include breakfast.

Moments **Tepoznieves: A Taste of Heaven**

Don't leave town without stopping at one of the many **Tepoznieves** locations; Av. 5 de Mayo 21 is one of the most convenient (✆ **739/395-3813;** www.tepoznieves.com.mx). The sublime local ice cream shop's slogan, *"nieve de dioses"* (ice cream of the gods), doesn't exaggerate. Almost 200 types of ice cream and sorbet, made only with natural ingredients, come in flavors that are familiar (vanilla, bubble gum), exotic (tamarind, rose petal, mango studded with *chile piquin*), and off-the-wall (beet, lettuce, corn). It's open daily 8am to 9pm.

Paraíso 3 (2 blocks straight up the hill from the town center), 62520 Tepoztlán, Mor. ✆ **739/395-0010.** Fax 739/395-0323. www.posadadeltepozteco.com. 22 units. 1,800–2,100 pesos double; 2,600–3,700 pesos suite. MC, V. Free parking. **Amenities:** Restaurant w/stunning view; small outdoor pool. *In room:* Hair dryer, no phone.

WHERE TO DINE

In addition to the two choices listed below, El Chalchi restaurant at the **Hotel Nilayam** (see above) offers some of the best vegetarian fare in the area. It's 3 blocks from the main square, with main courses priced around 60 pesos. Also, tame your chocolate fix with a visit to **Cacao,** Revolucion 9 (✆ **739/395-3770**), a charming chocolaterie, for some of the best bitter hot chocolate you'll ever taste. Imbibe or devour your cacao for 20 pesos and up.

El Ciruelo Restaurant Bar ★★★ GOURMET MEXICAN This long-standing favorite boasts beautiful flowering gardens set amid the striking backdrop of the Tepoztlán mountains. The large courtyard is filled with lush potted foliage and topped by a soaring band shell meant to keep patrons dry without obscuring the fantastic view of the mountains. The service is positively charming, and the regional food is divine. House specialties include cilantro soup with almonds, *chalupas* of goat cheese, chicken with *huitlacoche,* and a regional treat: milk-based gelatin with brown sugar. Try to get a seat on the outdoor patio, where a trio often serenades the crowd.

Zaragoza 17, Barrio de la Santísima, in front of the church. ✆ **739/395-1203.** Dinner 60–200 pesos. AE. Sun 1–7pm; Mon–Thurs 1–6pm; Fri–Sat 1–11pm.

Restaurant Axitla ★★ **Finds** GOURMET MEXICAN/INTERNATIONAL Axitla is not only the best restaurant in Tepoztlán, but it's also one of the finest in Mexico for showcasing the country's cuisine. Gourmet Mexican delicacies are made from scratch using the freshest local ingredients. Specialties include chicken breast stuffed with wild mushrooms in a chipotle chile sauce, *chiles en nogada,* pepper steak, grilled octopus, *chile Jarral* (stuffed chili with meat in an avocado sauce), and exceptional *mole.* There are also excellent steaks and fresh seafood. And if the food isn't enough—and, believe me, it is—the enchanted setting will make your meal even more memorable. The restaurant lies at the base of the Tepozteco Pyramid (about a 10-minute walk from the town center), surrounded by 1.2 hectares (about 3 acres) of jungle-like gardens that encompass a creek and lily ponds. The views of the Tepozteco Mountains are magnificent. Memo and Laura, the gracious owners, speak excellent English and are marvelous sources of information about the area.

Av. del Tepozteco, at the foot of the trail to the pyramid. ✆ **739/395-0519.** Lunch and dinner 80–150 pesos. MC, V. Wed–Sun 10am–7pm.

Fast Facts

1 FAST FACTS: SOUTHERN PACIFIC COAST

AREA CODES See "Staying Connected," p. 38.

BUSINESS HOURS Most businesses in larger cities are open between 9am and 7pm; in smaller towns many close between 2 and 4pm. Most close on Sunday. In resort areas stores commonly open in the mornings on Sunday, and shops stay open late, until 8 or even 10pm. Bank hours are Monday through Friday from 9 or 9:30am to anywhere between 3 and 7pm. Banks open on Saturday for at least a half-day.

DRINKING LAWS The legal drinking age in Mexico is 18; however, asking for ID or denying purchase is extremely rare. Grocery stores sell everything from beer and wine to national and imported liquors. You can buy liquor 24 hours a day, but during major elections, dry laws often are enacted by as much as 72 hours in advance of the election—and they apply to tourists as well as local residents. Mexico does not have laws that apply to transporting liquor in cars, but authorities are beginning to target drunk drivers more aggressively. It's a good idea to drive defensively.

It's illegal to drink in the street; but many tourists do. If you are getting drunk, you shouldn't drink in the street, because you are more likely to get stopped by the police.

DRIVING RULES See "Getting There and Getting Around," p. 10.

ELECTRICITY The electrical system in Mexico is 110 volts AC (60 cycles), as in the United States and Canada. In reality, however, it may cycle more slowly and overheat your appliances. To compensate, select a medium or low speed on hair dryers. Many older hotels still have electrical outlets for flat two-prong plugs; you'll need an adapter for any plug with an enlarged end on one prong or with three prongs. Many better hotels have three-hole outlets (*trifásicos* in Spanish). Those that don't may have loan adapters, but to be sure, it's always better to carry your own.

EMBASSIES & CONSULATES They provide valuable lists of doctors and lawyers, as well as regulations concerning marriages in Mexico. Contrary to popular belief, your embassy cannot get you out of jail, provide postal or banking services, or fly you home when you run out of money. Consular officers can provide advice on most matters and problems, however. Most countries have an embassy in Mexico City, and many have consular offices or representatives in the provinces.

The Embassy of the **United States** in Mexico City is at Paseo de la Reforma 305, next to the Hotel María Isabel Sheraton at the corner of Río Danubio (✆ **55/5080-2000**); hours are Monday through Friday from 8:30am to 5:30pm. Visit **http://www.usembassy-mexico.gov/** for information related to U.S. Embassy services. There are U.S. Consulates at Paseo de la Victoria #3650, Ciudad Juárez (✆ 656/227-3000.); Progreso 175, Col. Americana, Guadalajara (✆ 333/268-2100); Av. Constitución 411 Poniente, Monterrey (✆ 818/345-2120); Avenida Tapachula 96, Tijuana (✆ 664/622-7400); Calle Monterrey 141 Poiniente, Hermosillo (✆ 662/289-3500); Primera 200 y Azaleas, Matamoros (✆ 868/812-4402); Calle 60 No. 338 K x 29 y 31, Col. Acala Martin, Mérida (✆ 999/942-5700); Calle San Jose, Fraccionamiento "Los Alamos" Nogales (✆ 631/311-8150); and Allende 3330, Col. Jardin, Nuevo Laredo (✆ 867/714-0512). In addition, there are consular agencies in Acapulco (✆ 744/469-0556 or ✆ 744/484-0300); Cabo San Lucas (✆ 624/143-3566); Cancún (✆ 998/883-0272); Cozumel (✆ 987/872-4574); Ixtapa/Zihuatanejo (✆ 755/553-2100); Mazatlán (✆ 669/916-5889); Oaxaca (✆ 951/516-2853 or 951/514-3054); Puerto Vallarta (✆ 322/222-0069); Reynosa ✆ 882/823-9331); San Luis Potosí (✆ 444/811-7802 or 444/811-7803); and San Miguel de Allende (✆ 415/152-2357).

The Embassy of **Australia** in Mexico City is at Rubén Darío 55, Col. Polanco (✆ **55/1101-2200;** www.mexico.embassy.gov.au). It's open Monday through Thursday from 9:30am to noon.

The Embassy of **Canada** in Mexico City is at Schiller 529, Col. Polanco (✆ **55/5724-7900** or for emergencies 01-800/706-2900); it's open Monday through Friday from 9am to 1pm and 2 to 5pm. Visit www.dfait-maeci.gc.ca or www.canada.org.mx for addresses of consular agencies in Mexico. There are Canadian consulates in Acapulco (✆ **744/484-1305**); Cancún (✆ **998/883-3360**); Guadalajara (✆ **333/671-4740**); Mazatlán (✆ **669/913-7320**); Monterrey (✆ **818/344-2753; 818/344-3200**); Oaxaca (✆ **951/513-3777**); Puerto Vallarta (✆ **322/293-0098**); San José del Cabo (✆ **624/142-4333**); and Tijuana (✆ **664/ 684-0461**)

The Embassy of **New Zealand** in Mexico City is at Jaime Balmes 8, 4th floor, Col. Los Morales, Polanco (✆ **55/5283-9460**). www.

nzembassy.com. It's open Monday through Thursday from 8:30am to 2pm and 3 to 5:30pm, and Friday from 8:30am to 2pm.

The Embassy of the **United Kingdom** in Mexico City is at Río Lerma 71, Col. Cuauhtémoc (✆ **55/5207-2089** or 5242-8500; http://ukinmexico.fco.gov.uk/en). It's open Monday through Thursday from 8am to 4pm and Friday from 8am to 1:30pm.

The Embassy of **Ireland** in Mexico City is at Cda. Boulevard Manuel Avila Camacho 76, 3rd floor, Col. Lomas de Chapultepec (✆ **55/5520-5803**). See www.dfa.ie. It's open Monday through Friday from 9am to 5pm.

The **South African** Embassy in Mexico City is at Andrés Bello 10, Edificio Fórum, 9th floor, Col. Polanco (✆ **55/5282-9260**). It's open Monday through Friday from 8am to 4pm.

EMERGENCIES In case of emergency, dial ✆ **065** from any phone within Mexico. For police emergency numbers, turn to the "Fast Facts" sections in each of the individual chapters. The 24-hour **Tourist Help Line** in Mexico City is ✆ **01-800/987-8224** or 55/5089-7500, or you can now simply dial ✆ **078.** The operators don't always speak English, but they are always willing to help.

GASOLINE (PETROL) There's one government-owned brand of gas and one gasoline station name throughout the country—**Pemex** (Petroleras Mexicanas). There are two types of gas in Mexico: *magna,* 87-octane unleaded gas, and *premio,* which is 93-octane. In Mexico, fuel and oil are sold by the liter, which is slightly more than a quart (1 gal. equals about 3.8 liters). Many franchise Pemex stations have bathroom facilities and convenience stores—a great improvement over the old ones. Gas stations accept both credit and debit cards for gas purchases.

HOLIDAYS For schedules, see "Calendar of Events," in Chapter 1.

INSURANCE **Medical Insurance** Most U.S. health plans (including Medicare and Medicaid) don't cover travel to Mexico, and the ones that do often require you to pay for services upfront and reimburse you only after you return home.

As a safety net, you may want to buy travel medical insurance, particularly if you're traveling to a remote or high-risk area where emergency evacuation might be necessary. If you require additional medical insurance, try **MEDEX Assistance** (✆ **800/537-2029** or 410/453-6300; www.medexassist.com) or **Travel Assistance International** (✆ **800/821-2828;** www.travelassistance.com; for general information on services, call the company's **Worldwide Assistance Services, Inc.,** at ✆ **800/777-8710**; see http://www.worldwideassistance.com/pages/services/health/health_claims.html).

Canadians should check with their provincial health plan offices or call **Health Canada** (✆ **866/225-0709** or 613/957-2991; www.hc-sc.gc.ca) to learn the extent of their coverage and what documentation and receipts they must take home if they are treated overseas.

Travel Insurance The cost of travel insurance varies widely depending on the destination, the cost and length of your trip, your age and health, and the type of trip you're taking. Expect to pay between 5% and 8% of the vacation itself. You can get estimates from various providers through **InsureMyTrip.com.** Enter your trip cost and dates, your age, and other information, for prices from more than a dozen companies.

U.K. citizens and their families who make more than one trip abroad per year may find that an annual travel insurance policy is cheaper. Check **www.moneysupermarket.com**, which compares prices across a wide range of providers for single- and multitrip policies.

Most big travel agencies offer their own insurance and will probably try to sell you their package when you book a holiday. Think before you sign. **Britain's Consumers' Association** recommends carefully reading the fine print before buying travel insurance. **The Association of British Insurers** (✆ **020/7600-3333;** www.abi.org.uk) gives advice by phone. You might also shop around for better deals: Try **Columbus Direct** (✆ 0870/033-9988; www.columbusdirect.net).

For repatriation costs, lost money, baggage, or cancellation, seek travel insurance from a reputable company (www.travelinsuranceweb.com).

Trip Cancellation Insurance Trip-cancellation insurance will help retrieve your money if you have to back out of a trip or depart early, or if your travel supplier goes bankrupt. Trip cancellation traditionally covers contingencies such as sickness, natural disasters, and State Department advisories. The latest news in trip-cancellation insurance is the availability of **expanded hurricane coverage** and the **"any-reason"** cancellation coverage—which costs more but covers cancellations made for any reason. You won't get back 100% of your prepaid trip cost, but you'll be refunded a substantial portion. **TravelSafe** (✆ **888/885-7233;** www.travelsafe.com) offers both types of coverage. Expedia also offers any-reason cancellation coverage for its air-hotel packages. For details, contact one of the following recommended insurers: **Access America** (✆ **800/284-8300;** www.accessamerica.com); **Travel Guard International** (✆ **800/826-4919** or 715/345-0505 international collect); www.travelguard.com); **Travel Insured International** (✆ **800/243-3174;** www.travelinsured.com); and **Travelex Insurance Services** (✆ **800/228-9792;** www.travelex-insurance.com).

LANGUAGE Spanish is the official language in Mexico. English is spoken and understood to some degree in most tourist areas. Mexicans are very accommodating with foreigners who try to speak Spanish, even in broken sentences. See chapter 7, "Survival Spanish," for a glossary of simple phrases for expressing basic needs.

MAIL Postage for a postcard or letter is 11 pesos ($1); it may arrive anywhere from 1 to 6 weeks later. The price for registered letters and packages depends on the weight, and unreliable delivery time can take 2 to 6 weeks. The recommended way to send a package or important mail is through FedEx, DHL, UPS, or another reputable international mail service.

NEWSPAPERS & MAGAZINES The English-language newspaper, the *Miami Herald,* is published in conjunction with *El Universal.* You can find it at most newsstands. *The News*—a new English-language daily with Mexico-specific news, published in Mexico City—launched in late 2007. Newspaper kiosks in larger cities also carry a selection of English-language magazines.

PASSPORTS The websites listed provide downloadable passport applications as well as the current fees for processing applications. For an up-to-date, country-by-country listing of passport requirements around the world, go to the "International Travel" tab of the U.S. Department of State at **http://travel.state.gov**.See www.frommers.com/planning for information on how to obtain a passport.

For Residents of Australia You can pick up an application from your local post office or any branch of Passports Australia, but you must schedule an interview at the passport office to present your application materials. Call the **Australian Passport Information Service** at ✆ **131-232,** or visit the government website at **www.passports.gov.au**.

For Residents of Canada Passport applications are available at travel agencies throughout Canada or from the central **Passport Office,** Department of Foreign Affairs and International Trade, Ottawa, 125 Sussex Drive, ON K1A 0G3 (✆ **800/567-6868;** www.ppt.gc.ca). ***Note:*** Canadian children who travel must have their own passport. However, if you hold a valid Canadian passport issued before December 11, 2001, that bears the name of your child, the passport remains valid for you and your child until it expires.

For Residents of Ireland You can apply for a 10-year passport at the **Passport Office,** Setanta Centre, Molesworth Street, Dublin 2 (✆ **01/671-1633;** www.irlgov.ie/iveagh). Those under age 18 must apply for a 3-year passport. You can also apply at 1A South Mall, Cork (✆ **21/494-4700**) or at most main post offices.

For Residents of New Zealand You can pick up a passport application at any New Zealand Passports Office or download it from their website. Contact the **Passports Office** at ✆ **0800/225-050** in New Zealand or 04/474-8100, or log on to **www.passports.govt.nz**.

For Residents of the United Kingdom To pick up an application for a standard 10-year passport (5-yr. passport for children under 16), visit your nearest passport office, major post office, or travel agency or contact the **United Kingdom Passport Service** at ✆ **300/222-0000** or search its website at **www.ukpa.gov.uk**.

POLICE Several cities, including Cancún, have a special corps of English-speaking Tourist Police to assist with directions, guidance, and more. In case of emergency, dial ✆ **065** from any phone within Mexico. For police emergency numbers, turn to "Fast Facts," in the individual chapters.

TAXES The 15% IVA (value-added) tax applies on goods and services in most of Mexico, and it's supposed to be included in the posted price. There is a 5% tax on food and drinks consumed in restaurants that sell alcoholic beverages with an alcohol content of more than 10%; this tax applies whether you drink alcohol or not. Tequila is subject to a 25% tax. Mexico imposes an exit tax on every foreigner leaving the country by plane.

TELEPHONES See p. 38 in chapter 1, "Planning Your Trip to Southern Pacific Mexico."

TIME Central Time prevails throughout the Southern Pacific coast. All of Mexico observes **daylight saving time.**

TIPPING Most service employees in Mexico count on tips for the majority of their income, and this is especially true for bellboys and waiters. Bellboys should receive the equivalent of 50¢ to $1 per bag; waiters generally receive 10% to 15%, depending on the level of service. It is not customary to tip taxi drivers, unless they are hired by the hour or provide touring or other special services.

TOILETS Public toilets are not common in Mexico, but an increasing number are available, especially at fast-food restaurants and Pemex gas stations. These facilities and restaurant and club restrooms commonly have attendants, who expect a small tip (about 50¢).

VISAS See p. 8 in chapter 1, "Planning Your Trip to Southern Pacific Mexico."

Irish citizens can obtain up-to-date visa information through the **Embassy of the USA Dublin,** 42 Elgin Rd., Dublin 4, Ireland (✆ **353/1-668-8777;** or by checking the "Visas to the U.S." section of the website at **http://dublin.usembassy.gov**.

Citizens of **New Zealand** can obtain up-to-date visa information by contacting the **U.S. Embassy New Zealand,** 29 Fitzherbert Terrace, Thorndon, Wellington (✆ **644/472-2068**), or get the information directly from the website at **http://wellington.usembassy.gov**.

VISITOR INFORMATION The **Mexico Tourism Board** (✆ **800/446-3942;** www.visitmexico.com) is an excellent source for general information; you can request brochures and get answers to the most common questions from the exceptionally well-trained, knowledgeable staff

More information (15,000 pages' worth) about Mexico is available on the official site of Mexico's Tourism Board, **www.visitmexico.com.**

The **Mexican Government Tourist Board's** main office is in Mexico City (✆ **55/5278-4200**). Satellite offices are in the U.S., Canada, and the UK. In the **United States:** Chicago (✆ **312/228-0517**), Houston (✆ **713/772-2581**), Los Angeles (✆ **310/282-9112**), Miami (✆ **786/621-2909**), and New York (✆ **212/308-2110**).

In **Canada:** Toronto (✆ **416/925-0704**). In the **United Kingdom:** London (✆ **020/7488-9392**).

Online Traveler's Toolbox

Veteran travelers usually carry some essential items to make their trips easier. Following is a selection of handy online tools to bookmark and use.

- **Regional Travel** (www.travel-acapulco.com; www.go-oaxaca.com; www.go2huatulcobays.com; www.puertoescondidoinfo.com; www.zihua.net)
- **Expat Life** (www.mexonline.com; www.transitionsabroad.com)
- **Food** (www.airlinemeals.net)
- **Airplane Seating** (www.seatguru.com; and www.airlinequality.com)
- **Foreign Languages for Travelers** (www.travlang.com)
- **Maps** (www.mapquest.com)
- **Time and Date** (www.timeanddate.com)
- **Travel Warnings** (http://travel.state.gov, www.fco.gov.uk/travel, www.voyage.gc.ca, www.smartraveller.gov.au)
- **Universal Currency Converter** (www.oanda.com)
- **Weather** (www.intellicast.com; and www.weather.com)

State Tourism Boards The **Oaxaca Tourism Board** is at Independencia No. 607 and García Vigil, CP 68000, Oaxaca, Oax. (✆ **501-5000** ext. 11757; www.oaxaca.gob.mx). The **Guerrero Tourist Board** is at Av. Costera Miguel Alemán No. 4455 Centro Cultural y de Convenciones de Acapulco Fracc. Club Deportivo, CP 39850, Acapulco, Guerrero (✆ **744/484-2423;** www.guerrero.gob.mx).

WATER Tap water in Mexico is generally not potable and it is safest to drink purified bottled water. Some hotels and restaurants purify their water, but you should ask rather than assume this is the case. Ice may also come from tap water and should be used with caution.

2 AIRLINE, HOTEL & CAR RENTAL WEBSITES

MAJOR AIRLINES

THE MAJOR INTERNATIONAL AIRLINES The main airlines operating direct or nonstop flights from the United States to Mexico include **AeroMéxico** (✆ 866/275-6419; www.aeromexico.com), **Air France** (✆ 800/237-2747; www.airfrance.com), **Alaska Airlines** (✆ 800/252-7522; www.alaskaair.com), **American Airlines** (✆ 800/433-7300; www.aa.com), **Continental** (✆ 800/525-3273; www.continental.com), **Frontier Airlines** (✆ 800/432-1359; www.frontierairlines.com), **Mexicana** (✆ 800/531-7921; www.mexicana.com), **Northwest/KLM** (✆ 800/225-2525; www.nwa.com), **Taca** (✆ 800/400-8222; www.taca.com), **Delta** (✆ 800/221-1212; www.delta.com), **United** (✆ 800/241-6522; www.united.com), and **US Airways** (✆ 800/428-4322; www.usairways.com). **Southwest Airlines** (✆ 800/435-9792; www.southwest.com) serves the U.S. border.

BUDGET AIRLINES

Click Mexicana
www.clickmx.com

Frontier Airlines
www.frontierairlines.com

Interjet
www.interjet.com.mx

JetBlue Airways
www.jetblue.com

Volaris
www.volaris.com.mx

MAJOR HOTEL & MOTEL CHAINS

Best Western International
www.bestwestern.com

Courtyard by Marriott
www.marriott.com/courtyard

Crowne Plaza Hotels
www.ichotelsgroup.com/crowne plaza

Embassy Suites
www.embassysuites.com

Four Seasons
www.fourseasons.com

Hilton Hotels
www.hilton.com

Holiday Inn
www.holidayinn.com

Hyatt
www.hyatt.com

InterContinental Hotels & Resorts
www.ichotelsgroup.com

Marriott
www.marriott.com

Omni Hotels
www.omnihotels.com

Radisson Hotels & Resorts
www.radisson.com

Ramada Worldwide
www.ramada.com

Renaissance
www.renaissancehotels.com

Sheraton Hotels & Resorts
www.starwoodhotels.com/sheraton

Westin Hotels & Resorts
www.starwoodhotels.com/westin

Wyndham Hotels & Resorts
www.wyndham.com

7

Survival Spanish

Most Mexicans are very patient with foreigners who try to speak their language; it helps a lot to know a few basic phrases. Included here are simple phrases for expressing basic needs.

1 ENGLISH-SPANISH PHRASES

English	Spanish	Pronunciation
Good day	**Buen día**	Bwehn *dee*-ah
Good morning	**Buenos días**	*Bweh*-nohs *dee*-ahs
How are you?	**¿Cómo está?**	*Koh*-moh eh-*stah*
Very well	**Muy bien**	Mwee byehn
Thank you	**Gracias**	*Grah*-syahs
You're welcome	**De nada**	Deh *nah*-dah
Goodbye	**Adiós**	Ah-*dyohs*
Please	**Por favor**	Pohr fah-*bohr*
Yes	**Sí**	See
No	**No**	Noh
Excuse me	**Perdóneme**	Pehr-*doh*-neh-meh
Give me	**Déme**	*Deh*-meh
Where is . . . ?	**¿Dónde está . . . ?**	*Dohn*-deh eh-*stah*
the station	**la estación**	lah eh-stah-*syohn*
a hotel	**un hotel**	oon oh-*tehl*
a gas station	**una gasolinera**	*oo*-nah gah-soh-lee-*neh*-rah
a restaurant	**un restaurante**	oon res-tow-*rahn*-teh
the toilet	**el baño**	el *bah*-nyoh
a good doctor	**un buen médico**	oon bwehn *meh*-dee-coh
the road to . . .	**el camino a/hacia**	el cah-*mee*-noh ah/*ah*-syah
To the right	**A la derecha**	Ah lah deh-*reh*-chah
To the left	**A la izquierda**	Ah lah ees-*kyehr*-dah
Straight ahead	**Derecho**	Deh-*reh*-choh

English	Spanish	Pronunciation
I would like	**Quisiera**	Key-*syeh*-rah
I want to eat *a room*	**Quiero** **comer** ***una habitación***	*Kyeh*-roh koh-*mehr* *oo-nah ah-bee-tah-syohn*
Do you have . . . ? a book a dictionary	**¿Tiene usted . . . ?** **un libro** **un diccionario**	Tyeh-neh oo-*sted* oon *lee*-broh oon deek-syoh-*nah*-ryoh
How much is it?	**¿Cuánto cuesta?**	*Kwahn*-toh *kweh*-stah
When?	**¿Cuándo?**	*Kwahn*-doh
What?	**¿Qué?**	Keh
There is (Is there . . . ?)	**(¿)Hay** **(. . . ?)**	Eye
What is there?	**¿Qué hay?**	Keh eye
Yesterday	**Ayer**	Ah-*yer*
Today	**Hoy**	Oy
Tomorrow	**Mañana**	Mah-*nyah*-nah
Good	**Bueno**	*Bweh*-noh
Bad	**Malo**	*Mah*-loh
Better (best)	**(Lo) Mejor**	(Loh) Meh-*hohr*
More	**Más**	Mahs
Less	**Menos**	*Meh*-nohs
No smoking	**Se prohibe fumar**	Seh proh-*ee*-beh foo-*mahr*
Postcard	**Tarjeta postal**	Tar-*heh*-tah poh-*stahl*
Insect repellent	**Repelente contra insectos**	Reh-peh-*lehn*-teh *cohn*-trah een-*sehk*-tohs

MORE USEFUL PHRASES

English	Spanish	Pronunciation
Do you speak English?	**¿Habla usted inglés?**	*Ah*-blah oo-*sted* een-*glehs*
Is there anyone here who speaks English?	**Hay alguien aquí ¿ que hable inglés?**	Eye *ahl*-gyehn ah-*kee* keh *ah*-bleh een-*glehs*
I speak a little Spanish.	**Hablo un poco de español.**	*Ah*-bloh oon *poh*-koh deh eh-spah-*nyohl*
I don't understand very Spanish well.	**No (lo) entiendo muy bien el español.**	Noh (loh) ehn-*tyehn*-doh mwee byehn el eh-spah-*nyohl*

English	Spanish	Pronunciation
The meal is good.	**Me gusta la comida.**	Meh *goo*-stah lah koh-*mee*-dah
What time is it?	**¿Qué hora es?**	Keh *oh*-rah ehs
May I see your menu?	**¿Puedo ver el menú (la carta)?**	*Pweh*-doh vehr el meh-*noo* (lah *car*-tah)
The check, please.	**La cuenta, por favor.**	Lah *kwehn*-tah pohr fa-*borh*
What do I owe you?	**¿Cuánto le debo?**	*Kwahn*-toh leh *deh*-boh
What did you say?	**¿Mande?** (formal) **¿Cómo?** (informal)	*Mahn*-deh *Koh*-moh
I want (to see) . . . a room for two persons with (without) bathroom	**Quiero (ver) . . .** **un cuarto** or **una habitación** **para dos** **personas** **con (sin) baño**	*kyeh*-roh (vehr) oon *kwar*-toh, *oo*-nah ah-bee-tah-*syohn* *pah*-rah dohs pehr-*soh*-nahs kohn (seen) *bah*-nyoh
We are staying here only . . . one night. one week.	**Nos quedamos aquí solamente . . .** **una noche.** **una semana.**	Nohs keh-*dah*-mohs ah-*kee* soh-lah-*mehn*-teh *oo*-nah *noh*-cheh *oo*-nah seh-*mah*-nah
We are leaving . . . tomorrow.	**Partimos (Salimos) . . .** **mañana.**	Pahr-*tee*-mohs (sah-*lee*-mohs) mah-*nya*-nah
Do you accept . . . ? traveler's checks?	**¿Acepta usted . . . ?** **cheques de viajero?**	Ah-*sehp*-tah oo-*sted* *cheh*-kehs deh byah-*heh*-roh
Is there a laundromat . . . ? near here?	**¿Hay una lavandería . . . ?** **cerca de aquí?**	Eye *oo*-nah lah-*bahn*-deh-*ree*-ah *sehr*-kah deh ah-*kee*
Please send these clothes to the laundry.	**Hágame el favor de mandar esta ropa a la lavandería.**	*Ah*-gah-meh el fah-*bohr* deh mahn-*dahr* *eh*-stah *roh*-pah a lah lah-*bahn*-deh-*ree*-ah

NUMBERS

1 **uno** (ooh-noh)
2 **dos** (dohs)
3 **tres** (trehs)
4 **cuatro** (kwah-troh)
5 **cinco** (seen-koh)
6 **seis** (sayes)
7 **siete** (syeh-teh)
8 **ocho** (oh-choh)
9 **nueve** (nweh-beh)
10 **diez** (dyehs)
11 **once** (ohn-seh)
12 **doce** (doh-seh)
13 **trece** (treh-seh)
14 **catorce** (kah-tohr-seh)
15 **quince** (keen-seh)
16 **dieciséis** (dyeh-see-sayes)
17 **diecisiete** (dyeh-see-syeh-teh)
18 **dieciocho** (dyeh-syoh-choh)
19 **diecinueve** (dyeh-see-nweh-beh)
20 **veinte** (bayn-teh)
30 **treinta** (trayn-tah)
40 **cuarenta** (kwah-ren-tah)
50 **cincuenta** (seen-kwen-tah)
60 **sesenta** (seh-sehn-tah)
70 **setenta** (seh-tehn-tah)
80 **ochenta** (oh-chehn-tah)
90 **noventa** (noh-behn-tah)
100 **cien** (syehn)
200 **doscientos** (do-syehn-tohs)
500 **quinientos** (kee-nyehn-tohs)
1,000 **mil** (meel)

TRANSPORTATION TERMS

English	Spanish	Pronunciation
airport	**Aeropuerto**	Ah-eh-roh-*pwehr*-toh
flight	**Vuelo**	*Bweh*-loh
rental car	**Arrendadora de autos**	Ah-*rehn*-da-doh-rah deh *ow*-tohs
bus	**Autobús**	Ow-toh-*boos*
bus or truck	**Camión**	Ka-*myohn*
lane	**Carril**	Kah-*reel*
nonstop (bus)	**Directo**	Dee-*rehk*-toh
baggage (claim area)	**Equipajes**	Eh-kee-*pah*-hehss
intercity	**Foraneo**	Foh-rah-*neh*-oh
luggage storage area	**Guarda equipaje**	*Gwar*-dah eh-kee-*pah*-heh
arrival gates	**Llegadas**	Yeh-*gah*-dahss
originates at this station	**Local**	Loh-*kahl*

English	Spanish	Pronunciation
originates elsewhere	**De paso**	Deh *pah*-soh
Are seats available?	**Hay lugares disponibles?**	Eye loo-*gah*-rehs dis-pohn-*ee*-blehss
first class	**Primera**	Pree-*meh*-rah
second class	**Segunda**	Seh-*goon*-dah
nonstop (flight)	**Sin escala**	Seen ess-*kah*-lah
baggage claim area	**Recibo de equipajes**	Reh-*see*-boh deh eh-kee-*pah*-hehss
waiting room	**Sala de espera**	*Sah*-lah deh ehss-*peh*-rah
toilets	**Sanitarios**	Sah-nee-*tah*-ryohss
ticket window	**Taquilla**	Tah-*kee*-yah

2 DINING TERMINOLOGY

MEALS

desayuno Breakfast.

comida Main meal of the day, taken in the afternoon.

cena Supper.

COURSES

botana A small serving of food that accompanies a beer or drink, usually served free of charge.

entrada Appetizer.

sopa Soup course. (Not necessarily a soup—it can be a dish of rice or noodles, called *sopa seca* [dry soup].)

ensalada Salad.

plato fuerte Main course.

postre Dessert.

comida corrida Inexpensive daily special usually consisting of three courses.

menú del día Same as *comida corrida.*

DEGREE OF DONENESS

término un cuarto Rare, literally means one-fourth.

término medio Medium rare, one-half.

término tres cuartos Medium, three-fourths.

bien cocido Well-done.

Note: Keep in mind, when ordering a steak, that *medio* does not mean "medium."

MISCELLANEOUS RESTAURANT TERMINOLOGY

cucharra Spoon.

cuchillo Knife.

la cuenta The bill.

plato Plate.

plato hondo Bowl.

propina Tip.

servilleta Napkin.

tenedor Fork.

vaso Glass.

IVA Value-added tax.

fonda Strictly speaking, a food stall in the market or street, but now used in a loose or nostalgic sense to designate an informal restaurant.

INDEX

See also Accommodations and Restaurant indexes, below.

General Index

ACCOMMODATIONS

Restaurants